TERRITORIES IN RESISTANCE

A Cartography of Latin American Social Movements

Raúl Zibechi
Translated by Ramor Ryan

AK
PRESS

EDINBURGH • OAKLAND • BALTIMORE

Territories in Resistance:
A Cartography of Latin American Social Movements

© 2012 Raúl Zibechi
Translated by Ramor Ryan

This edition © 2012 AK Press (Oakland, Edinburgh, Baltimore)
ISBN: 978-1-84935-107-2 | eBook ISBN: 978-1-84935-102-7
Library of Congress Control Number: 2012937710

AK Press	AK Press
674-A 23rd Street	PO Box 12766
Oakland, CA 94612	Edinburgh, EH8 9YE
USA	Scotland
www.akpress.org	www.akuk.com
akpress@akpress.org	ak@akedin.demon.co.uk

The above addresses would be delighted to provide you with the latest AK Press distribution catalog, which features the several thousand books, pamphlets, zines, audio and video products, and stylish apparel published and/or distributed by AK Press. Alternatively, visit our websites for the complete catalog, latest news, and secure ordering.

The interview that comprises this book's Epilogue first appeared in *South Atlantic Quarterly* 2012 Volume 111, Number 1: 165–191, and appears with their kind permission.

Visit us at:
www.akpress.org
www.akuk.com
www.revolutionbythebook.akpress.org.

Printed in the USA on acid-free, recycled paper.

Contents

Foreword, by Dawn Paley   1
Introduction   7

Section I. Movements as Bearers of "Other Worlds"

1. Latin American Social Movements: Trends and Challenges   13
2. Social Movements as Spaces of Learning   21
3. The Healing Power of the Community   31
4. Recreating the Social Tie: The Revolution of Our Days   37
5. Collective De-alienations   51

Section II. Latin America in Movement

6. Subterranean Echoes: Political Resistance from Below   61
7. Recuperated Factories: From Survival to Self-management   91
8. Another World is Possible: Zanon Ceramics   101
9. Chile: The Long Mapuche Resistance   109
10. Landless Workers Movement: The Difficult Construction of a New World   121
11. The Other Campaign, or Politics from Below   127
12. Colombia: Militarism and Social Movement   159
13. Where the Asphalt Ends: School and Community in Bogotá's Peripheries   171
14. Ecuador: A Prolonged Instability   179

Section III. The Peripheries of Latin America: Territories of Hope

15. The Urban Peripheries: Counter-powers from Below?   189

Section IV. Progressive Governments and Social Movements

16. The Art of Governing the Movements   267
17. Governments and Movements: Autonomy or New Forms of Domination?   299

Epilogue

Interview by Michael Hardt and Alvaro Reyes   307

Reference List   335
Index   349

Translator's Acknowledgments

Ramor Ryan wishes to thank Chuck Morse who copy-edited the text, Charles Weigl for layout, and Raúl Zibechi who offered assistance throughout. Additional gratitude goes to the following who helped during various stages of the process— Luigi Carlos Calentano, Esteban Véliz Madina, Nancy Lucita Serrano, Alvaro Reyes, Dawn Paley, Don Tomás de San Ramón, Cuitláhuac, Michael McCaughan, Tauno Biltsted, James Mary Davis, Ana Nogueira, Erez Gudes, Vikki Law, Eddie Yuen, Timo Russo, Zach Blue and Muireann de Barra.
Gracias compañer@s.

My work is dedicated to Ixim Dagge-Hernández.

Foreword

Before Occupy Wall Street, there was La Victoria.

La Victoria, a shack settlement turned bustling, permanent neighborhood, was born when 1,200 families living in desperate poverty in Santiago de Chile took over an undeveloped sector of the city. The new residents of La Victoria erected houses and buildings without government permits, communally organized a security system, and within months, were running their own school. This year, La Victoria will turn fifty-five.

Raúl Zibechi, a writer whose work on social movements is widely read in Spanish, suggests that La Victoria may have been the first mass organized land occupation in Latin America. "In this new kind of movement, self-construction and self-determination take the place of demands and representation," writes Zibechi, reflecting on the occupation of La Victoria. "This pressure from below transformed the course of social struggles and the cities."

The language Zibechi uses to describe the establishment of the encampment at La Victoria over fifty years ago finds echo in the words and practice of Indigenous sovereigntists, members of France's Invisible Committee, and anti-authoritarian supporters of Occupy Wall Street. Throughout *Territories in Resistance: A Cartography of Latin American Social Movements*, readers will find a close and compelling resonance between the movements Zibechi describes and various struggles in North America.

There are, of course, many differences between Occupy Wall Street and urban movements south of the US-Mexico border. Unlike the long term occupation carried out in Santiago de Chile, Occupy Wall Street and similar encampments didn't make it through their first winter. But at the same time, the Occupy movement, which has its origins in crisis and is based in a firm rejection of the political and economic system, shares other important similarities with the movements documented by Zibechi.

Maybe, as in the case of La Victoria, the experience of Occupy will inspire new community-level urban movements in North America to stage and defend public occupations, transforming the course of social struggle. Or maybe not. The future of autonomous, grassroots struggles (including, but not limited to, Occupy) is contested. The aspirations of these struggles could be quelled by state enforced exploitation and repression on the one hand, or by the coercive power of the established left, linked to electoral politics and unions, on the other.

It is at this very juncture that the English translation of Raúl Zibechi's *Territories in Resistance* has arrived, and the timing couldn't be better. Honing in on enduring anti-authoritarian, anti-state, and anti-capitalist social movements in Latin America, Zibechi explores the successes of these struggles, and their challenges, which, he emphasizes, often come from unexpected quarters.

Let's go back to Chile for a moment, back to the hard scrabble settlement founded by women, men, and children determined to live with dignity. Over time, La Victoria evolved into a stronghold of resistance against the dictatorship of Augusto Pinochet. Eleven national protests against the regime were organized out of the neighborhood in 1983–84, and repression was fierce: at least seventy five protestors were killed, while thousands more were injured and jailed. "The leaders were primarily young people who used barricades and bonfires to demarcate their territory and attack the closest symbols of order such as municipal buildings, traffic lights, etc," writes Zibechi. But despite the repression, there was no defeat; instead, it was this movement that forced the dictatorship to retreat.

It wasn't until the transition to democracy in 1990, writes Zibechi, that the movement began to wane.

Zibechi takes a fifty-year view on La Victoria and Chilean social movements, from which he draws three lessons: first, that communitarian movements cannot be defeated by repression, except by mass slaughter; second, these same movements *can* suffer defeat at the hands of the left, who can soften and fragment the movements, making them more amenable to the state; and third, that this kind of defeat requires the co-optation of key individuals or collectives within movements.

Though the circumstances are distinct, different versions of the same issues continually surface with regards to grassroots movements in North America, as anti-authoritarians are continually forced to calibrate their relationships with reformist groups, which are often well funded, media savvy, and purport to be allies. INCITE Women of Color Against Violence's 2007 book *The Revolution will Not be Funded* is the seminal North American text on the mechanisms through which grassroots collectives and others are reined in using state and foundation funding. "The non-profit industrial complex is a system of relationships between: the State (or local and federal governments), the owning classes, foundations and non-profit/NGO social service & social justice organizations that results in the surveillance, control, derailment, and everyday management of political movements," INCITE writes.

In North America, activists accepting foundation and government funding has become somewhat of a norm. "One century after it began, corporate philanthropy is as much part of our lives as Coca Cola," writes Arundhati Roy in her recent essay "Capitalism: A Ghost Story." Though Roy acknowledges that some NGOs do good, she points out that "corporate or Foundation-endowed NGOs are global finance's way of buying into resistance movements, literally like shareholders buy shares in companies, and then try to control them from within. They sit like nodes on the central nervous system, the pathways along which global finance flows. They work like transmitters, receivers, shock absorbers, alert to every impulse, careful never to annoy the governments of their host countries."

Territories in Resistance describes how social movements in Latin America have been impacted by U.S. style democratization and corporate/foundation funded co-optation, and examines how collectives and groups have responded in order to maintain their autonomy.

But Zibechi pushes beyond the notion of co-optation, bringing to light the mechanics of statecraft as practiced by left-governments of South America, which have developed increasingly sophisticated methods to control movements. He calls this the art of governing movements: "This is not a form of governmentality constructed by the state and assumed by the movements, but actually a joint construction in shared space/time," writes Zibechi. "To oversee this strategy, it is not necessary to co-opt individuals, which could even be counterproductive. There must be a will to construct it together." He traces the roots of this form of movement governance from within (and above) to the insertion of leftist activists into the state apparatus of countries including Uruguay, Argentina, Brazil, Ecuador, and Mexico in the 1990s.

Zibechi also takes a critical position on the governments of Ecuador, Venezuela, and especially Bolivia. "Progressive governments are necessary for the preservation of the state… In this new situation, they are the most effective agent at disarming the anti-systemic nature of the social movements, operating deep within their territory and as revolt brews," he writes. "Under progressive governments, current movements are weaker, more fragmented, and more isolated than ever." His positions in relation to these governments aren't based in sectarian arguments or more-radical-than-thou posturing, but instead are informed by his ongoing commitment to and long term connections with grassroots Indigenous and popular movements.

Territories in Resistance also includes stories from social movements in Colombia and Peru, countries that have avoided (or in the case of Peru, been late to join) the "pink tide" of so-called leftist presidents. These movements, which are generally overlooked by activists, journalists, and Latin Americanists in North America, according to Zibechi, constitute some of the most vibrant, innovative, and active social movements in the hemisphere today.

Territories in Resistance is a valuable, accessible text that will be of interest to community activists or readers looking for a critical, informed take on goings on in Latin America. Our understanding of movements and new forms of repression generally will be strengthened through a careful consideration of Zibechi's position on progressive governments and their impacts on movements, a perspective that is too rarely articulated in English. His unflinching attention to autonomous and communitarian movements merits a close read, as he hones in on the challenges these movements face and the means they devise to survive and to stay autonomous. Such reflections are often disparaged by the established left as sectarian or radical. It is in these uncomfortable spaces, which are often left unexplored—even by grassroots groups—for fear of unnerving a funder or a powerful "ally," where Zibechi is at his strongest.

"In essence, left parties accomplish tasks that the Right could not achieve through repression: an historic defeat of popular forces, without massive bloodshed but every bit as effectively as authoritarian states of yesteryear," he writes. It's not just states and the electoral left that pose challenges to movements, however, because "just as left-wing professionals and trade unions played a role in reinstalling constitutional democracies with restricted freedoms in the Southern Cone, some armed leftist groups contributed to weakening popular forces, particularly the urban poor."

Zibechi's gaze in scrutinizing movements in Latin America prioritizes "fleeting insurrectionary moments," and he asks if it is not "time to change our perspective and focus our attention on dynamics that escape academic conceptualization but clearly have the potential to change the world?"

And though organizing a rebellion is, according to Zibechi, a contradiction in terms, he thinks it is also problematic when a movement lacks structure. His view of how that structure might take place runs counter to received movement knowledge: "the debate about articulation/structure should focus on: avoiding centralization and unification; avoiding converting the structures and or diffuse or informal networks into apparatuses with their own life; strengthening the new world which is born in the movement."

In this sprawling, comprehensive book, Raúl Zibechi captures processes often hidden from view, adding a unique texture to our understanding of social movements (or, societies in movement) in Latin America. *Territories in Resistance* brings to life a host of valuable examples for English language readers wishing to develop new spaces for debate and discussion about popular movements in their own regions.

Dawn Paley
San José del Cabo, Mexico.

Introduction

A continent on the move, in flux, and at boiling point. Two decades of crisis, hardship, and repression; two decades of structural adjustment driven by the Washington Consensus and intended to impose a vertical, authoritarian society. But also two decades of resistance, of popular organization, of "overflows" that delegitimized the model imposed from above. Ultimately, the powerful failed in their attempt to dominate the popular sectors of our continent and plunder their riches. This has produced an unstable equilibrium shaped by three critical forces: global and local elites, governments' struggle to move beyond neoliberalism, and social movements. The power or the limits of these three forces will be decisive when charting the path of social and continental emancipation.

In the last two decades, there have been profound and long-lasting changes in the Latin American popular world, which represent a radical shift with respect to earlier periods. This set of changes, which I touch upon in this volume, presents an enormous challenge to the revolutionary and social theory inherited from the previous period, defined by the centrality of the union movement and the nation-state.

Entire societies, not just social movements, have been put in movement. Millions of men and women from below, driven by necessity, have mobilized for two decades and, by doing so, have changed not only the world but also themselves. As a result, Latin America has become a beacon of hope for many around the world.

However, the concepts and words used typically to describe and understand our realities are inadequate to the task of interpreting, and accompanying, those societies in movement. It is as if the capacity to name has been trapped in a period transcended by the active life of our peoples. Many of the assumptions and analyses that shaped us during the struggles of the sixties and seventies have become, to borrow a phrase from Braudel, "long-term prisons." Quite often, they stifle creative capacity and condemn us to reproduce what is already known and has failed.

A new language, one that is capable of talking about relationships and movements, must break through the tangle of inherited concepts to analyze structures and organizational frameworks. We need expressions capable of capturing the ephemeral, the flows that are invisible to the vertical, linear eye of our masculine, legalistic, and rational culture. That language does not exist, and thus we must invent it in the heat of the various resistances and collective creations. Or, better yet, pitch it out from the underground of popular sociability so that it can grow out onto the great avenues, where it can become visible and, thus, be adopted, altered, and transformed by societies in movement.

In short, we need to name ourselves in such a way that is faithful to the spirit of our movements and that turns fear and poverty into light and hope; a magical gesture reminiscent of the *zumbayllu* (spinning top). Ernesto, the forlorn protagonist of Arguedas's book *The Deep Rivers*, uses the zumbayllu as a means to escape the violence of his boarding school into what Cornejo Polar calls an "unusual movement of brotherhood." I employ the image of the zumbayllu as a reflection of societies in movement that, in order to exist, to ward off death and oblivion, must move themselves from their inherited place. These societies must keep moving, because to stop means falling into the abyss of negation, to cease to exist. At this stage of capitalism, our societies only exist in movement as the Zapatista communities teach us so well, as well do the Indians throughout the Americas, the landless farmers, and, increasingly, those condemned to the margins of the urban world.

Images like the spinning top brings us closer to the magic world of movements, which can move quickly from horror and hatred to fraternity, and vice versa. The double movement, the rotation on its own axis and the passage across a plane, are two complementary ways of understanding social change: displacement and return. Indeed, it is not enough just to move, to vacate its inherited material and symbolic place; a type of movement is also necessary that is a dance, circular, capable of piercing the epidermis of an identity that does not let itself be trapped because with each turn it reconfigures itself. Displacement and return can be understood as repetition and difference. The zumbayllu, as a reflection of the other society, is, philosophically speaking, committed to intensity over representation, destined always to sacrifice movement to the altar of order.

The spinning top of social change is dancing for itself. We do not know for how long or to where. The temptation to give it a push in order to speed up its rhythm can bring it to a halt, despite the good will of those trying to "help." Perhaps the best way to promote it is to imagine that we ourselves are part of the zumbayllu—spinning, dancing, all and sundry. To be a part of it, without any control over the final destination.

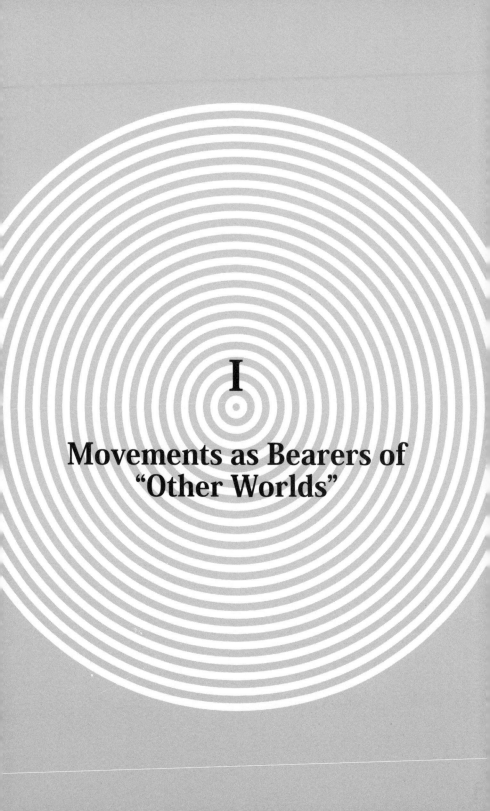

I

Movements as Bearers of "Other Worlds"

Latin American Social Movements: Trends and Challenges[1]

The social movements of our continent are traversing new routes, ones that separate them from the old labor movement as much as the new movements in the core countries. Building a new world in the breaches that have erupted in the model of domination, they are responses to the social earthquake caused by the neoliberal wave of the eighties. This wave ruptured the territorial and symbolic forms of production and reproduction upon which popular sectors' world view and daily activity rested.

Three major political and social currents born in this region form an ethical and cultural frame of the great movements: the grassroots Christian communities linked to liberation theology; the Indian insurgency, with its non-Western cosmology; and Guevarism, the inspiration for revolutionary militancy. These currents of thought and action converged, giving rise to a rich "mestizaje" or mix that is one of the distinguishing characteristics of the Latin American movements.

Since the early nineties, social mobilizations have brought down two presidents each in Ecuador and Argentina; one each in Paraguay, Peru, and Brazil; and wrecked corrupt regimes of Venezuela and Peru. In several countries, social mobilizations have slowed down the privatization process through massive street actions that sometimes led to outright popular insurrections. In this manner, the social movements have forced elites to take their demands into account and negotiate, and they have helped install progressive governments in Venezuela, Brazil, and Ecuador. Neoliberalism crashed into the tide

---

1   This article was originally published in *Observatorio Social de América Latina* (*OSAL*), no. 9 Clacso, Buenos Aires, January 2003.

of social movements that opened up more or less deep cracks in its model.

These new paths represent a long-term shift. Up until the seventies, social action revolved around demanding rights from the state, establishing alliances with other social sectors and political parties, and developing plans of struggle designed to change the balance of power on a national scale. These ultimate objectives were implemented in programs that guided the movements' strategic activity. In essence, social action sought access to the state in order to change property relations, and that goal justified the state-centric forms of organization, based in the organizational concept of centralism, the division between leaders and led, and a pyramid structure within the movements.

Common Trends

Alternative lines of action had gained strength by the late seventies, reflecting the profound changes brought about by neoliberalism in the daily life of the popular sectors. The most significant movements (the landless and rubber tappers in Brazil, indigenous Ecuadorians, neo-Zapatistas, water warriors and coca farmers in Bolivia, and unemployed in Argentina) possess common features, despite their spatial and temporal differences, since they respond to problems shared by all social actors on the continent. In fact, together they form part of a family of social and popular movements.

One common factor is the territorialization of the movements—that is, they have roots in spaces that have been recuperated or otherwise secured through long (open or underground) struggles. This reflects a strategic response of the poor to the crisis of the old territoriality of the factory and farm and to capital's reformulation of the old modes of domination. The de-territorialization of production (spurred by dictatorships and neoliberal counter-reforms) ushered in a crisis for the old movements. It debilitated subjects that were part of disappearing territorialities in which they had previously acquired power and meaning. This defeat opened up a still-unfinished period of rearrangement that was reflected in the reconfiguration of physical space. The result in each and every country, though with different intensities, characteristics, and rhythms, is the relocation of the popular sectors into new territories that are often on the fringes of cities and areas of intensive rural production.

Territorial rootedness is a feature of the landless movement in Brazil, which created an infinity of small, self-managed islands: by the Ecuadorian Indians, who expanded their communities to rebuild their ancestors "ethnic territories," and by the indigenous of Chiapas, who populated the Lacandon jungle (Fernandes 2000; Ramón 1993; Garcia León 2002, 105). This strategy, which originated in rural areas, began to appear on the desolate urban fringes: the excluded created settlements on the margins of large cities by taking and occupying plots of land. Across the continent, the poor have recuperated or conquered millions of hectares, creating a crisis within the territorial order and remodeling the physical spaces of resistance (Porto 2001, 47). From their territories, the new actors consolidated long-term projects, most notably the capacity to produce and reproduce life, while establishing alliances with other fractions of the popular sectors and the middle class. The experience of the Argentine *piqueteros* [unemployed workers] is significant, since it is one of the first instances of an urban movement with these characteristics.

The second common characteristic is that they seek autonomy from the state as well as from political parties. Their political autonomy rests on their material autonomy—the movements' growing capacity to provide their own subsistence. Just half a century ago, *concierto*[2] Indians living on farm estates, factory workers and miners, and the underemployed and unemployed were entirely dependent on the bosses and the state. However, the communards, coca growers, landless farmers, and especially the Argentine piqueteros and urban unemployed all work consciously to build their own material and symbolic autonomy.

---

2   "Concerted": Indians in the Andean region are those "in concert with"—in agreement with—the landowner, which involves a relationship of servitude and income in kind.

Thirdly, they work for the re-valorization of the culture and the affirmation of the identity of their people and social sectors. Both the old and new poor valorize the affirmation of ethnic or gender difference, which plays an important role in indigenous and women's movements. Their de facto exclusion from citizenship seems to have prompted them to build a fundamentally different world. Understanding that the concept of citizenship has meaning only if some are excluded has been a painful lesson learned over the past decades. Hence the movements tend to press beyond the concept of citizenship, which was useful for two centuries for those who needed to contain and divide the dangerous classes (Wallerstein 2001, 120–135).

The fourth common feature is the formation of their own intellectuals. The Andean indigenous world lost its intellectual dimension during the repression that followed the anti-colonial uprisings in the late eighteenth century. As a result, the popular and labor movements that came in its wake depended on intellectuals who brought socialist—specifically Leninist—ideology "from outside." The struggle for education allowed Indians to access tools used previously only by the elite and resulted in the formation of professionals from Indian and impoverished backgrounds, a small part of whom are still linked culturally, socially, and politically to the sectors from which they originated. Parallel to this, sections of the middle classes that had secondary education and sometimes even university training sank into poverty. Thus, people appear among popular sectors who are armed with new types of knowledge and capacities that facilitate self-organization and self-training.

The movements are taking the education and training of their leaders into their own hands and often employ educational criteria inspired by popular education. In regard to this, Ecuadorean Indians have lead the way by starting up the Intercultural University of Indigenous Peoples and Nationalities, which draws upon the experience of bilingual, intercultural education in the nearly three thousand Indian-run schools. Also leading the way is the Landless Movement of Brazil, who run their own schools in some 1,500 settlements, as well as multiple spaces dedicated to training educators, professionals, and activists (Dávalos 2002; Caldart 2000). Other movements, like the piqueteros, are gradually recognizing the need to take responsibility for education, not least because national states tend to overlook the matter. In any case, it has been a long time since intellectuals from outside of the movement spoke on their behalf.

The changing role of women is the fifth common feature. Indian women serve as elected parliamentarians, guerrilla commanders, and social and political leaders; rural and piquetera women occupy important positions in their organizations. And this is just the visible part of a much broader phenomenon reflecting the new gender relations established in social and territorial organizations that emerged from the restructuring in recent decades.

Women and children have a decisive presence in all activities related to the daily subsistence of popular and indigenous sectors, both in rural areas and the peripheries of cities—from farming and selling in the markets to education, health, and productive enterprises. The instability of couples and the frequent absence of men means that women have become responsible for organizing in the domestic sphere and in the broader tapestry of relationships woven around the family. In many cases, families have become productive units in which everyday labor and family activities come together. In summation, new familial and productive forms have emerged in which women constitute a unifying pillar.

The sixth trait the new movements share is a concern for the organization of work and the relationship with nature. Even in cases where the struggle for agrarian reform or the recuperation of shut-down factories take prominence, the activists know that ownership of the means of production does not solve most of their problems. They tend to see land, factories, and settlements as spaces in which to produce without bosses or foremen, as spaces to promote egalitarian relationships with a minimal division of labor and based on new techniques of production that do not generate alienation or destroy the environment.

Current movements also shun the Taylorist kind of organization (hierarchical, with a division of labor between those who direct and execute), in which the leaders are separated from the bases. The organizational forms of the current movements tend to reproduce family and community daily life, often taking the form of territorially based self-organizing networks. The Aymara uprising in September 2000 in Bolivia showed how community organization was the starting point and foundation of the mobilization, including the system of rotation that ensured the maintenance of roadblocks, and became the framework for an alternative power (García Linera 2001, 13). Successive uprisings in Ecuador were based on a similar premise: "They come together and remain united in the 'taking of Quito,' and do not even dissolve or disperse in the mass marches; they stay cohesive and return to their zone, where they continue to maintain collective life" (Hidalgo 2001, 72). This description also applies to the behavior of the landless movement and the piqueteros during large mobilizations.

Finally, self-affirming forms of action through which the new actors make themselves visible and assert their distinctive identities tend to replace the older forms, such as the strike. The "taking" of cities by the indigenous represents the material and symbolic re-appropriation of an "alien" space, thereby giving it new content (Dávalos 2001). For landless peasants, land occupations represent the emergence from anonymity and reunion with life (Caldart 2000, 109–112). The piqueteros feel that the only time that the police respect them is when they block a road. The Mothers of Plaza de Mayo are named after a space appropriated more than twenty-five years ago, where they deposit the ashes of their comrades.

Of all the characteristics mentioned above, the new territorialities are the most important distinguishing feature of Latin American social movements and what offers them the possibility of reversing their strategic defeat. Unlike the old worker and peasant movements (in which Indians were subsumed), the current movements advance a new organization of geographic space, in which new practices and social relations emerge (Porto 2001; Fernandes 1996, 225–246). They see land as more than a means of production, thereby going beyond a narrow economist conception of it.

Territory is the space in which to build a new social organization collectively, where new subjects take shape and materially and symbolically appropriate their space.

New Challenges

The current movement is also immersed in intense debates that affect its organizational forms and attitude toward the state, political parties, and left and progressive governments. The orientation that predominates in the coming years will determine how these issues are resolved.

Although much of the grassroots are attached to territory and establish predominantly horizontal relationships, the articulation of the movements beyond their local regions raises unresolved problems. Even well-established organizations such as the Confederation of Indigenous Nationalities of Ecuador (CONAIE) have had problems with leaders elected as deputies, and during the brief "takeover" of January 2000, a significant fissure occurred between the bases and the leadership, who appeared to abandon the organization's historical project.

Establishing all-embracing, permanent forms of coordination implies entering into the field of representation, and this places the movement in a difficult position. In certain periods, it cannot afford to make concessions to visibility or escape intervening on the political stage. The debate on whether to opt for a centralized, highly visible organization or a diffuse, discontinuous one presents the two extremes of the question, although there are no simple solutions to the matter and it cannot be settled for once and all.

Finally, the question of the state remains at the forefront of the movements' debates, and everything indicates that the issue will become more urgent as progressive forces occupy national governments. There is a need for an appraisal of the manner in which the movements have become transmission belts for political parties and have found themselves subordinated to national states, mortgaging their autonomy. However, the idea of forging clear boundaries between social and political forces seems to be gaining strength, as is already evident in Brazil, Bolivia, and Ecuador. While the former tend to support the latter, aware that progressive governments can promote social action, it seems unlikely that subordinate relations will be re-established.

It is not fundamentally an ideological debate, but is rather about looking at the past in order not to repeat it. Above all, it is about trying to look inward, into the interior of the movements. The picture that appears, one that becomes increasingly intense, is that the long-awaited new world is being born in the movements' spaces and territories, embedded in the gaps that are opening up in capitalism. It is "the" real and possible new world, built by indigenous people, peasants, and urban poor on conquered lands, woven into the base of the new social relations between human beings, inspired by ancestral dreams, and recreated through the struggles of the past twenty years. This new world exists; it is no longer merely a project or program but rather a series of multiple realities, nascent and fragile. The most important task that lies ahead for activists over the coming decades is to defend it, to allow it to grow and expand. To do this, we must be ingenious and creative in order to combat our powerful enemies who are hellbent on destroying it; we must have patience and perseverance in the face of our own temptations to cut corners that, as we know, lead nowhere.

Social Movements as Spaces of Learning[3]

Latin America has become a symbol, a place where, more exemplary than elsewhere, this struggle between the logic of the "first class" and the logic of emancipation is present.

Jacques Rancière

Social movements are taking the training of their members and education of their families' children into their own hands. Initially, this was a response to the state's retreat from providing social services: education, health, employment, housing, and other provisions linked to the survival of popular sectors that had been degraded through two decades of neoliberal policies. Later, movements began to consider how to they could accomplish tasks previously overseen by the state: Would they simply try to do it better, in a more complete and "inclusive" manner, or would they begin from these experiences and take a route that would lead in other directions? In short, would they be able to integrate health, education, and production into the broader emancipatory process?

In many poor neighborhoods in large cities, school is the only place where the state has a presence, which was previously the case in remote, rural communities. And it is not a neutral presence. On many occasions, the state's presence creates divisions within communities; in other instances, state schools transmit values that are different from those found in popular culture and among indigenous peoples, facilitating the spread

---

3   Paper presented at the International Congress of Sociology of Education. Buenos Aires, August 25–28, 2004.

of individualistic attitudes that go hand-in-hand with neoliberalism. Nevertheless, the struggle for education has always been and remains a struggle for the recognition of people's rights.

What is new in the last decade is the intensity with which some movements have assumed responsibility for education. They view it as a way of building movements and as an essential aspect of everyday life. Movements are also creating educational spaces in their territories, where they determine how the schools function, thereby challenging a key premise of the national state's dominance. In view of this, it is appropriate to pose the question: To what extent can social movements reconstruct the arenas of knowing and understanding? (Dávalos 2002, 89). They appear to be in a position to reconstruct forms of knowledge destroyed by neoliberalism.

Education in Movement

The landless movement in Brazil (Movimiento dos Trabalhadores Rurais Sem Terra, or MST) is likely working with greater intensity on education than any other Latin American social movement. Although indigenous movements had previously fought struggles around school issues, they mostly did not go beyond building schools that were managed by the state and did not implement different educational practices. For the Indians, mastering the skill of writing was a way to get knowledge of "the other" world, the dominant sector, so as the better to neutralize the state's influence. There were, however, some educational experiences designed and overseen by the Indians themselves, the so-called "Indian school," which allowed them to concentrate "cultural energy" and renew collective memories that became the core of ethnic identity, facilitating processes of organization, mobilization, and even the formation of their own political projects (Ramón 1993, 112).

For Brazil's landless movement, the self-managed school is one of the most unique features for the movement, although the efforts were only consolidated in the nineties. There are about 2,000 schools in the settlements, in which about 4,000 teachers serve some 200,000 children; the educational criteria have been designed by the movement itself, stressing that

education is "an important political activity for the transformation of society" that should have its starting point in the
reality of the settlements and camps around the children and
that families should be involved in both school planning and
administration. MST schools are governed by two basic goals:
developing students' critical awareness through studies that
"lead to reflection and the acquisition of a broader world view,
differentiated from official discourse," and the "understanding
of the history and meaning of the struggle for land and agrarian reform that led to the creation of the settlement" in which
the school is situated and the students live. They also concentrate on developing students' technical, productive skills,
which they see as "alternative techniques" and "practical exercises in arenas of knowledge needed for the development of
the settlement" (Morissawa 2001, 241).

Important as this is, it is just one aspect of the MST's education program. We could talk much more about this process,
detailing the most advanced pedagogical experiences, as well
as the movement's incursion into remote areas or technical
training and work in the university. However, I think one of
the most interesting aspects is that the movement itself has
become an "educational subject." This is much more than intervention in educational practices and community involvement in schools. It means that the social movement itself has
become an educational subject, and therefore all its spaces,
actions, and ideals have a "pedagogical intention." I think
this represents a revolutionary change in how we understand
education and also how we understand the social movement.

Considering the "social movement as an educational
principle" (Salete 2000, 204) implies going beyond the traditional role accorded to the school and teacher: it ceases to be
a specialized space for education for which one sole person
is responsible. Instead, all spaces and actions, and all of the
people involved, are pedagogical space-times and subjects.
Among the many other consequences, education under these
conditions has no end or objective beyond re-producing the
movement and cultivating a new world, which means "producing human beings." In short, "to transform oneself by

transforming" is the pedagogical principle that guides the movement (Salete 2000, 207).

So what does it mean to say that the movement is the educational subject? It means that education is an education *in movement*. This notion challenges our most basic conceptions. How can you educate in movement? It is one thing to educate *for* the movement or *in the* movement, but another is to do it *in* movement. What matters here is neither what pedagogy is utilized nor what model of schooling is pursued, but the *climate* and human *relationships*. Education is no more and no less than a social climate embedded in social relations, and the result of the educational process will depend on the kind of climate and character of social relations. If the climate is competitive and the relationships are hierarchical, the educational space will be closed, separated from the environment, and the human beings that emerge will tend to have the same values. But a different conception, such as the one represented in the slogan "to transform oneself by transforming"—an education in movement—does not guarantee the results that will be achieved. We can assume that individuals *in* collectives, in line with the movement for social change in which they were formed, will arise and that the result will broaden and strengthen the movement. But perhaps it will not be so, and hopefully one of the "lessons learned" will be learning how to live with uncertainty.

It seems necessary to point out four reasons why the movement is a pedagogical subject, which Roseli Salete refers to as "educational matrices": the movement not as an institution but as a capacity to move itself; the atmosphere of community fraternity; production as a central aspect to the transformation of our world; and the forms of life that emerge from these daily practices.

- By "social movement" we mean the human capacity, individually and collectively, to modify the assigned or inherited place in a social organization and to seek to expand spaces of expression (Porto Gonçlaves 2001, 81). That movement-in-motion (while the movement lasts) is a permanent process of self-education. It tries to do so consciously, so as to enhance and strengthen itself. We can also understand the movement as "transforming itself by transforming." If the social struggle fails to change the place it occupied beforehand, it is doomed to failure, since it reproduces the oppressive roles that presumably gave birth to it. But the change of roles/places can be stopped with the adoption of a new identity that replaces the old or may tend to settle in a sort of fluidity, by which the subject is continuously transforming itself. As we shall see, school and movement, institution and change are contradictions.

- This vortex of constant change, which can accelerate or slow down, can only be contained within a strong human community, by strong bonds of brotherhood, in which "family style" links are key to the continuity of the experiences and processes. In this respect, the foundation is not a fixed identity, a physical place, or a social role, but the human relations through which we share life. Salete calls this "pedagogy as rooting in a collective." This is why it is so important that the movement organization work as a lattice and a space of affective ties, which implies eradicating the hegemonic idea embedded within left-wing thought that sees the organization solely as the instrument to achieve goals.

- Productive work is educational if it is transformative; that is, if it is not only productive but a way of building human relationships. In this sense, the social movement should not advocate for work that reproduces hierarchies and Taylorist divisions of labor, but should appeal to cooperation, and reject a notion of time imposed by the system for the sake of an internal time. How can we organize ourselves to work and produce so that we can establish pedagogical relations? This question should replace those relating to efficiency, in the economic as much as the political field.

- Finally, everyday forms of life in the movement should be imbued with values and attitudes that encourage people to become the creative subjects of their own lives. That is, there should be an *emancipatory climate*. We know what constitutes an oppressive, authoritarian climate, but defining emancipatory human relations is not easy. Emancipation does not allow for prescriptions or models; it is a process that is always unfinished and must be experienced individually. But it has an additional "difficulty": As Rancière says, "The logic of emancipation only deals with, ultimately, individual relationships" (Vermeren et al 2003, 52). Does this mean that there can be no collective emancipation? Certainly Rancière-Jacotot does not go that far. The guiding idea is that "one can only be emancipated by oneself," but if there is a space-time marked by the logic of emancipation and not the logic of "the first in the class"—that is, a climate conducive to emancipation—that climate does not fall from the sky but will have been created by the collective activity of the social movements that are, to paraphrase Braudel, the "home of the common people."

Within this approach, there are no recipes or pedagogical methods or educational models ready to install. The experiences of the landless movement show that the movement has no place in school, that the one and the other are contradictory, and that "putting the school in movement" represents a huge challenge because it is a space operating within an institutional logic (Salete 2000, 240 et seq.). This contradiction can only be resolved within the movement, understood not as an institution but with the logic of the movement in motion mentioned above. "The identity of the [state] school depends on the daily opposition to the idea of process, of transformation, of life happening in its unpredictability and fullness, which contradicts its own social work of making education" (Salete 2000, 242).

To create an education in movement implies that schools and movements must co-exist, despite their differences. This means the school must be part of an "integral" pedagogical subject, becoming part of the climate and the learning process of the social movement. Doing this presents a huge challenge: having to convert each space, each instance, every action, into spaces for growth and collective learning. To convert the movement into a pedagogical subject involves placing reflection and ongoing evaluation of what is happening at the forefront of activities, to open up spaces of self-reflection, and, of course, to take "internal" time, which naturally does not coincide with the time of the political parties and the state. There are several examples of this approach within the piqueteros movement: the "philosophy workshop" of the Movement of Unemployed Workers (MTD) in La Matanza (Lee 2004), the "reflection groups" of the MTD Solano (Ferrara 2004), and Ronda de Pensamiento Autónomo (Autonomous Thinking Group), in which some piquetero groups, neighborhood assemblies, and students participated.[4] In these instances there is a total and complete break from the traditional training space for the sake of a more appropriate space for the community/movement.

In addition to these experiences of the MST and the MTD, one can add the experiences of the Ecuadorian Indians who have created the Intercultural University of Indigenous Peoples and Nationalities. In Ecuador, there are 2,800 indigenous-run schools, with some of them forming part of the intercultural, bilingual education system, although CONAIE initiated "a different kind of school, one which is mostly based on the participation of the community, *a pedagogy that was practiced by our elders*" (Macas 2000, 2; emphasis added). The Intercultural University is an example of this process of appropriating education for the "Indians in movement"—it is not housed in great buildings, it promotes the oral tradition, and it is guided by "a shared learning process, which can be informal [i.e., not regulated by academic formalities in the classroom] and itinerant, to facilitate the incorporation of students in each village or community" (Macas and Lozano 2000, 3).

The trend within these movements is to reintegrate different aspects of life, to bring together various aspects that

---

4   See www.lavaca.org.

had previously been separate and split apart. In the neighbor-hoods, this begins with the "de-institutionalization of space," which means, in effect, "generating communal and flexible places" and also an "integration of time," wherein there is a dissolution of the divide between working time, leisure time, domestic time, and so on (Sopransi 2004). This "appropria-tion" of time and space, for the community in movement, de-structures instituted and institutionalized knowledge that usually lies in the hands of specialists.

It is not easy to see where this is leading. If, as we can gather intuitively, education is life itself or that life should be an act of education, this means recovering life in its integral character—overcoming division and fragmentation. And if what educates is life itself, then the educational act must af-firm, empower, expand, and set *in movement* the "knowledge" that already exists in popular sectors' daily life.

School, State, Territory

How can we conceive of schooling as a differentiated educa-tional space within the social movement? At this point, Clas-tres argues, war breaks out between the community school and the state. In other words, school is a key location in the battle between the community and the state, and so the battle takes on a territorial character.

The current movements tend to develop territorial roots, which they understand as the space in which to allow non-capitalist social relationships to unfold while they resist the neoliberal model. The new territories—here I am thinking of piquetero barrios, the landless movement's settlements and camps, among other examples—are spheres for the crystal-lization of new social relations, which introduce new territo-rialities based on the reconfiguration of previous ones. Move-ments "mark" the space with their daily presence, doing so through their unique connections and relationships. The new schools are being born in these territories.

The MST aspires to take control of education, and some-times it manages to get the community to assume responsi-bility for it. "The school is an achievement of the settlement or camp. All of the families are involved, not just those with children currently attending classes. Whenever possible, the base groups must discuss the operation and the direction of the school" (MST 1999). Nevertheless, it is ultimately the movement that decides the direction of the school.

The experience in Indian communities is somewhat different. The community controls a territory and usually builds a school in it that ends up becoming the only place that the state has a presence in their territory. However, the state's presence often leads to conflict, especially when the community persists in maintaining and affirming its cultural difference. In Bolivia, schools are an inheritance of 1952 revolution: the communards allocated land for the school that they themselves would build, which included planting plots for the subsistence of the teachers. The relationship seems clear: The school is on "our territory," say the Indians.

Nevertheless, state school inevitably bears a hidden curriculum, one that only the social struggle succeeds in making visible. One point of conflict is the difference between the logic of the school and the logic of the community: "To what degree can the logo-centric logic of the state be made compatible with the logic of the oral textuality of the community?" (Regalsky 2003, 168). It is difficult to transfer the community knowledge by means of the state school because there is an irresolvable tension between the two: "Any transfer of knowledge through the state school immediately undergoes a change of format and lose its metaphorical charge, becoming logos—the word is only its literal meaning, while the significant context vanishes within the four walls of the classroom" (169).

This is a power struggle that usually resolves itself in favor of the state's authority, which means, in this case, the school. For Regalsky, state schooling in the community is a space "perforating the jurisdiction of the community, weakening it and shifting the balance of power in favor of the regional Creole authorities" (Regalsky 2003, 170). In short, the school is a space for a confrontation between the strategies of the peasant Indians and the state. In this sense, school is an instrument of the state intended to dismantle Indian territoriality and restructure it in its favor.

I am referring to the experience of the struggle for land and education among communities in Raqaypampa in the Cochabamba zone of Bolivia. To put a brake on their efforts, the Bolivian state set out to reorganize the educational institutions, employing the concept of "multiculturalism" as an instrument—that is, "using the ethnic demands of the CSUTCB [a peasant confederation]—appropriating them and making them part of its own platform" (Regalsky, 175). The inevitable conflict of jurisdictions erupted in Raqaypampa when the communities withdrew all their children from the local schools. They only accepted re-opening them on the condition that authorities allowed "indigenous teachers" selected in community assemblies to serve as the official teachers. The community even clashed with the teachers' union, who defended the outside creole teachers, who were graduates from a state institute.

In the end, the Communal Council of Education imposed a solution with the support of the peasant community, and even went so far as to modify the regional school calendar so as not to interfere with seasonal agricultural labor. In one memorable assembly in 1992, a Quechua peasant farmer said, "we're showing them that we can teach our children better than the state teachers can" (Regalsky, 191). The indigenous had the capacity to question the "autonomy" of the school and its teachers because they had employed an alternative logic, with a strong territorial and cultural base.

The experience of Raqaypampa raises an important question: that of defining the school's principal actor. The response to this question will determine whether the educational aspirations of the popular sectors in movement form part of the new world that we want to build or whether they remain subordinated to the logic of the state, which is the logic of the accumulation of capital.

The Healing Power of
the Community[5]

A community has an emancipatory approach to health care when it recovers its own healing powers, which have been expropriated by the medical industry and the state, and liberates itself from the control that capital exercises over health care through multinational pharmaceuticals. Zapatista health care practices, as well as those of many indigenous peoples and piqueteros groups, share many commonalities despite their enormous cultural differences.

Indigenous peoples often recover their ancestral knowledge, which goes hand-in-hand with recognizing the wisdom of traditional health practitioners while not discarding modern medicine. In fact, they attempt to combine the two. Much like when communities decide to construct a school, so too the first step in community health care is constructing a local dispensary capable of dealing with those emergencies that cause the highest mortality rates.

But Indian peoples have their own long tradition of health care.

In the traditional indigenous cosmovision, there is no separation between health and lifestyle or, that is, the community. Therefore, "the health of individuals as physical bodies, depends, at root, on the health of the community" (Maldonado 2003). The concept of healing in indigenous medicine is identical to the concept of healing in that society and it is based on a dense network of reciprocal social relations: *minga*

5   This text was originally published as part of the article, "La emancipación como producción de vínculos," by Raúl Zibechi, published in Ana Esther Ceceña's, *Los desafíos de las emancipaciones en un contexto militarizado*, Clacso: Buenos Aires, 2006.

(community work), community assemblies, and collective fiestas. These are spaces for "harmoniously liberating the sub-
conscious, both of the individual and the collective" (Ramón
1993, 329).

In indigenous societies, the capacity to heal emerges
from self-generated structures, unlike Western society, which
has medical bodies that are separate from society as a whole
and that control and monitor health care. Indigenous health
practitioners have organized in various regions to recover and
enhance indigenous medical knowledge (Acero and Dalle
Rive 1998; Freyermuth 1993). This is part of the emancipatory process of the indigenous peoples of our continent and
part of the lengthy process of constituting these peoples as political subjects. In some cases, indigenous organizations (such
as CONAIE in Ecuador and the Regional Indigenous Council of Cauca in Colombia, among others) have created their
own health programs, with the support of doctors and nurses
trained in Western medicine, and with some support from the
state (CRIC 1988).

The Zapatistas have set up a system of health care in the
five *Caracoles* that cover all rebel communities. Some eight
hundred of *casas de salud* [community health centers] are
operating, served by a similar number of health promoters,
alongside a dozen municipal clinics and two hospitals that
perform surgery (Muñoz 2004). The San Jose hospital near
La Realidad was built in three years by thousands of indigenous locals working in shifts. There is also a training school
for health promoters there, as well as dental care facilities, an
herbalist center, and a clinical laboratory. Several volunteers
hailing from the communities work full-time in the hospital;
they do not receive a salary but are supported by the Good
Government Council, which "provides them with food, travel
expenses, footwear, and clothes"(Muñoz 2004). The Zapatistas
have set up an herbal laboratory there as well:

> This dream started when we realized that the knowl-
> edge of our elders and our elderly was being lost. They
> know how to cure bones and sprains, they know how

to use herbs, they know how to oversee the delivery process for pregnant women, but all of that tradition was being lost with the use of medicines purchased in the pharmacy. So we came to an agreement among the people and brought together all the men and women that know about traditional healing. It was not easy to bring everyone together. Many *compañeros* [comrades] did not want to share their knowledge, saying that it was a gift that cannot be transferred because it is something they carried within them. But then a sense of awareness and understanding grew among the people, the heath authorities held discussions, and they convinced many to change their way of thinking and to participate in the courses. They were some twenty men and women, older people coming from the communities, who acted as teachers of traditional health and about three-hundred-fifty students signed up, most of them Zapatista compañeros. Now they have increased the amount of midwives, bonesetters, and herbalists in our communities (Muñoz 2004, 319).

In the autonomous regions, there is a functioning network of community health centers and clinics, dental consultants, clinical analysis and herbal laboratories, where eye and gynecolological services are available, and pharmacies. Consultations cost a nominal fee for the Zapatista base and are often given free of charge. Anybody in the communities, Zapatista or not, can avail themselves of the medical services; the medicines are dispensed without cost if they have been donated and sold at cost if they were purchased; traditional medicines are free. In some Caracoles, infusions and ointments are made from local medicinal plants. All this has been accomplished through the work of indigenous communities as well as through national and international solidarity efforts. Significantly, the Mexican state has not been involved at all.

Autonomous piqueteros groups organize health care around the same principles, despite the differences between Mayan cultures and popular sectors in a huge city like Buenos

Aires, birthplace of the Latin American labor movement and a showplace of global consumerism. During the health workshop held at the Autonomous January gathering in 2003, groups concluded was that "the cure is within the movement itself." The MTD has organized preventative health clinics in many of the neighborhoods where they have a presence, staffed by professionals working in solidarity. This is true of other piquetero groups as well. The MTD Solano in Buenos Aires and MTD Allén in Neuquén supply their members with free medicines and eyeglasses. This illustrates what can be accomplished beyond the market: Thanks to a sympathetic optician, discarded or out-of-style frames are paired with lenses bought at cost and now all the movement's members in need have affordable glasses.

The MTD also mixes, packages, and distributes medicinal herbs purchased directly from local producers. Now the movement is proposing to take it a step further by developing homeopathic tinctures from plants cultivated in small community plots. The result is that piquetero families are discovering the advantages of alternative medicine and using conventional medicine less frequently, or doing so only in emergencies. In some neighborhoods people have begun working with Chinese therapies such as acupuncture and have organized workshops dealing with native herbs in order to broaden the use of alternative cures (Salud Rebelde 2004).

The movement has also set up "reflection groups" in every neighborhood "to deal with personal problems, relationships, feelings, and collective growth." In these groups, according to one participant, "one learns to lose fear; that fear is a sickness."

Indeed, with respect to dependency on doctors and specialists, these groups believe that "verticality induces sickness" and that "wellness is finding ourselves" (Enero Autonomo 2003). The story of one of these groups' meetings, as told by a social psychologist who participates in the movement and who coordinated their first meeting (which was held in a very poor neighborhood under MTD Solano influence), speaks for itself:

After the presentations, we began the meeting with an open question: Does anybody want to say anything? It was like turning on a tap. Almost immediately an anguished woman began telling us that she had been sexually abused as a girl by her father. Between sobs, she told a story of overcrowding, promiscuity, males and females sleeping in the same room, and the subsequent violations as part of family life, a situation all too common for poor households in the townships spread through the peripheries of big cities.

When she had finished her painful story, the silence in the room was powerful, a silence made from seventy-odd, quietened people, the silence of not knowing how to react together when so much deep pain was exploding forth in the room, seeking a response forty or fifty years after the event, a resonance, or some kind of understanding or forgiveness or just simply to be heard. Those assembled seemed uncertain how to express the compassion they felt toward the companera. In the end, the group focused on the most basic fact: that the companera had shared her pain with them and now they must begin to consider what can be done about it. Really it was just a simple notion, but one that opened the way for the participation of other voices. Words of comfort flowed out, understanding, hugs, gestures of solidarity, in many instances from others who recognize in themselves a similar kind of suffering (Ferrara 2004).

Certainly, as indicated by the indigenous and piqueteros, it is the movement and community itself that has the power to heal. But the paths were different for each.

Indigenous peoples are recovering their traditional medicinal practices, which had been suppressed by the conquerors; the ex-workers and unemployed, molded by the culture of consumption, have had to de-institutionalize work, space, time, and politics to reinvent their lives. In summary, this has included:

- self-managed productive projects, or production "for itself."
- opening up spaces in the "galpones"[6] and in movement territories in order to have permanent and free meeting places in which new relations are practiced.
- "the integration of the various temporal spheres of everyday life and respect for time itself," meaning an attempt to reunite time fragmented and parceled up by the system.
- and practices of horizontality, autonomy, collective participation, dignity, cooperation-based solidarity, and direct democracy as opposed to representation, hierarchy, and the instrumentalization of the traditional political practices (Sopransi and Veloso 2004).

---

6   A garage, shed, or warehouse, with or without walls.

Recreating the Social Tie:
The Revolution of Our Days[7]

Addressing the issue of social ties is to return to the concerns of the early socialists, for whom change meant primarily the creation of new social relations and did not depend on the ties between movements and states. It also emphasizes the centrality of the question of emancipation, which is inseparable from changing social ties.

Secondly, speaking of the achievements and difficulties, of the powers and limits of the social movements, requires an inward gaze. It involves exploring the question of *how* relations are built among members of the movement and also between them and the surrounding environment. In my view, it is of great strategic importance whether or not the movement uses Taylorist forms in organizing daily life, with a division between intellectual and manual work or between those who give and those who obey orders, or goes beyond that and searches for non-capitalist forms of relations. I would argue that much of the current movement does indeed seek non-capitalist forms and that, by doing so, we are not only showing that socialism or some other, more humane society is possible but also that it is presently being built.

Potentialities and Achievements

Elsewhere I have pointed out seven characteristics commonly found in current Latin American movements: *territorial* rootedness in spaces won through long struggles; *autonomy* from states, political parties, churches, and unions; the affirmation of *identity* and *difference*; the capacity to assume control for

---

7   Paper presented at the seminar "De la exclusión al vínculo," organized by the Goethe Institute, Buenos Aires, June 2005.

education and to form intellectuals from within their own
ranks; the increased role of *women*—and therefore the whole
family—who are often the mainstay of the movement; a non-
hierarchical relationship with nature and *non-Taylorist forms*
of division of labor in their organizations; and the movement
of instrumental forms of action toward *self-assertiveness.*

Of these common characteristics, the new territorialities created by the movements are the most important differ-
entiating feature with respect to older movements and those
currently existing in the First World. It is also their existence
that offers the possibility of reversing the strategic defeat of
the labor movement wrought by neoliberalism. It is within
these territories that the movements are collectively building
a whole new organization of society.

Having first emerged in rural areas among peasants and
Indians, in recent years the new territorialities have begun
appearing in large cities such as Buenos Aires, Caracas, and
El Alto. They are spaces in which the excluded ensure their
daily survival.

This means that the movements are now beginning to
take the everyday life of their people into their own hands.
There has been a major shift in the urban areas mentioned
above: The people do not only survive on the "leftovers" or
"waste" of consumer society but have also begun to produce
their own food and other products for sale or exchange. They
have become producers, which represents one of the movements' greatest achievements in recent decades, in terms of
autonomy and self-esteem. This step was the result of their
own "natural" development and was not a consequence of
advanced planning by leaders.[8]

Secondly, the social movements have adopted organizational forms based on the family. A feature of the movements
that have challenged the system most seriously (i.e., Indian
communards, peasant farmers, the landless and homeless
movements in Brazil, piqueteros, and non-territorialized
women and youth movements) is that they have forms of

---

8   I use the term "natural" instead of "spontaneous"—the latter is often used
critically to describe movement actions that occur without planning or leaders.

organization built upon the family—not nuclear family units, but new, stable, and complex forms of extended family relationships.[9] Within this extended family form, women often play a central role, and not always one that mirrors the dominant role of the male, but in the context of new relationships with children and other families. For instance, in the landless movement, the basic nuclei are groups of families living under the same roof or as neighbors in the camps; in the homeless movement (*Sin Techo*), there are often clusters of families living together in occupied spaces; and among piqueteros there are forms of extended families revolving primarily around women.

The role of the family in these new movements is embodied in new social relations in four areas: the public-private relationship, the new family forms, the creation of a domestic space that is neither public nor private but something new that includes both, and the re-production of life. At the root of these processes is the breakdown of patriarchy; neoliberalism fostered this phenomenon, but it began much earlier. Patriarchy has been in crisis since the sixties, as is visible in numerous sites, from the family to the factory, and this has affected education, the military, and other disciplinary institutions. It will be difficult for capitalism to survive if it fails to consolidate new forms of control and subjugation.

The role of family seems to respond to a feminization of the movements and social struggles, which is clearly part of a feminization of society as a whole. By feminization, I refer to increased agency among women and a new balance among the genders that affects all areas of society (Capra 1992).

These changes, defined primarily by the increased role of the family in anti-systemic movements, leads to a reconfiguration of the political. They affect the form it takes, the channels through which it is transmitted, and even the ends sought. Among indigenous people in Bolivian cities, "the political exists not so much in the streets but in the more intimate

---

9   Immanuel Wallerstein points out that the domestic units are not frequently studied, even though they are institutional pillars of our societies, just like the state, businesses, and social classes.

sphere of markets and households, spaces in which women undoubtedly dominate" (Rivera 1996, 132). Female leadership and the new domestic units are modifying the political in ways that have still to be fully comprehended.[10]

In this way, the movements are beginning to turn their spaces into alternative spaces. There are two reasons for this: first, they are converting them into spaces for survival and socio-political action (as we have seen), and, second, they are constructing non-capitalist social relations within them.

The approach to health care or education, and how to produce and distribute food does not simply mimic the capitalist pattern. Indeed, we see a tendency in many of these enterprises to call into question the inherited ways of doing things.

How was it possible to create non-capitalist "islands"? It was possible thanks to the movements' efforts to open spaces or gaps in the dominant system, physical and symbolic spaces of resistance that became spaces of survival. And, furthermore, necessities of survival prompted them to begin producing and reproducing their lives in new ways:

- Education tends to be self-education; the educational space is not only the classroom but also the whole community; it is not only teachers who teach but also everyone in the members of the community, even children at times; the whole movement itself is an educating space.

- In production, they seek self-sufficiency and diversification in order to lessen dependency on the market; they try to produce without pesticides or contaminating products; they try to sell outside of the claws of the market; they attempt to ensure that all the producers are familiar with all stages of production; they try to ensure that the technical division of labor does not generate social hierarchies in gender or age; they are working to reduce the division between mental and manual labor

---

10 Wallerstein understands a domestic unit as "a unit that puts the income of its members in a common pool to ensure its maintenance and reproduction," in *Capitalismo histórico y movimientos antisistémicos* (Wallerstein 2004, 235).

as well as that between those who give orders and those who obey.

- In health, the social movements are seeking alternatives to the pharmaceutical industry by recovering lost knowledge; they are increasing their reliance on medicinal plants and alternative medicine; they try to ensure that doctors or medical supervisors do not become a power separated from the community; they try to eliminate the traditionally passive, dependent "patient" relationship; they try to encourage community members to re-appropriate medical knowledge and to play a role in health care.

The above descriptions represent only *tendencies, aspirations, or attempts* in the midst of the social struggles. They are not conclusions, but flows and movements. After all, is a movement but to move-oneself? "Every social movement derives from those who break with social inertia and begin to move themselves, which is to say, *they change place*, rejecting the place that they were historically allocated within a given social organization and seeking to broaden their spaces of expression" (Porto Gonçalves 2001, 81).

We are dealing with a set of activities that are based on new types of social ties that are present, somewhat unevenly, in the various movements. However, it is nevertheless a kind of barometer through which we can visualize the degree of anti-capitalism in the movement. Anti-capitalism no longer reflects only the place that one occupies in society—worker, peasant, Indian, etc.—or the program that advances it, or declarations of intent, or the intensity of the demonstrations; it also comes from *this kind of practice, from the character of the social bonds among activists.*

There are many political leaders and academics that argue that the social movements suffer from fragmentation and dispersion. Both these "problems" should be overcome, they assert, through centralization and unification.

However, we should applaud the fact the movements have not "fallen" into some kind of centralized structure.

Unstructured, non-unified movements have repeatedly demonstrated their capacity to bring down governments, liberating large zones and regions from the state, creating different forms of life, and undertaking crucial daily battles for the survival of the oppressed. I contend that social change—the creation and recreation of the social bond—does not need structure or unification. Indeed, emancipatory social change runs counter to the structures advanced by the state, academia, and political parties.

We must consider the meaning of dispersal or fragmentation. What assumptions are implicit in our argument when we make this claim about a movement? To claim that a movement, a social subject, or a society is fragmented implies looking at it from a state-centered perspective, which presupposes the homogeneity of the social and therefore of the subject. Moreover, it presumes that to be the subject involves a degree of non-fragmentation. It assumes that the state, academia, and political parties already know why the subjects exist and that they can define when they exist and when they do not.

Second, proponents of structuring movements—generally, those who argue for the centrality of state politics—fail to take stock of the last hundred years of the labor and socialist movement. An overview can be summarized thus: "A controlled and organized transition tending to involve some continuity of exploitation" (Wallerstein 1998, 186). To repeat, this is not a theory, but only a reading of a hundred years of socialism.

Nevertheless, the left and academics assure us there is not the slightest chance of victory without structure, or that the movement's triumphs will be ephemeral and that any disarticulated or fragmented movement marches toward its own certain defeat. This type of argument brings us back to major questions about the course of the twentieth century. Was it not the unification and centralization of past movements that allowed the state and capital to neutralize them? Furthermore, how does one explain popular rebellions in Latin America, at least since the Venezuelan Caracazo in 1989, that achieved very important victories without being formally organized?

However, coordination does exist in practice. All movements tend to have more or less stable links with related groups and collectives. And these are not only links created by militants—there are links in everyday life, in the daily reality of peoples' lives. Broadly speaking, I think it is possible to distinguish two types of coordination:

One is *external* and born of necessities outside the movement. This refers to the perspective of political parties and academics who contend that the movement needs a unified and centralized structure or a network of networks to be complete. This other structure is imposed on the existing one, squashing it. This kind of external structure always seeks to link the movement to the state or with political parties, and in the process, the movement loses its autonomy. Daniel Bensaid, invoking Laclau and Žižek, points out that "the political struggle does not dissolve in the social movement" (Bensaid 2005).

We might ask about the coordination of the December 19/20, 2001 rebellion in Argentina, the April 2003 popular uprising in Venezuela organized to reverse the coup against Hugo Chávez, and the popular uprisings in Bolivia in 2003 and in 2005. If we are honest, we must reply that we do not know. However, dwelling on this question is far more productive than picking from the gallery of ready-made answers drawn from the academy and political parties.

On the other hand, the movement constitutes types of *internal* coordination in order to meet objectives that, once these goals are met, stop working or give way to other forms of coordination. Although these structures of organization may be more or less lasting, their relative permanence is not necessarily a virtue.

Writing about the October uprising of 2003, Silvia Rivera emphasizes the role that women played and how they morally defeated the army (2004). She points out how the women were capable of "organizing in minute detail the daily quota of rage, by converting the private matter of consumption into a public issue, by making their rumor-mongering arts into a game that would 'destabilize' the repression." Rivera further points out that while the uprising was led by indigenous women and youth, when the debate about solutions arose, "male voices, western and articulate," became prominent. Nevertheless, this "democracy of the women and men from below" that organized the insurrection "is lost again in the *manqhapacha* [internal space-time], returning to the languages of symbol and ancestral idioms" (2004).

I contend that only by paying attention to fleeting insurrectionary moments—when the unfeasible becomes visible for a moment, like lightning illuminating the night sky—can we attempt to understand the world of those from below. On the other hand, I think we have given scarce attention to "abnormal" cases, those that challenge prevailing norms, as if they were somehow exotic, even though if looking at our Latin American reality demonstrates that they are much more common than those we can consider "normal." Leftwing parties and academics interested in the social movement continue to uphold the supposed centrality of the political and assert that the absence of "a detailed plan" (as Ranajit Guha, a historian of subaltern groups, notes), and therefore a direction, shows that the movement is in some way non-political. Why neglect the "rumor-mongering arts" and "the interior space-time" of women and young people and grant them a lower political status in relation to the space-time of professional politicians? Is it not time to change our perspective and focus our attention on dynamics that escape academic conceptualization but clearly have the potential to change the world?

Difficulties and Limits

When we speak of the difficulties or the limits that movements encounter, we often think of the need to confront external problems: the state, capital, political isolation, organizational weakness vis-à-vis enemies, the fragmentation and dispersion of the struggles, and so on. However, the concept of limits implies that limitations are primarily internal.

What are the main difficulties that movements experience? I will concentrate on just a few, aware that they are not the only ones:

Excessive visibility. There is a belief that a movement will be more efficient if it is more visible, because it will be able to reach a larger population. However, this makes it more dependent on the space-time agenda of the system and more vulnerable in its early years, when it is weaker and has fewer defenses. For this very reason, the Zapatistas needed ten years gestation before appearing in public.

On the other hand, excessive visibility tends to lead to the situation in which movements see themselves through the eyes of the "lord." This has always been a problem for the dominated: the lack of autonomy—with respect to cosmovision as well—is closely related to the movement's inability to set its own priorities and its dependence on the established agenda.

Intensification/expansion. Another common sense affirmation says that the way to extend a movement's influence is through coordination and organization and the formulation of a common program. This promises the largest possible mobilization.

However, in the light of the principal social struggles of the past fifteen years (the Caracazo, etc.) we can say *we do not know how a movement produces and generalizes itself.*

I think the movement needs to expand its action to change the balance of power, but reality indicates that what really produces change is the intensification of experiences. And that intensification—making them more profound—can hopefully resonate within other people and thus help the movement expand. But of course it is not enough to merely wish for the expansion of a movement for it to happen. There needs to be more. Nevertheless, no matter how well things are planned or how rigorous the analysis behind the action, the cause and effect relation does not function in the social realm, and we should be thinking seriously about why this is failing.

"To organize rebellion" is a contradiction in terms—to organize means to impose order, to discipline, to institute. This runs counter to rebellion; when an action is ordered, it is no longer rebellion. This is one of the most serious problems for anti-systemic movements. Many scholars have pointed out that the more organized a movement is, the less it is able to mobilize and vice versa.

Although we do not know how to solve this dilemma, we should take two things into account: First, we should not deny it, and second, we need to expand the concept of organization and recognize that chaos is also a form of organization.

Finally, I would emphasize that it is problematic when a movement lacks structure. While non-capitalist social relations are not created beginning from an articulation, it is nevertheless necessary to defend and protect what has been created. I believe it is useful to understand articulation in the sense that a seed must be protected as it germinates—that is, to protect is not to create, it is not the articulation that creates the new world, but it helps it to survive until it can be born.

As we all know, the problem is that the articulations, or structures that we are familiar with (Communist Parties, one-party party, etc.) not only have not protected the new world but in reality have prevented it from being born, aborted it, or acted as its grave diggers. In my view, the drama of the twentieth century can be summed up in the Soviet or Chinese experience.

Therefore the debate about articulation/structure should focus on avoiding centralization and unification; avoiding converting the structures and or diffuse or informal networks into *apparatuses with their own life*; strengthening the new world that is born in the movements.

These problems have no easy answers. Looking at the current state of the development of the social movement, I think it would be a decisive step forward if truly alternative social relationships could be created. Creating non-capitalist relations in the movement—in schools, bakeries, health sites, or free radio stations—is an area in which we have less experience and *where we have historically failed*.

Secondly, it seems necessary to create temporary and horizontal spaces for the exchange and sharing of knowledge regarding alternative experiences. The circulation (a better term than "communication") of experiences within the movement is important.

Instead of focusing our attention and our activity on the state, political parties, and capital, and so on, it is better to focus on the experiences that create new social ties. This needs to be our central concern. The key to our struggle is to look within, to grow inside, and thus to create the new world. To resist and struggle in this day and age is fundamentally about creating those ties and thus a new, "other," world.

On the question of structure, it may be useful to reflect on a meeting that Colectivo Situaciones[11] and MTD-Solano organized on this topic in which the idea of a diffuse network is brought up:

> The diffuse network allows for the many different types of encounters, many partial or explicit, bound, or over-lapping networks, each with different modes of articulation and coordination; in the end, many networks in formation can open the experience in question. In this regard, it is essential not to be trapped within one single core network, one that would tend to organize and hierarchize the multiplicity of the different experiences that we are opening up.... When one of these structured networks claims to be "the" strategic network, the one that organizes all the others, so begins a process of centralization and hierarchy that excludes networks and situations that are not subordinated to it (MTD Solano and Colectivo Situations 2002, 220–222).

Revolution and Social Change

It seems useful and even necessary to proceed with some hypotheses about social change without attempting to configure a closed, finished social theory—hypotheses based on assumptions and beliefs about how to change the world. Intuitions are also useful—intuitions born and fed off social action and the reflections of those who want to change the world without asking permission to do so.

Movements produce change not only because they change the balance of power within society but also because they weave social ties that are born and grow and germinate

---

11   Colectivo Situaciones is an autonomous group of political actors and theorists from Argentina.

and become the mortar of the new world—not the new world itself, but the seeds of that world.

Referring to the Paris Commune, Marx said the following about social change and revolution:

> The workers have no ready-made utopias to introduce *par decret du peuple* (by decree of the people). The workers know that in order to work out their own emancipation, and along with it that higher form to which present society is irresistibly tending by its own economical agencies.... They have no ideals to realize, but to set free the elements of the new society with which the old collapsing bourgeois society itself is pregnant (Marx 1980).

To set free means "to liberate." Marx's hypothesis about revolution—which some elevate to the rank of "revolutionary theory"—is that revolution is an act of force, similar to giving birth, and what it gives birth to are "the elements of the new society" that already exist in bourgeois society. To visualize the revolution as a birth—as a setting free, as a liberation— signifies two things: that social relationships already exist among workers that negate capitalism; and secondly, that the revolution does not create the new world, but gives birth to it.

In short, Marx never believed that the state could create this new world but, at most, that the state machinery destroyed and reconfigured by workers could be used as a kind of forceps, a device to help give birth to the new world and new social relations struggling to emerge.

The Zapatistas also asserted that the state does not construct the new world when they stated that their goal is to change the world, not to take power. I contend that this is an idea born of social practice and not the result of abstract theoretical reasoning. In fact, this Zapatista proposal is spreading fast among various social movements, especially those who act and think for themselves, autonomous from the state and the political parties. The coordinator of the MST, Joao Pedro Stédile, told the recent Social Forum in Porto Alegre, "The question of power is not resolved by taking the government palace—which is the easiest solution and has been done many times—but by transforming social relations." I use the MST as an example because it is has huge differences from the Zapatistas, but also has something very important in common: It is changing the world from below.

Collective De-alienations[12]

Up to now we have only mentioned a few aspects of the everyday experiences of various movements, without describing them in detail and without addressing the question of their limits or shortcomings. Critics wary of the movements' "spontaneity" and "incompleteness" see these limits as one of their greatest "sins." What is the goal of this approach to critique? What kind of methodology do critics employ that allows them not to analyze but to merely describe? How is it that instead of rigorously examining the limitations, they are content to merely present them? Before addressing these issues, it is worth taking the following points into account:

First of all, I do not intend to establish new theories or alternative methodologies. Far from trying to fill in gaps in classical revolutionary theory and critical theories, formulating "better" or more accurate ones, the response I will give to the criticism outlined in the opening paragraph heads in a different direction. I will try to reveal the aspects of social practices that demonstrate emancipatory sensibilities, with the conviction that emancipation is always, as with any process, an incomplete process: an uncertain road, a journey that never reaches its destination. Why? Because emancipation is not an objective but a way of life.

Still, it can be rightly said that emancipatory practices have their limits. This is true. But where do we set their limits?

---

12 This text was originally published as part of the article, "La emancipación como producción de vínculos," by Raúl Zibechi, published in Ana Esther Ceceña's, *Los desafíos de las emancipaciones en un contexto militarizado*, Clacso: Buenos Aires, 2006.

And who fixes them? An external agent? The party? The state? The academy? I do not want to overlook the fact that emancipatory practices, which exist mainly in social movements and, in my opinion, always outside the institutional framework, are often partial, incomplete, and reversible: they do not offer any guarantee of continuity or permanent expansion and growth. This is so, and this is a general limitation of the human species, or life. There are no guarantees. But we are on the wrong path if we seek assurances from the state, political parties, or academic theory, because the space for emancipatory practices is not to be found there.

What can we do faced with the "limits" of these social practices? I can think of nothing better than to strengthen them, intensify them, fertilize them so that they may be more emancipatory, *to use these very practices to shatter their limits from within*. I know this may seem insufficient, but I see no other emancipatory alternative.

This brings me to the second question, which is "methodological." We strengthen and expand social movements by understanding the meaning of the actual social practices, of the "historical movement that is unfolding before our eyes" (Marx). Understanding is a creative act, as Keyserling notes. Creation is a social practice, individually and collectively, which implies going beyond what exists. Creating is also a poetic act (from the Greek *poieo*, which means "to create," but also *kreas*, which means "flesh"—in short, the biblical "to create the flesh"), fundamental (to go to the bottom, deep), generous, and uncertain.

But the process of understanding is a form of action; one understands only what one lives. Hence we can only understand the meaning of social practices *in* and *with* them—from within. This presents a fundamental epistemological problem for established theory. This is not a new discovery, but a simple return to Marx's famous eleventh thesis.

Within the movements, the fabric of the tapestry of the "other" world are social relations that facilitate learning, healing, and production, without reproducing the molds of the system. These relationships are part of the emancipatory climate, which is conducive to the construction of the new world. While the system separates, splits, and fragments, we can say, paraphrasing Subcomandante Marcos, that the movements build, bring together, include, and remember.[13] Transmuting death into life can only be done by enhancing the capabilities buried within the people. And this, I argue, is precisely what some movements are doing in their territories, albeit in different, even contradictory ways, and almost always groping, because there are no recipes or working models for this endeavor.

New ways of thinking emerge from this other world. Up to now, the production of theory was undertaken by agencies of the state, the academy, and political parties. Now the movement itself produces theories that are embodied in non-capitalist social relations. This, in my view, is an epistemic turn and represents a difficult challenge for us in the movement.

The emergence of new subjects constituted in the social margins, the so-called excluded, turns upside down the knowledge and practice of the specialists. This is especially true for those specialists who believe that the knowledge of the "other," whether it is Indians, peasants, or the poor, "was not only considered irrelevant, but also as one of the obstacles to the transformational task of development" (Lander 2000, 31).

When these "obstacles" become subjects, and begin to change the course of history and produce forms of knowledge that call into question the monopoly of the specialists—when the "objects" become subjects—then the established powers face a dilemma.

The specialists can either deny the new reality or accept the birth of a different but no less important epistemic subject, which inevitably leads to a loss of their power and privilege. It comes as no surprise that the social sciences were "founded in Europe during the eighteenth and nineteenth centuries,

---

13 "This country is lucky. Where others destroy, the indigenous construct. Where others separate, they bring together. Where others exclude, they include. Where others forget, they remember. Where some are a burden for others, here they take the burden of among other things, of our own history. And the EZLN is lucky to have been taken on by these people." Subcomandante Marcos, 2004.

mainly to support and strengthen the construction of nation-states" (Walsh 2004b).

The movements call into question what is perhaps modernity's most perverse heritage: the subject-object relation. This relationship is a colonial imposition in Latin America and probably all over the Third World, part of "the coloniality of power" that classifies and ranks differences (Quijano 2000). It simultaneously determines the epistemic place from which it enunciates and legitimizes the colonial power. The debate about the coloniality of knowledge and power (Lander 2000; Mignolo 2003) is of particular importance here given that neoliberalism has introduced a sort of re-colonization of our societies. Under neoliberalism, large sections of the working class that were integrated during the period of the welfare state have since been excluded, thereby joining historically excluded sectors (Indians, African Americans, etc).

In fact, the original cultures did not know the subject-object relation because their cosmovision was based on inter-subjective relations, in which all are subjects: the plurality of subjects is their most outstanding characteristic (Lenkersdorf 1996). Among the urban popular sector, or at least among the "excluded," ways of life are organized around "convivial" relations, in which the relational aspect is the determining factor; one "cannot be understood as an individual—and to think and characterize them as such is a fiction elaborated from outside—but as a relationship that is happening or just taking place" (Moreno 2000, 171).

What is new is that the "subaltern" is being constructed as a cultural, political, and theoretical subject. I would like to emphasize *how* new ideas are produced in the movements, because these processes illuminate the type of relationships that are being born and also reveal their opposite: the relations of domination/subordination imposed by colonialism and reinforced by neoliberalism.

This theoretical activity not only emerges from different places of enunciation and different subjects, but also bears different assumptions that disrupt the fundamental distinctions of state-centered Western thought: subject-object, rationality-emotions, science-myth, past-present, and so on. In general, the new thinking is the product of a series of exchanges produced in situations of poverty and exclusion. The physical place is on the margins of capitalist space and the social place is in the subterranean level of society: rural areas or on the peripheries of cities, the weak links in the chains of colonialism, or, in Mignolo's words, "anti-neoliberal concentration zones" (Walsh 2004a).

The new movements *approach the question of knowledge through their own ethical assumptions.* Bolivian Aymara anthropologist Silvia Rivera states that "knowledge, fetishized and turned into an instrument of prestige and power, can tip against the needs and interests of the community studied, and the researcher can become an unconscious agent of their defeat or disintegration" (Rivera 1990). The author goes even further when asserting that revealing the secrets of the "other"—not only the Indian but also of any subaltern group of society—can be such a severe transgression that it can be considered "the equivalent of treason."

What is demanded is that the research have a commitment to the excluded, not as a consequence of an asymmetrical relationship (it does not matter whether the researcher is from the academy or a political party) but as a relation among equals. This is the true meaning of intercultural relations, when a commitment to the poor takes priority over questions of method and discipline. Rivera addresses this in a discussion about the epistemic potential of oral history and the interaction between the researcher and his or her subject:

> Oral history in this context is, therefore, much more than a "participatory" methodology or an "action": it is an exercise in collective de-alienation, as much for the researcher as for his or her subject. The results will be much richer if, during this process, efforts of conscious interaction are made between the different sectors and the exercise is conducted on the basis of mutual recognition and honesty about each ones place in the "colonial chain."... Therefore, recuperating the cognitive

status of human experience, the systematic process takes the form of a dialectical synthesis between two (or more) *active* poles of reflection and conceptualization, and not between a "cognoscente ego" and a "passive other," but between two subjects that are reflecting together on their experience and the vision that each has of the other (Rivera 1990).

It speaks to the needs of the social movement when the educator or researcher defines the agenda of popular education and research.

However, more is required of the educator, researcher, or activist than just commitment—it is necessary "to subject oneself to the social control of the community being 'investigated'" (Rivera 1990). Commitment, which is often an instrumental relation, gives way to an affective link that allows the movement to control the researcher.

So we come to a crossroads: "Is an investigation possible that does not unleash a process of *falling in love*? How could a link between two experiences be possible without a strong sense of *love* or *friendship*?" (MTD Solano and Colectivo Situations 2002, 15).

We are witnessing the reversal of the process in which the militant investigator remains immune to "contact" with the movement for the sake of political purity or scientific objectivity. And, fortunately, such experiences are increasingly common. Perhaps the best known case is that of rebel insurgent Subcomandante Marcos and the group of militants that went with him into the Lacandon jungle. The road they traveled is not very different from that of the catechists of the diocese of San Cristóbal de las Casas and Bishop Samuel Ruiz himself. The indigenous communities transformed them over time. Indeed, for the Zapatistas, the decisive factor is not who is talking but "from where it is spoken" (Subcomandante Marcos 2004).

The Zapatista slogan, "asking we walk," can be read *in* movement, emphasizing the interplay of both terms. We walk because we are in movement and we can only but ask questions while moving, or resisting. But in turn we are asking, which suggests the existence of a plurality of voices and subjects that displaces relations of power and appeals to the *how* of the political (Holloway 1997). However, it is necessary to go one step further, because asking *in* movement also implies answers *in* movement. In my view, this indicates that the movement is the determining factor, which would be in line with Marcos's affirmation in the sense that the most important thing is the "from where" it is spoken. The answer is *in* movement.

This does not refer to a place, like a political party or the academy, or a movement understood as an institution, but *in* movement, in resistance. And this is how the new subjects develop theory, the Zapatistas say.

In Argentina, Colectivo Situaciones and the MTD Solano have developed the concept of "the militant researcher." This is being part of the social movement—not just integrating into the organization, but participating in the disengagement or place shifting that the whole movement pursues, an act of moving-oneself that captures and reconfigures. This also presents a new kind of challenge. People do not emerge from the margins to think and act like the "included" think and act. The new subjects—Indian movements, the landless movement, the piqueteros, etc—do not continue the uninterrupted march of labor, farmers, or student movements of the sixties. They have no proposals to resume the tasks interrupted by the dictatorships. They are the result of other genealogies that take them on another path, their own path, one that is different from those preceding it.

Those paths of the new movements strive to make intercultural learning an art of understanding and translation, allowing us to fertilize our thoughts with different agendas, arising from different cosmovisions that are not intended to be all embracing, but rather local experiences that are just as important as those considered "central." One of the theoretical challenges that arises from the margins pertains to the concept of synthesis—a colonial inheritance, in my view— which is always exclusive and flattens differences. Synthesis,

II
Latin America in Movement

6
Subterranean Echoes: Political Resistance from Below

The insurgency was a conscious initiative of the rural masses. The conscious aspect, however, seems to have received little attention in the literature on this subject. The omission is hidden in most accounts behind metaphors that treat peasant revolts as natural phenomena.... Alternatively, there is an attempt to explain the cause of the rebellion as a kind of automatic response. In either case, the insurgency is considered something external to peasant consciousness, and the Cause is presented as a ghost of Reason.

Ranajit Guha

It is a regrettable characteristic of the Western mind to relate expressions and actions to exterior or transcendent ends, instead of evaluating them on a plane of consistency on the basis of their intrinsic value.

Gilles Deleuze and Félix Guattari

In the last fifteen years in Latin America, the movements capable of challenging the system—launching revolts, uprisings, and mobilizations that threaten elite domination—have been born on the "margins" of society and have been led by the poorest, by those deprived of social and political rights. The movements of those "without"—without homes, without land, without work, without rights—have such vigor that they have leaped to the center of the political stage.

These new protagonists have displaced the union movements in many countries from their traditional leading role as a force for social transformation. But the current movements have also displaced the left, especially during the moments of extreme crisis that occurred when the neoliberal model started to break up. This was seen quite clearly in the revolts in Argentina (between 1997 and December 2001) and Bolivia (September–October 2003), and also in incipient form during the crisis in Uruguay in the winter of 2002. In all these cases, the poorest sectors reacted to the passivity of the union movement by undertaking widespread looting.

These new actors have also been at the center of profound upheavals in other countries, notably Ecuador, Venezuela, Paraguay, and Mexico. In Brazil "the excluded" (landless, and to a lesser extent, homeless) have mounted serious challenges to successive governments, including that led by Luiz Inácio Lula da Silva. What is certain is that the new protagonists— which include some more traditional but revitalized oppositional forces along with the new poor produced by neoliberalism—have succeeded in changing the social and political map of the continent, putting the neoliberal model on the defensive for the first time.

Finally, as shown by the insurrections in Argentina and Bolivia and by the mobilizations in Peru, Venezuela, and Ecuador, there is a new urban activism in big cities, which had previously been sites of acquiescence to the neoliberal model. In the early nineties, resistance came from rural areas and small towns, where the social structure making resistance possible had not been dismantled, but more recent urban uprisings indicate that opposition now emerges from sectors that are more heterogenous than the traditional working class.

That this set of challenges has emerged from the "margins" (or from the basement of society invoked by Subcomandante Marcos) has profound implications for social and political change.[1] On the one hand, the current movements have created new spaces of organization and resistance—the Caracoles, ethnic territories, Aymara headquarters—that are essentially autonomous territories, whether they define

---

1   I use the words "margins" and "marginality" in a merely descriptive sense. The term "exclusion" refers to persons or social sectors that were not granted social rights within the welfare state.

themselves as such or not.[2] But these spaces are no longer limited to rural areas, as evidenced by the profound urban transformations that the poor have created in the Aymara city of El Alto and in settlements in cities such as Buenos Aires, Montevideo, and Asunción (to mention just those in the Southern Cone).

Who are these new protagonists? How have they moved from apparent passivity to shaping their own lives and challenging the powerful? Is this a third wave of movements? A new category of activism from the poor and marginalized?

These new actors not only challenge the state and the dominant classes, but also call into question the political and theoretical framework of the old left and that characteristic of the "new social movements" (despite sharing traits with the latter). They pose important questions about the future of social struggles. The welfare state and import-substitution industrialization allowed for the creation of a broad, well-organized union movement, in which left-wing parties had an active presence. The unitary, centralizing logic of the state inspired the structure of these groups; they saw the state as the point of reference, object, and target of their action. They used forms of struggle intended to increase their bargaining power (primarily strikes and demonstrations); this enabled them to organize workers on the basis of class solidarity and encouraged the birth of a pattern of instrumental action that produced good results.

What forms of organization and action are emerging in this new period? How will the new protagonists relate to the state and to left-wing parties? Will they give priority, as did the workers' movement, to fighting to install governments sympathetic to their interests? Will they become institutionalized? In short, what is, or will be, the politics of those on the margins of the system, the "non-taylorized"? And, to pose an even more unsettling question, what kind of politics can be pursued in fragmented societies, with nation-states in decline and for subjects on the margins of society?

---

2   On the "ethnic territories" in Ecuador, see Ramón Valarezo (1993); on the Aymara barracks, see Patzi (2003).

Only time and the intensification of social action can answer these questions. I only hope to show their relevance and that the new forms of struggle will not necessarily be "carbon copies" of those that the left and the union movement employed in the sixties. We have seen the possibility of a different path for the Zapatista communities in Chiapas[3] and, to a lesser extent, for the indigenous movements on our continent, but not yet for the new actors in the cities.

Underlying all this, perhaps little is new. Nevertheless, we are wittnessing a crisis of the states and ruling circles and the strengthening of social movements—in short, "the breaking up of the system, combined with subaltern insurgencies, bring to light the accumulation of underground forces" that were invisible up until recently (Hylton and Thomson 2003, 17).

The Creation of Spaces

We are moving toward a new relationship between people and territories. In the period of hegemony of the workers' movement, the concept of territory was vague in contrast to the centrality of production relations. Class distinctions seemed to dissolve outside the factory, and the idea of working-class power would have been incomprensible without certain counter-hegemonic bastions in the peripheries of the large cities, where workshops and communities were tightly linked (Lojkine 1988). At the same time, the discourse of equality— woven with threads of citizenship that the welfare state offered in exchange for recognition of its legitimacy—hid a reality of latent (and disguised) differences that today emerge with their full disintegrative effect.

However, profound changes occurred in the territorial basis of national states, local industries, and the classes that supported them. Capital flight led to massive emigration within national boundaries and particularly within the different urban networks, be it among cities or even within the same city.

In any case, and this is one of the most notable changes that have occurred in Latin America: The power emerging in

---

3   Subcomandante Marcos's text "Un mundo nuevo" is a good summary of the Zapatista responses to these questions.

the new insurgent bastions does not appear to be connected to the factory or the municipality, which, although shaped in part by the new subjects, does not wish to integrate them and can no longer represent them, seeking at best to neutralize them through clientelism.

The new relationships between territory and subject emerge from the prior deterritorialization, which represents a wound in the urban fabric. Capital flight is simultaneously a flight from the spaces in which the working class constrained capital's power, and it leaves devastation in its wake, because "capital, by its nature, creates physical environments in its own image for the sole purpose of destroying them afterward, when it seeks temporary geographic expansion and displacement, in an attempt to resolve the crises of overaccumulation which affect it on a cyclical basis" (Harvey 2004). In Latin America, this devastation takes the form of unemployment, extreme poverty, and the out-and-out expulsion of millions of workers from the city into inhospitable, fetid, often flood-prone outskirts. In the Southern Cone, we have three relatively recent examples: the expulsion of 200,000 poor from the city of Buenos Aires to the periphery in 1977 by the military dictatorship; the expulsion of 24,000 miners and their families in 1985 in Bolivia, some of whom ended up in the city of El Alto and some, after an extensive journey, in El Chapare as coca farmers; and the expulsion, over two decades, of 17 percent of the population of Montevideo from their old working- and middle-class neighborhoods to the periphery, where 280,000 unemployed and under-employed live in shanty towns. From the integrated city to the segregated city.

However, the habitat is the space that grounds culture— "where the social subjects are formed who shape the geographic space, appropriating it, endowing it with their meanings and practices, their senses and sensibilities, with their tastes and pleasures" (Leff 1998, 241). The spatial fracturing represents a cultural fracturing based on pre-existing differences, a matter that is of particular importance in countries once believed to be relatively homogenous such as Argentina, Chile, and Uruguay. Now we discover that their supposed social homogeneity concealed, under the mantle of a generic working-class culture, a certain "extra something" that turns out to be similarly fragmented. Thus, what European and North American "social history" told us about "working-class culture" could not account for the peculiarities and differences of the working classes in this part of the south.[4]

And what happens to the subjects who are formed in the segregated territories? Reflecting on the *Seringueiros,*[5] Porto Gonçalves notes astutely that "new subjects emerge by instituting new territorialities" (2001, 208), a relevant consideration provided we recognize that we are talking not only of other territories but also of other subjects—not the same subjects in a different form, changed to suit the new spaces and strategies for survival.

Non-citizens—those stripped of their citizenship in neoliberal society—are opening up their own spaces in a process of struggle in which they develop as subjects; spaces that they create, design, and control. Understanding this requires reversing one's perspective: rejecting the negative and state-centered viewpoint—that defines people by what they lack—and adopting another way of looking that starts with the differences that they have created in order then to visualize other possible paths. In this sense, the urban poor become part of the experience already lived by the rural poor—both Indians and landless peasants—who in a prolonged process of struggle have created or broadened their spaces, seizing millions of hectares from landowners, and consolidated spaces that they already had (in the case of the Indian communities) by recovering control over their own communities.

---

4   What is certain is that, as E.P. Thompson and other social historians have pointed out, cultural homogeneity never existed. But now we face an even bigger problem. The changes that have taken place in our societies are of such scope that traditional social history (working-class history, basically) cannot comprehend them. Everything indicates that we must now turn—even in countries and regions where the original populations have almost disappeared—to so-called "subaltern studies," since the complexity of a society fragmented by "neocolonialization" calls for more appropriate analytic instruments than the ones we have been using up to now, at least in the Río de la Plata region.

5   Translator's note: *Seringueiros* is Portuguese for the itinerant rubber tappers in Brazil's Amazon forest.

The occupants have created forms of organization close-ly tied to territory: the basic unit for day-to-day purposes is the block [*manzana*], which elects a person responsible, or *manzanero*; the *manzaneros* meet as a body of delegates who then elect an executive committee. All the people in the settle-ment gather to decide the most important issues. This type of organization involves "the existence of a whole communi-tarian movement where domestic life seemed to merge with the community" (Merklen 1995). In this respect, the new ur-ban movements are in tune with the indigenous and landless movements, operating with a very different logic from that of narrow, interest-based workers' associations.

The challenges to the system are unthinkable without spaces beyond the control of the powerful. According to James Scott, the first condition for the subordinate groups to speak openly is "a separate social space where neither con-trol, surveillance nor repression by the dominant forces can reach" (Scott 2000, 149). The spaces controlled by the op-pressed are always "far from," which guarantees a certain au-tonomy; they emerge and grow in "the weak links of a chain of socialization" (52).

Until a few years ago, Indians were the only social sec-tor to enjoy autonomously controlled spaces, particularly after consumerist society destroyed or disfigured classic working-class spaces like the tavern, and after industrial reorganization neutralized opportunities for communication at the work-place. However, the violent shocks caused by neoliberalism, particularly the accelerated internal migration during the last two decades, have created new rifts and fissures, in which the poor have been able to create new forms of sociability and resistance.

Many of the recent challenges to neoliberalism have emerged from the "new" territories, which are uniquely au-tonomous and independent: El Alto in Bolivia; the neighbor-hoods and settlements of the unemployed in Argentina; the camps and settlements of the landless in Brazil; the popular neighborhoods in Caracas, and the indigenous regions in Chiapas, Bolivia, and Ecuador. Later we will see that the crisis of the old territorialities implies an equal crisis in the systems of representation.

(Self)-Affirmation Through Difference

We know that there are no subjects or social movements or social change without difference. In this period of capitalism, the dynamics of class struggles seem to have been inverted. In the period of the welfare state, the struggles had an integrative effect because, independently of any concrete demands that might be raised, the model of development could offer a place to popular sectors. In that period, it was unthinkable to struggle without making demands on the state. The unions, with their state-centric structures, their rules and forms of representative democracy, reinforced that tendency, and the impoverished and excluded learned to act as citizens. By contrast, in the present exclusionary period of capitalism, the social struggle of the marginalized tends to reinforce difference.

The distance between the old worker and unionist movement and the current actors has two distinct dimensions: the relationship to territory and the relationship to reproduction. The first entails a progression from external control [*heteronomía*] to relative autonomy, as evidenced in the insurrectionary moments. The second, intimately connected to the former, involves a transition on the part of the subjects from dependence on capital to control over the production and reproduction of their living conditions. Both involve a Copernican shift in the urban social movement and constitute the main difference between Latin American movements and those in the First World (Zibechi 2003a).

The territorial foundation of the new movements accounts for a number of their characteristics. One of the most notable is that "space is the site *par excellence* for difference" (Porto 2001, 45). Different uses of spaces produce different situations. In opposition to the older city controlled by capital, where the design and construction of the working-class neighborhoods is directed by the state or through private initiative (with spaces for living, socializing, and leisure governed by the rhythms of manufacturing and the logic of accumulation), now there is a new city produced by the disengagement-movement-flight of a significant portion of the working class toward spaces outside the control of capital, or at least where capital has a limited and distant presence.

Although such settlements tend to reproduce the structure of the consolidated city, they have unique characteristics, the most notable being that they have constructed their own habitat, from homes to public spaces and streets. Here there are a range of distinct features: from the spaces within the home (with a large, central family area) compared to the classic working-class home (inspired by the functionality of small compartmentalized rooms, just like in middle-class homes), to the urban and architectural peculiarities in cities such as El Alto, where there was the birth of a mestizo, Baroque style that some architects call "postmodern Baroque" (Limpias 2002). The very design of the new settlements, where single-story dwellings dominate, reveals an important difference from the big city: "While some huddle and pile together uncomfortably, others spread out generously. This difference marks different paths in urbanism, architecture, and culture" (2002).

In short, concentration versus dispersion. The "dispersed" use of space offers the new subjects other possibilities. Among the most important of these is the prevention of panoptic control (which requires a certain degree of concentration of the population).[6] While the city constructed in the image of capital—following the logic of concentration—negates the autonomy of the subjects, the dispersed city opens itself up to difference; but it is a difference rooted in social ties of a communitarian character (going beyond the traditional meaning of community). In any case, the territory enables a convergence of difference with communitarian ties that may turn—particularly during moments of rebellion—into an exclusive (and exclusionary) political unity (Clastres 2003, 43–45).

---

6   During the Bolivian insurrection of October 2003, the rebels destroyed pedestrian overpasses from which the military surveilled and fired on the population. To control the settlements—flat spaces spread out over wide areas—authorities must now gain entry into the barrio, as there are no longer any "high points" from which they can keep watch.

This is one of the reasons why the Argentine and Uruguayan states sought to undermine the kind of exclusionary territoriality successfully deployed in El Alto. The settlements and poor neighborhoods on the periphery of Buenos Aires were subject to a police operation during the rebellion of December 19–20, 2001, intended to pit one neighborhood against another, spreading rumors through local leaders or directly through the police. The same was done in Montevideo July 31–August 1, 2002, at the peak of the financial and social crisis. I want to stress that subjects act by affirming and building on their differences. If the workers' movement negated difference ("externally," by converting the worker into a citizen, and "internally," by reproducing the centralist, unitary logic of the capitalist state within their organizations), the new subjects reject both attitudes. The trajectory has also been different: Worker resistance within the workplace neutralized Taylorism and dissolved it as a system of production and control; the consequent flight of capital reflected the workers' insubordination, or flight from capitalist relations of production. This gave rise to a parallel dissolution of all spheres of control and discipline, from the family to the school. The destruction of the spaces created by capital, which caused its flight (Harvey 2004), freed the terrain for new forms of appropriation by the rebels, which meant a transition from the struggle for land (understood as an exchange value and means of production) to the struggle to affirm a territoriality (territory as use value, as space to establish a culture). This re-territorialization, however, is not produced on the same bases but comes about in the opposite manner: It comes from within the subjects in formation, the bearers of an "other" culture/way of life, which is forged in the process of resistance and insubordination.

The groups that emerge as movements do so by building new political and cultural identities. In this sense, the term "social movement" should be understood as a rejection of an assigned or imposed place in society—as a change in social place, as a sliding, in the strict sense, that causes "geography and sociology to mix" (Porto 2001, 198). But if a class is, as E.P. Thompson notes, a set of historical relations, those "changes of place" implicitly involve changes in relations. Thus, the different relation to territory contributes to generating, in each case, different subjects. But these subjects affirm their differences, which leads—not in a linear but in a circular fashion—to increases in difference over time. The struggle is, therefore, different from the worker/union struggle, and in the deepest sense: the struggle is by and for the defense and strengthening of difference.

Producing their livelihood in the territories signals a second radical break from the industrial past. For the first time, popular sectors have erected a set of independently controlled forms of production in an urban space. Although these remain connected to and dependent on the market, vast sectors now control their forms and rhythms of production and are no longer dominated by the rhythms of capital and its division of labor.

The new poor initially concentrated their survival strategies on services—recycling materials discarded by consumer society or setting up small or family-owned retail shops in unused areas—but gradually started manufacturing. El Alto must be one of the most carefully analyzed cities by the state and non-governmental organizations: 70 percent of the working population is engaged in family (50 percent) or semi-entrepreneurial (20 percent) undertakings.[7] This type of undertaking predominates in the sales or restaurant sector (95 percent of those employed in that sector), followed by construction (80 percent), and manufacturing (75 percent). Young people predominate in these sectors: More than half of the employees in manufacturing are between the ages of twenty and thirty-five, with women being the overwhelming majority in retailing and restaurants in the family and semi-entrepreneurial categories.

In El Alto, the main protagonist in the labor market is "the family, whether as economic unit generating employment or as contributor of the greatest number of salaried workers"

---

7   Semi-entrepreneurial units have fewer than four workers, one or two of them being relatives, including the owner (who also works) and the other(s) being employees.

(Rojas and Guaygua 2003, 75). In these spaces, a "new social and labor culture" arises, marked by nomadism, instability, and changed work relations.

A qualitative investigation into the family units, where half of the active population of El Alto works, concludes that there is no separation between ownership and management. The division of labor in the workshop, even in those cases where merchandise spans various processes, is minimal; with few exceptions, all those who work can rotate without the production process being affected. In family units, non-remunerated family work predominates; in a good proportion of the cases studied, the members teach each other how to do the work and the time allocated to the task is left up to the person working, so long as deadlines for orders are met (Poveda 2003, 22f). In many cases, the study points out that some micro-businesses combine a large number of family units, but the "owner" who pays wages tends also to give the family "assistance" or "loans in times of need" (2003, 17).

Álvaro García Linera notes "a greater autonomy of work management" in these workshops, given that this is "a production activity not directly supervised by the owner" (García 1999, 118). He adds that these forms of production are non-capitalist (although "refunctionalized" by the market and capital) and insists that they are not transitory but are "the historic and medium-term form of expanded reproduction of capital in Bolivia" (201). I want to stress that the overwhelming majority of the workers in El Alto, and in the country as a whole, are not subject to the Taylorist division of labor; they control production times and practice an almost undivided organization of labor, with the possibility of rotation among the different tasks. It is this young workforce, with a high proportion of women, very poor but educated (there is only an 8 percent illiteracy rate in El Alto and 52 percent have at least one year of secondary school), with a great deal of autonomy in their work and highly integrated with the family, that was the key protagonist in the insurrection of September–October 2003.

My question is whether there is some connection between this kind of autonomous family-based work and the fact that these same sectors were capable of mounting an insurrection without leadership or leaders. The relevance of this question lies in the fact that when workers formerly left the organization of their work to employers and the management of society to the state, they had to organize with hierarchical, centralized structures and depended on their leaders—union and political—to represent them and make decisions.

The autonomy of such persons vis-à-vis capital runs in tandem with their autonomy vis-à-vis the state. In fact, they have created an impressive network of organizations to maintain basic aspects of their daily existence, from the construction and maintenance of their environment (dwellings, water and waste service, and streets) to essential aspects of education and health. In El Alto alone there are between 400 and 550 neighborhood councils, with one for every 1,000 inhabitants over the age of ten.

In this regard, the experience of Bolivia's excluded differs little from that of other countries of the continent (Zibechi 2003b). Even in a highly industrialized country like Argentina, the Central de los Trabajadores Argentinos (CTA) maintains that wage increases have reached only 19 percent of the active population, which is barely 8 percent of the total population.[8] This is why the CTA asserts that union action cannot be centered on wage issues alone: 60 percent of the active population are unemployed, self-employed, or informal unregistered wage-workers (Nochteff and Güell 2003).

The same logic of dispersion that we saw in the territorial construction of habitat operates in production. Dispersion should not be confused with decentralization, the latter being a state-based logic, which operates from the top and is external to the subjects. The logic of dispersion is an internal logic in which the sectors involved adjust their way of life by establishing a different relationship to territory. This logic suggests that, in order to survive, the subjects must

---

8   The Argentine Workers' Central Union is a trade-union federation in Argentina. It was formed in 1991 when a number of trade unions disaffiliated from the General Confederation of Labor (CGT). Though the CTA is a multitendency organization, it is led by unionists with a Social Christian viewpoint. There are also Peronists, Communists, and Trotskyists in the CTA.

deploy themselves in the territory on the basis of family/ communitarian considerations.

A series of questions still remain about how social, cultural, and economic undertakings are carried out among subjects living on the "margins" of the system. The most important factor pertains to the role of the family, particularly the new extended family. It seems clear that family-based relations structure how people produce and reproduce their lives, but they also mold the forms that collectives use to defend themselves from attacks and combat their adversaries. Do we see a new mode of domestic production here? Are there new territorialities that rely on a "domestic and productive space" (Porto 2001, 203), inducing new types of conduct in social space?

If, as I think, the latter is true, we are witnessing the creation of new situations marked by the deepening of differences. The unemployed from the popular sectors who live in urban settlements affirm their difference by turning themselves into piqueteros and later into autonomous producers. The route is very similar among other groups in the region that combine the flight from capitalist relations with the creation of relations of dispersion as a way of affirming difference.

Politics from the Margins

We have seen that during the period of industrial development, sovereign nations, welfare states, and unions occupied center stage. The social movement in that period had a unitary and centralized apparatus; it demanded rights of workers as citizens and it directed this demand at the state. The preferred forms of struggle were the strike, the demonstration, and insurrectional uprisings when the state took on dictatorial contours. The union expressed the unity of the workers against capital; class identity superimposed itself over other identities, just as national identity subsumed identities that existed within the limits of the nation-state. In short, these were societies of culturally homogenous citizens (in the official discourse at least) permeated by an irreconcilable class division that played out and dissolved in the political field.

In that supposedly integrated society, citizens spent their lives in controlled, disciplined spaces: from the patriarchal family to the school, from military service to the Taylorist-Fordist factory. Of course, not all the inhabitants were citizens but in formal terms the great majority were, while the "marginalized" were expected to at least take some initial steps along the path toward citizenship. The last two decades, as we know, have reversed this tendency, generating the exclusion of about half of the population, at least in the continent's Southern Cone. Moreover, the prospects of integration and equality have ceased to be tempting, since the socio-cultural tolls required to reach the status of citizen have proved to be too heavy for those who are "different": They are required to give up their culture, which is precisely the factor upon which their survival depends.

Will the eruption of the marginalized follow the same path as the workers' struggles and revolts? How can we deduce or decipher the political methods of the excluded? The key moment that fleetingly illuminates the shadows—that is, the margins as seen from the point of view of the state—is the insurrection, the moment of rupture when the subjects deploy their strategies. Reflecting on the Bolivian insurrection, Silvia Rivera points to the contradiction between the space/time of capital (public and visible, patriarchal, and colonial) and that of the subjects in rebellion (invisible, immanent):

> If during the uprising it was mainly the women and young people of Bolivia's most indigenous city that gave moral fire to the uprising and provided it a sense of collective dignity and sovereignty, when the time came to discuss solutions, it was once again only the men's voices that were heard—western and educated.... Meanwhile, the society and democracy that excluded women and men constructed, who painstakingly organized the rage and broke the silence, is lost again in the *manqhapacha* [internal space-time], returning to the languages of symbol and ancestral idioms (Rivera 2004).

In the daily life of divided societies, public time dominates the scene; the only audible voices are those of the economic, political, and union elites. This is why the Argentine insurrection was both "unexpected" and "spontaneous" to those elites, who could not hear the subterranean sounds, despite the fact that the voices from below had been echoing for more than a decade in anticipation of the approaching event.

Our task is not to state what the political action of the excluded should be (that is a task for party leaders or academics), but to determine what is happening among the social groups—comprising at least half of the population of the Southern Cone—that feed into the most active movements. Certainly some of those mobilized reproduce essential aspects of the capitalist system in their action and organizations. However, if we focus our attention on the most critical moments—the Argentine and Bolivian rebellions or the efforts of the excluded in Uruguay during the crisis of July–August 2002—we will be able to see that there is indeed politics on the margins.

I find that there are four significant characteristics of political action on the margins. I don't believe that there is a hierarchy in the traits that I shall outline, but I do find that they are all interconnected in some fashion.

The first characteristic is *the politicization of social and cultural differences*. This is the key to carrying out a process that is unconscious, to a degree. It is what happened in Bolivia with the *Manifesto of Tiahuanaco* (1973),[9] where "ethnic differentiation clearly took on a political path"—politicization defined as "ethnic awareness" (Regalsky 2003, 115), a fluid process of resistance involving territorialization and the structuring of political space by the rural communities and the Aymaras and Quechuas who have emigrated to the cities.

In Argentina, the piqueteros politicize their social differences when they opt to form collectives of autonomous

---

9   On September 15, 1973, a group Aymara-speaking men and women gathered at the famous archaeological site of Tiahuanaco about ten miles from Lake Titicaca in Bolivia, where they read a manifesto that was to transform the politics, economics, and culture of Bolivia.

producers without a division of labor rather than going back to work for a boss for a miserable wage (Zibechi 2003b); when they decide to take care of their health by trying to break their dependence on medication and on allopathic medicine; or when they deal with education using their own criteria and not those of the state (*Página 12* 2004). Even in Uruguay, where it is difficult to find autonomous spaces because of an all-embracing statism (of which the left is the greatest exponent), the marginalized have been able to create hundreds of self-managed, organic community gardens (*Brecha* 2003).

Politicizing difference means becoming conscious of it. Collective self-awareness is what gives the community a vision of its role in the world. It is what Marx created for the working class. In a journey of self-awareness (to understand and name what one is and what one is doing), popular education plays an important role, given that without self-instruction one cannot overcome dependence. But there is more. It also involves understanding that "nothing is irrational from the point of view of the person involved" (Wallerstein 1999, 29). This leads us to question the existence of a universal rationality that might exist above concrete beings and mark out a path for them, even that of socialism. Hence the necessity, according to Wallerstein, to understand that "everyone is formally rational"—that is, capable of combining the irreducible subjectivity of human conduct with lucid and intelligent choices. This affirmation has enormous implications if, as I believe, the excluded are building a new world (for them), neither better nor worse, but, above all, different. To think that the excluded "are not able" is to think that there still exists one formal rationality: that of the parties and the academy (i.e., that of the state).

The second characteristic of political action of the excluded has to do with the crisis of representation or the active presence of those represented. I do not intend to enter the already well-worn debate over this issue, but only to point out what is happening in certain movements. Certainly, we can confirm that "the breakup of inherited territorialities takes place through a deep crisis in the systems of representation"

(Porto 2000, 51). Indeed, the flight of capital provokes a territorial crisis that becomes a crisis of representation, given the latter's connection to territory.

Let's see. The worker does not control the space in which he or she labors, but is controlled via the microscopic organization of work. Deindustrialization, capital flight, destroys those spaces in which the worker was controlled. Something similar might be said of the urban crises provoked by capital flight (Harvey 2004). The flight ruptures the panopticon-like urban structure. In its place, as we have seen, popular sectors create new forms of self-organization in order to produce and to appropriate space. Capital flees from sites where new subjects are emerging and being insubordinate, and these subjects "insinuate themselves by setting up new territorialities" (Porto 2000, 208) in both urban and productive settings. Does this mean that they are carriers of new forms of representation? It is possible. But representation is a "structure of domination" (Weber 1993, 235) that, in the form in which we know it today, was created by capitalism and is integrated into the state-form.

Some movements utilize delegates as alternative to the representative, although more and more reject this (Williams 2000, 282), and the new habitat brings other forms of connecting and new cultural practices with it. In the spaces being created and occupied by the subjects in formation, encounters and relationships occur that may give rise to new potentials. In short, the new territories are spaces in which relationships are formed that can displace old forms of representation. But that is not all. While old forms of mediation vanish, new ones appear. Thus, as Porto Gonçalves points out on the subject of the Seringueiros, the movements are formed with tension and contradictions—"con/contra" (with/against)—which challenge the powerful, but also "with/against the church, the unions, the political parties, and their intellectuals" (Porto 2000, 215). This "with/against" dynamic involves the recognition that where there is a "below" there is also an "above," and that in this dynamic "their" new mediators—representatives or even delegates, that is, those who speak instead of them— should continue to be pressured, perhaps in different ways from those used to pressure the state. "In the case of those who by the nature of their activities are not given to speak or to write, their strength is greatly associated with their physical presence in space" (214). To be recognized, they need to occupy the space, to disturb the given order so as to gain visibility, to "make themselves present" in order to remove those who represent them.

As we have seen, the crisis of representation is closely linked to the "new social protagonism" (Colectivo Situaciones 2002, 145–162). In effect, representation is counterposed to expression, given that "beneath the relations of representation—the classic ones of political subjectivity—there is an expressive dimension at work" (145). Whereas the logic of representation is separation and transcendence, that of expression is one of experience and immanence. So the key categories of representation are: consensus, articulation, opinion, explicit networks, communication, and agreement. Those of expression are encounters, composition, disarticulation, resonances, and diffuse webs:

> Expression works in terms of composition, that is, of constituting time, forms, and *an autonomous space in which to unfold one's existence.* Expression thus permits us to explain the production of the world as an "ethic without a subject," i.e., as the process—unconscious and delocalized—of producing the values of a new sociability, based on a *multitude of experiences* that participate in the production of vital meanings *without any kind of conscious or voluntary coordination* (Colectivo Situaciones 2002, 146: emphasis mine).

This is a non-state-oriented reading from within the movements that emerged in the Argentine insurrection of December 19–20, 2001. Social action undermines representation. Similarly, Silvia Rivera locates the Bolivian insurrection[10]

10 The timing of the insurrection was linked to the proximity of Christmas, a period of bigger family expenditures that the popular sectors had to confront without resources because of the financial crisis.

in the annual cycle that begins in October, the *awti pacha* ("time of hunger, time of endurance"): "The moment in the annual cycle when people tighten their belts and *retreat to* a phase of non-consumption, falling back on reserves of potato starch, grain, and dried meat that enable them to survive until the time of abundance comes again" (Rivera 2004; my emphasis). In short, cyclical and interior time lines shape the timing of insurrection and this calls into question the monolithic— and virtual—time-line of representation.

It seems obvious that social action built upon communitarian ties supersedes the relationship of representation. Representation reflects the logic of the state as "consummate sign of division in society"; its functioning depends on its being the expression of "a fragmented social body, a heterogenous social being" (Clastres 2004, 75). Representation operates in the absence of social ties.

Finally, the expressive presence of social ties ruptures the state panopticon and, in its place, multiplicity develops. In other words, the emergence of the multiple—multiplicity of expressive space/times that cannot be represented—breaks apart representation as state-centric synthesis: revolt against separation; autonomy, "rejection of submission" (Clastres 2004, 76).

The third characteristic of the political action of the excluded is that it is *non-statist*, that is, it not only rejects the state form, but it acquires a *non-state form*. Having destroyed the welfare state, elites not only weakened their ability to maintain their hegemony but also weakened the presence of the state-form in the social movement of the oppressed and exploited, which facilitated the cooptation or neutralization of the dangerous classes. If indeed revolt illuminates power relations among the dominated, it is revealing that Latin America has seen a whole set of leaderless revolts, "without organizational memory or central apparatus" (Deleuze and Guattari 1994, 26). Power relations within the space of the uprising tend to be based on other forms. The mortar that binds and drives those in revolt does not correspond to the state-form, which is vertical and pyramidal, but rather rests upon a set of ties that are more horizontal and unstable than bureaucratic systems.

The best known instance of this rejection of representation is the slogan "que se vayan todos" ["they all should go"] that emerged in the course of the December 19–20 events in Argentina. In the neighborhood assemblies, in piquetero groups, and in occupied factories, this slogan has concrete expressions: "entre todos todo" ["among everyone, everything"], which is very similar to the Zapatista "entre todos lo sabemos todo" ["among everyone we know everything"]. Both statements point to the non-division of labor and thought and action and also the absence of leaders existing separate from the groups and communities.

Correspondingly, this non-state form has a great deal to do with generational and gender rebellion. In El Alto, in October 2003 the insurrection looked like this:

> The role of the women was absolutely crucial. By organizing in minute detail the daily quota of rage, by converting the private matter of consumption into a public issue, by making their art of rumor-mongering into a game to "destabilize" the repression, by reintroducing bartering networks and people's kitchens for the marchers, they succeeded in morally defeating the army, providing not only physical sustenance, but also the ethical and cultural fabric that enabled everyone to remain furiously active, the domestic wall having been broken down and the streets transformed into a space of collective socialization (Rivera 2004).

Indigenous people have defined a "back seat driver" style of doing politics as one in which "a group designates representatives in order to put them forward, so that they can be controlled and guided" (Gilly 2003, 26).

Once again, we note striking similarities between distant movements: The "back seat driver" style seems to be the twin of the Zapatistas' "walking at the pace of the slowest." But it would be a mistake to attribute these forms of action exclusively to the "indigenous movement" or to particularities of the cosmologies of native peoples. Similar forms are being practiced in very different social spaces. The common denominator that facilitates this kind of collective experience seems to be related to the re-construction of communitarian ties by displaced protagonists (youth, women, the old, and the new poor).

The tendency of some movements to eschew institutional forms—that is, the weakening of the state-form within the world of the oppressed—manifests itself very unevenly in different countries and regions, and especially in different circumstances. Thus, in countries where the nation-state maintains a strong presence (e.g., Brazil), the movements tend to form more stable and hierarchical structures. Conversely, in situations of acute state disintegration (Argentina 2001–2002 or Bolivia between February and October 2003), the non-state orientation found in domestic spaces tended to extend into public spaces very broadly. As it turns out, activists were surprised to see that when they ruptured the "domestic wall" and occupied public space, they did so using the very articles and practices associated with domestic space (pots and pans in Buenos Aires; rumor-mongering in El Alto). Thus, in Buenos Aires, residents came to the local assemblies with their pets and chairs from their homes, while in El Alto they watched over their dead in the dusty streets built by the community.

These brief examples (there are thousands in every demonstration that is not organized vertically)[11] illustrate the power that domestic spaces are acquiring at the very moment that statism is going through phases of weakness and crises. There are significant differences between the forms of action that unions embraced during the heyday of the workers' movement and the current forms of protest advanced by the so-called excluded. It seems premature to draw conclusions about this, but

---

11 Ranajit Guha, referring to colonial India, compares the politics of the elite with "the politics of the people." He points out that "mobilization in the sphere of elite politics was carried out vertically, while that of the subalterns was carried out horizontally." He adds that the former was "more cautious and controlled," whereas the latter was "more spontaneous" and was based on traditional territorial and kinship organization (Guha 2002, 37).

the differences are notable: The workers movement cloaked itself in the respectable guise of representative democracy, on the public stage, and accepted the rules of capital in the workshop, of patriarchy in the family, and of hierarchy generally. The acceptance of hierarchical customs went hand in hand with submission to the state, and the forms of action (strikes and street demonstrations) were directed at propping up "a strategy of bureaucratic pressure to which the other forms of pressure were subordinated" (García 1999, 49).

By contrast, in the current period, marked by the weakening of the national states, I see the more disruptive movements acting in a self-defined way: from the election of mandated representatives to the adoption of self-affirming forms of struggle (Zibechi 2003b, 31). When comparing Bolivia's recent "gas war" to the peasant mobilization twenty years ago, some said, "Now the Indians *do not ask for anything*, they demand sovereignty over a strategic resource, all under the heading of territory" (Mamani 2004, my emphasis). There is a new similarity between Bolivia and Argentina: They say that "they all should go," which amounts to asking for nothing, "only" demanding sovereignty (from a state whose legitimacy they do not recognize).

As can be seen, this non-state orientation of political action opens a Pandora's box. Waging a struggle that is without but not against the state involves positioning ourselves in ways unheard of and unthinkable just a short time ago. We can see the Bolivian revolt as "a revolt of common sense, as the upsetting of the invisible architecture of daily social interaction" (Rivera 2004)—a revolt with its own center that depends neither on external schedules nor on official bodies nor on state-based political rationality. Revolts like this flow from internal needs and time and were underground long before "going out" into public space. Indeed, the bold and sweeping acts that impress authorities "were perhaps improvised on the public stage, but had been rehearsed at length in the hidden discourse of popular practice and culture" (Scott 2000, 264).

The fourth characteristic I find is the defense and affirmation of differences. The new forms of action—roadblocks, pickets, and communitarian uprisings—are "natural" for people who intend to assume control over their own territories.

The roadblock (a *bloqueo* for Bolivians and a *piquete* for Argentines) is perhaps the most widespread form of action among the movements we are considering. First used in Bolivia in a 1974 protest known as the "masacre del valle" in Cochabamba, the action opened up a new phase of the peasant movement and the emergence of "a new generation of leaders with greater access to higher education and wider contacts." This, combined with the spread of the katarista current,[12] formed "the axis of the autonomous reorganization of peasant unionism" (Rivera 1983, 144). The mobilization of the peasants of Cochabamba (harshly repressed by the Hugo Bánzer dictatorship) triggered the breakdown of the military-peasant pact completed five years later. In this mobilization, roadblocks were incorporated into the repertory of forms of action, becoming henceforth the most important resource for rural mobilizations and, later, for urban actions after the "water war" in Cochabamba in April 2000.

In Argentina, the use of the roadblock emerged from a transformative crisis with strong territorial overtones: in 1996, in Cutral Co, a small town in the Neuquén province in the south, and in the town of General Mosconi in the north. In both cases, one-time oil workers—the oil industry had provided employment and living quarters in these towns—went from "lifetime job security" to absolute precariousness, from a secure wage to poverty, and thereby transformed themselves from workers to piqueteros in the short period between 1992 (when YPF, the state oil company, was privatized) and 1996–97 when roadblocks started. In both cases, the appearance of this new form of action was part of a process of profound reshaping of social subjects.

The roadblock is a technique with multiple uses. It ranges from interruption of the flow of merchandise and the protection of regions or cities to, in its "aggressive" version, a gradual fencing off with the threat of isolating the municipal or state

---

12 Followers and activists that coalesced around the Centro Cultural Tupaj Katari with the goal of creating an autonomous indigenous movement.

bodies. I believe that the widespread use of the roadblock reflects the territorialization of protest and the social movement. The roadblock is the best way to defend spaces controlled by the new subjects, and they mostly use it defensively and not as a means of taking power from the state. However, the roadblock does evolve as a method, as is happening in Argentina and Bolivia.

The Zapatistas have taken steps that confirm this analysis. The main objective of the EZLN's "military" activity is to defend the caracoles and autonomous municipalities and regions built up by the rebels. In Argentina, in Bolivia, in large regions of Ecuador, and less visibly in other countries of the continent, the long decade of uprisings, revolts, and mutinies has broadened spaces of de facto autonomy; though not institutionalized as in they are Chiapas, they are no less efficient in their daily functioning. The Bolivian region around Lake Titicaca, where the Aymara headquarters were set up; in the town of El Alto; in the "ethnic territories" of the Ecuadoran sierra, at an altitude of more than 3,000 meters (Galo 1993); in the conurbations of Buenos Aires; and in incipient form in marginal areas in Montevideo[13]—these are territories with some degree of autonomy and in which the national state has little or no impact (having been expelled as in the Bolivian case) or replaced by popular survival networks. The existence of these spaces has enabled popular sectors to survive the destructive effects of neoliberalism, when everything would indicate—if we look at economic indices and the decline in incomes—that "we should be seeing people dying of hunger in the streets."[14]

The rebels use the roadblock to protect and defend the spaces that allow them to survive and maintain their differences and use it as a platform from which to launch formidable challenges against the powerful.

---

13 On the steps being taken by the "marginalized" of Montevideo, see Liscano (2000) and Contreras (2003).

14 Statement of Venezuelan economist Asdrúbal Baptista, cited by Moreno (1993, 173) to explain how the popular sectors can go on with their lives despite all predictions to the contrary. For Moreno, the explanation is that "the people have their own forms of survival based on the system of relations centered on the family, which in turn has its own very distinct characteristics."

The Hidden or Subterranean
Agenda of the Movements

The moments of crisis provoked by popular uprisings shed a special light on the subterranean world. They illuminate the inner creative spirit of the movements, which typically operates in the shadows, far from the eyes of the media. Certainly not all risings have the same characteristics—not even consecutive uprisings with the same protagonists in the same space. The substantial differences among the half-dozen uprisings that CONAIE in Ecuador has led since 1990 are proof of this. However, the revolt illuminates the hidden agenda of the different participants, if only partially.

The terms "project" and "agenda" refer to a type of activity that is different from the traditional unionist/left concepts of "program" or "strategy." A subterranean or implicit "project" becomes clear only after the fact and over time.[15] A subterranean agenda or project is the path that the oppressed must follow to survive. In a period of systematic disintegration, this "project" has a greater chance of success, given that it is not an abstract construction but the course that the popular sectors pursue as a consequence of a series of choices made over time, with the objective of staying alive.

It would be a serious mistake to think that the words "hidden" or "subterranean" refer to some deliberate concealment on the part of the protagonists, with the intent to deceive their adversaries. The term "hidden" refers also to the perspective the protagonists have of themselves. Reflecting on the history of the Bolivian Peasant Confederation (CSUTCB), Pablo Regalsky points out that "the true movement of the people followed a hidden agenda, different from that imagined by the leaders but also *different from that imagined by the people themselves* when they started to act" (Regalsky 2003, 130; my emphasis). To make this visible, we must understand the internal logic of the movement—the movement in its immanence. This includes any long-term changes generated by its internal logic (the long term is the only time-scale in which the immanence can unfold).

---

15   In the Ecuadoran case, the long-term, subterranean project of the Quechuas of the Sierra was the "reconstruction of ethnic territories" (Galo 1993, 188–203).

From this point of view, we can say that the long-term strategy of those living on the social margins is that of building a different world starting with the place that they occupy. In this sense, they refuse—now explicitly and consciously—to accept the role of subordinates or "excluded" that the system has reserved for them. Evidently the change in social position has already occurred. The most decisive moment of this change was the breakup of the welfare state, as the Taylorism-Fordist regime gave way to globalization, with capital fleeing insubordinate workers, penalizing each wave of protagonists with deindustrialization, thereby pushing them into the margins while also feeding the latter's development.

Nor should we think that popular sectors act in a blind or "spontaneous" fashion. Spontaneity does not exist in the long term. It is one of the ways that the state (and left-wing parties) judge their subordinates when they do not act as they are expected to do. They are often accused of not having a plan for replacing the current system. However, we can agree with Ranajit Guha that

> The peasant knew what he was doing when he rose up. The fact that he focused particularly on destroying the authority of the elite that stood above him and did not have a detailed plan to replace that elite does not place him outside of the political realm. On the contrary, the insurgency affirmed its political character precisely through this negative act with which it tried to invert the situation (Guha 2002, 104).

It is very likely that the subterranean project of the popular movements that are born in the "basement" is to disperse and break up the neocolonial and neoliberal state and, in fact, to break up the state as such. But we will not find this out by placing a microphone in front of the protagonists because, as already suggested, they are not even formulating the project in this way, at least presently. We know, however, that "the movement unfolding before our eyes" (Marx) consists of a gigantic effort for daily survival by the oppressed and that this effort involves strengthening the communitarian spaces and ties that they are creating and re-creating. The logic of the "re-creation" of links in distinct spaces seems to consist of affirming differences, given that only in this way can the dominated survive, or rather they can only survive by being different (and through difference).

In the last two decades, the movements have followed paths that often point in similar directions. There is not "one" movement or path, but there are parallel tendencies that follow non-unified paths, based on internal rather than external time, and without leadership bodies that take them in a pre-determined direction.

The way that the movements follow their paths is in itself a social project that reveals elements of a new society. Whether these elements expand, deepen, and strengthen or weaken and disappear depends in good measure on whether or not the participants of the movements are aware of their internal difference. It is in the way of walking/moving that they can develop (or not) their distinctive features. Although I postulate that the way of moving is the true "program" of the movements, this is not a model applicable to everyone everywhere. Correspondingly, there is neither a permanent nor a continuous path to follow, nor identical ways of following it. In some cases, paths are taken that seem to go nowhere; sometimes there is simply no permanent path (external and visible) although there may be a flow (or silences instead of words and action, as the Zapatistas teach us).

We must trust that the oppressed are gaining experience; they are even learning to communicate without speaking, to walk without moving, to fight without fighting—all of which challenge our capacity for comprehension, which is anchored in binary and external concepts, and ruled by the linear time of capitalist production.

Among the many challenges we face is that of thinking and acting without the state. This involves thinking and acting as a movement; but movements, as we have seen, tend toward dispersion, with regard not only to the state but to any point of reference, resulting in a condition of fluidity that dissolves the

subject. Perhaps this is what Marx meant, in the "Manifesto
of the International on the fall of the Commune," when he
pointed out that we have "no ready-made utopia to introduce"
but that we simply "set free the elements of the new society
with which old collapsing bourgeois society itself is pregnant."
"To set free": to strengthen, to affirm, to expand, to shine a
light on the new world that already lives within the world of
the oppressed.

Recuperated Factories: From Survival to Self-management[1]

Factories "recuperated" by their workers are one response to two decades of neoliberalism and deindustrialization. In a movement unprecedented in Latin America, workers have taken direct control of production and operated without bosses—sometimes even without foremen, technicians, or specialists—in about 200 factories and workplaces in Argentina, some 100 in Brazil, and more than 20 in Uruguay. The worker takeovers came not as a result of ideological debates, as has generally happened in the history of oppressed movements, but out of urgent need. The massive closure of factories and companies supplying the domestic market prompted a handful of workers to prevent at least some of these plants from becoming abandoned warehouses.

Though this new workers' movement is heterogeneous, it has some common problems that are evident in both small and mid-sized factories and those in different productive sectors. These include legal struggles for the recognition of worker ownership, securing the supply of raw materials, the lack of working capital, marketing, and technical difficulties stemming from obsolete machinery or the exodus of technicians and managers. Such problems have been addressed and have often been resolved by the workers themselves, who have taken their destiny into their own hands.

A Predatory Model

The demise of military dictatorships (1983 in Argentina, 1985 in Uruguay and Brazil) gave birth to democratic regimes, but

---

1   Originally published by the Americas Program of the International Relations Center (americas.irc-online.org).

economic, political, and social structures inherited from the authoritarian period put tight constraints on these governments from the outset. That legacy—characterized by huge foreign debts—led these governments to accept the recommendations promoted by the Washington Consensus. These included rolling back economic regulations and dismantling the feeble welfare states that had been built in most of the countries of the region.

Beginning in 1990, financial and economic deregulation, privatization, and the shedding of protective tariffs caused many factories to close. This led to unemployment for many workers and more precarious working conditions for those who still had jobs. When import restrictions were lifted, it opened the floodgates to imported products, and local industries often could not compete. Hardest hit were small and medium-sized enterprises that supplied the domestic market.

The massive closure of these companies was but one aspect of the deep restructuring of production undertaken in the nineties. Meanwhile, leading industrial sectors became highly concentrated. This aggravated unemployment, which soon became a permanent structural feature of the economy. The process of deindustrialization in Argentina, Uruguay, and Brazil was followed by renewed growth based on the simplification of production strategies and the transformation of the technical and social organization of labor. Restructuring not only raised unemployment rates—to above 10 percent of the economically active population in nearly every Latin American country and above 20 percent at the end of the decade in Argentina—but also prevented most former workers from being rehired at the automated or robotized plants, since they lacked the training for the new positions created in such plants. Moreover, this type of modernization exacerbated trends toward social exclusion and the isolation of popular sectors.

For many workers, the closure of the companies where they worked condemned them to a lifetime of marginalization. This was especially true for workers over forty, who had very little chance of re-entering the formal labor market. Unemployment meant not only a loss of income but also the forfeiture of benefits such as health insurance, retirement pensions, and housing. This explains why some workers chose to fight to recover their source of employment—to keep their factories operating even without the owners.

A New Type of Movement

In Brazil, the movement to recuperate factories preceded similar efforts in Argentina and Uruguay. In 1991, *Calzados Makerly* in São Paulo closed its doors, eliminating 482 jobs. With the support of the Footwear Workers' Union, the Inter-union Department of Studies and Statistics, and grassroots activists, *Calzados* workers led a fight for worker-managed production.

In 1994, the Asociação Nacional dos Trabalhadores em Empresas de Autogestão [National Association of Worker-Managed Enterprises, or ANTEAG] was formed to coordinate the various efforts that emerged in the wake of the industrial crisis. ANTEAG currently has offices in six states and seeks to support worker-management projects by linking them to initiatives undertaken by nongovernmental organizations and state and municipal governments. Solving the movement's serious funding problem is one of the association's most important tasks. ANTEAG now works with 307 worker-managed cooperative projects that employ some 15,000 workers; of those, 52 are companies that were recuperated by their workers. The worker-managed companies are found in all branches of industry from mineral extraction (*Cooperminas*, for example, has 381 workers) to textiles (which includes scores of small companies, nearly all operated by women), to tourism services.

ANTEAG sees worker management as an organizational model that combines collective ownership of the means of production with democratic participation in management. The model also implies autonomy, in the sense that workers are responsible for decision making and control of the companies. This model discourages the hiring of professional managers, and if professionals are hired, they must always be under the control of the collective.[2]

---

2   See www.anteag.org.br.

Argentina's case is different. There, the recuperated factories movement emerged at the peak of the economic crisis and progressed very rapidly. The creation of these enterprises in Argentina was linked to grassroots experiences within the resistance movement spawned by the crisis. The worker-run factory movement grew out of a combination of workers' efforts to keep their jobs, organization among middle-class groups (professionals, employees, technicians) in neighborhood assemblies, and meetings of piqueteros. All of these groups continue to advance their own demands and proposals while building links with worker-run enterprises.

The vast majority of recuperated factories in Argentina are small or medium-sized and most were hurt by the economic liberalization policies that Carlos Menem's government imposed in the nineties. Let's look at the data. They cover a wide range of sectors: over 26 percent are in the metal industry; 8 percent are in refrigeration; 8 percent are electrical appliance manufacturers; printing presses, transportation, food processing, textiles, glass, and health companies each represent under 5 percent of the total. Half of the workplaces have operated for more than forty years and, when reclaimed by their workers, had an average of sixty employees. Only 13 percent had more than 100 workers (Fajn 2003).

Some 71 percent of worker-run factories distribute income in an egalitarian manner (e.g., janitors earn the same as more highly skilled workers), and only 15 percent have maintained the wage policies that were in effect before they were occupied. Though the factory-recuperation process began in the mid-nineties, workers took over two-thirds of the enterprises during the socially cataclysmic years of 2001 and 2002. This underscores the close tie between the grassroots resistance movements that emerged during the economic crisis and the factory takeovers. Seven of every ten factories were recuperated only after fierce struggles—physical takeovers in nearly half the cases and prolonged sit-ins at factory gates in 24 percent of the cases. In these instances, occupations lasted for an average of five months, which reveals the intensity of the conflict waged by workers before gaining control of the plants.

Surveys indicate that the factories recovered through long, intense conflicts are more likely to have egalitarian wage scales and to take part in neighborhood assemblies in middle-class neighborhoods. Only 21 percent of recuperated firms have maintained their former foremen and only 44 percent have kept their administrative personnel. Thus, manual workers began production in more than half of the reclaimed plants. Despite the intense and often exhausting battles fought to recover them, factories where highly combative struggles were waged have been the most successful—these factories operate at an average of 70 percent capacity compared with the 36 percent capacity found in those secured through lesser conflicts. Likewise, facilities abandoned by supervisors and managers have a higher productive capacity than those in which supervisors and managers have remained (70 percent versus 40 percent).

Creating New Linkages

A quick overview of specific experiences reveals one of the most interesting aspects of the Argentine movement—the close ties being forged between the workers in recovered companies, residents organized in neighborhood assemblies, and piquetero groups. These forms of collaboration have enabled workers to extend their networks well beyond the factory doors.

Two recuperated businesses—Chilavert (a graphics shop) and El Aguante (a bakery)—have survived thanks to the leading role played by neighborhood assemblies in taking over the facilities. In late May 2002, the management of Chilavert, located in the Pompeya neighborhood of Buenos Aires, called in the police to evict the workers who were occupying the plant. The Popular Assembly of Pompeya, as well as other assemblies and groups of residents, got involved by calling meetings to discuss the problem and then used phone and word-of-mouth communication to mobilize residents to help the workers resist the repeated eviction attempts (Cafardo and Domínguez 2003). Similar situations arose in other factories. In many cases, the alliance between workers and neighborhood residents proved crucial, whether the neighbors were organized in assemblies or not formally organized at all.

Panificadora Cinco (as the El Aguante Cooperative was formerly known) shut down in October 2001, laying off eighty workers without severance pay. In April 2002, the Carapachay neighborhood assembly, seeking ways to obtain cheaper bread, linked up with a group of twenty of these workers fired by the bakery. Following a joint meeting, residents and former workers took over the plant. They resisted eviction attempts for forty-five days, as local residents camped out with workers in a tent outside the bakery in an *aguante*,[3] until they finally gained ownership of the plant. Neighborhood solidarity was decisive: assembly members, piqueteros, and leftist activists in charge of security patrols held three festivals, a march through the neighborhood, a public denouncement of the owner, a May Day ceremony, talks, debates, and cultural activities. This exceptional case reveals how a social struggle can redraw territories and establish linkages where indifference was once the norm.

In the case of IMPA, a metallurgical company, the workers' organization helped consolidate the local neighborhood group and cemented a stronger alliance with it. The employee-run factory enjoyed the support of local residents even before its workers had organized assemblies in the zone. Then the workers decided to create a cultural center as a way of reaching out to the community and building solidarity with the neighborhood and social movements.[4] The center was a success and paved the way for efforts now being undertaken by other recovered factories whose workers realize how important it is not to be isolated within their plants and warehouses.

Similarly, in the midst of a conflict at a bakery cooperative called New Hope, a group of neighborhood assembly members, psychologists linked to *Topía* magazine, and local artists submitted a proposal to the workers' assembly for the creation of an arts and culture center as means of garnering the support

---

3   *Aguante* literally means "endurance" or "patience," but in recent years grass-roots movement have used it to refer to active solidarity in difficult situations.
4   *IMPACTO* newspaper, published by IMPA workers.

of neighborhood residents and raising the cooperative's social profile. Now the cultural center hosts daily workshops on music, theater, dance, puppetry, literature, and gardening; presents recitals and plays; features movies for both adults and children; and sponsors lectures by prominent intellectuals.

These examples demonstrate a novel characteristic of the workers' movement: an incipient but growing territorial rootedness. The link between worker-run enterprises and neighborhood assemblies points to society's growing interest in the success of these companies and workers' willingness to go beyond the factory gates and participate in the broader social movement. In some cases, this is manifested by a factory's commitment to hire unemployed neighborhood residents to fill job openings. Thus, by maintaining community activism, rebuilding social ties, and tending toward the territorialization of the struggle, the factory-recovery movement seeks to address one of the main problems it faces: distribution or, to put it differently, relations with the market.

Commerce and the Market

Solidarity begins when collaboration arises among neighbors (acting individually or through assemblies), worker-run factories, student groups, and piqueteros. When a factory begins operating under worker-control, this solidarity usually takes one of two paths: It may be institutionalized through large, stable organizations (such as ANTEAG in Brazil) or, as has occurred at many Argentine workplaces, horizontal links may be established with other initiatives, such as cultural centers in factories (about a half dozen operate) or initiatives aimed at addressing the needs of the overall movement, particularly its relationship with the market.

Brazil has developed a broad movement organized around economic solidarity, with an entire distribution network of products made by landless peasants and production cooperatives. In Argentina, these links that had been bureaucratized are now re-emerging at the grassroots level. At the peak of the economic crisis, barter networks grew exponentially, at one point involving two to five million people.

Although the barter movement later declined and fell into crisis, it helped initiate the debate about how to trade outside of the monopolist market. New projects are emerging in Argentina that favor "face-to-face" relationships and seek to avoid the creation of large structures beyond the control of grassroots collectives.

After the mass protests of December 19–20, 2001, that led to the fall of Argentine President Fernando de la Rúa, productive links among recuperated factories, piqueteros, peasants, and neighborhood assemblies multiplied. A common trait of these social sectors and movements is that they tend to produce for their own needs. Groups of piqueteros plant crops, bake bread, and produce other articles, and some are setting up hog and rabbit farms or fish hatcheries. A few neighborhood assemblies bake bread, cook meals, manufacture cleaning and cosmetics products, or collaborate with *cartoneros*.[5]

Some neighborhood assemblies are doing work that blurs the division between production and consumption. There are sixty-seven assemblies in Buenos Aires and well over half are autonomous and coordinated at the territorial level. This sector actively promotes "fair trade" and solidarity though conscientious consumption. Their activity puts rural producers, piqueteros, assembly members, and recovered-factory workers into contact with one another, and they are beginning to weave ties that are not mediated by the market. In a sense, these experimental endeavors are recuperating the original nature of the market, which Fernand Braudel and Immanuel Wallerstein believe was characterized by transparency, modest profits, controlled competition, and freedom, and was always the domain of "common people" (Wallerstein 1998).

There are multiple examples of this: Palermo, a suburb of Buenos Aires, holds a fair-trade market two days a week with more than a hundred stalls. The market only sells products made by the neighborhood assemblies (e.g., bags made of recycled material, cleaning articles, bread, diapers, recycled

---

5   *Cartoneros* are jobless residents of large cities who salvage cardboard and sell it to wholesalers.

computers and paper, homemade pastas, handcrafts, and marmalade's, etc.), piquetero groups, and recuperated factories (Muracciole 2003). In another instance, workers and residents work together to produce and distribute a brand of yerba maté known as Titrayjú (the acronym for *Tierra, Trabajo, y Justicia* [Land, Work, and Justice]). An organization of small rural producers in northern Argentina known as the Agrarian Missions Movement produces the tea. To avoid exploitation by intermediaries, over the last year, neighborhood assemblies have sold and distributed the tea directly in Buenos Aires, assisted by piqueteros and other grassroots organizations.

Utilizing the creative space opened by the protests against Argentina's economic crisis, assemblies in the middle- and upper-income neighborhoods of Nuñez and Saavedra founded the Cooperativa Asamblearia [Assembly Cooperative]. The assemblies first began with community purchasing, then organized a cooperative that distributes products from five recovered factories, an agrarian cooperative, and several other neighborhood assemblies. Workers at El Tigre, a worker-managed supermarket in Rosario that sells products from recovered factories, community gardens, and small growers throughout the country, are doing something similar.

Although the Argentine movement is in its early stages, it has already invented forms of exchange that go far beyond the early barter arrangements. The purpose of bartering was to create a currency that could facilitate a massive, alternative economic system. The new efforts, on the other hand, prioritize ethical and political issues in the production and marketing of goods, and seek to close the gap between producers and consumers by promoting direct, face-to-face relationships. The Cooperativa Asamblearia, for example, seeks to "promote the production, distribution, marketing, and consumption of goods and services from worker-managed factories, that is, products that are the fruit of the labor and the collective property of workers," according to a brochure introducing the cooperative.[6] Three basic principles guide the group's actions: worker-managed production, responsible consumption, and

---

6   For more information, see http://www.asamblearia.com.ar.

Another World Is Possible: Zanon Ceramics

On some rare occasions, the slogan "another world is possible" becomes a reality. The workers that took control of a ceramics factory and have been running it as a cooperative for the last four years demonstrate that it is possible to create another life even in the context of a large, high-tech business.

"The poetry of life can be greater than the poetry of paper," said the Argentine poet Juan Gelman after examining "a square meter of poetry" impressed into ceramic tile that the workers of Zanon take wherever they go as a gift. When he learned that his poetry decorated the twenty-five squares of ceramics, he excitedly wrote, "Never in my life did I imagine that I would see my poems published on ceramics. Never in my life did I imagine that the workers of a recuperated factory would interrupt their work in order to make it happen. It appears my imagination fell short."

The more-than-five-year struggle of the workers of Zanon Ceramics have the makings of a lyric poem. They had to confront a successful Italian businessman, labor unions from the Neuquén Province (in southern Argentina, two kilometers away from Buenos Aires), and government authorities and the police before they became the country's largest reclaimed factory, and the most successful from a "business" standpoint.

Zanon is Argentina's largest ceramics factory, occupying almost twenty acres (80,000 square meters) and utilizing the latest technology: mobile production lines for transporting the tiles, mechanical caterpillars and robotic cars that slide along rails, robots to print patterns into the clay, gigantic funnels for mixing, and automatic kilns. Nevertheless, the firm operates through cooperative, rather than hierarchical, structures.

The Gaze from Outside

At first glance, the experience at Zanon Ceramics is scarcely different from that of other businesses taken over by their workers—a total of two hundred in Argentina. The recuperation of the labor union by the workers may be the most important feature. In Argentina, labor unions do not defend the laborers, but rather the businessmen, and the Sindicato de Obreros y Empleados Ceramistas de Neuquén [Labor Union of Workers and Ceramics Employees of Neuguén], which operates in four factories in the province, was not the exception. The company paid an extra salary to the union leaders and made donations to the union to ensure that there would be no conflict.

Fears ran high within the factory, recall workers Mario Balcazza and Jose Luis Urbina (2005): "If the boss told a worker that he had to work for sixteen hours one day, he had to do it, because otherwise they suspend him the next day." When workers began to put together a list of alternative candidates to run in the 1998 union elections, internal repression increased dramatically: "If you spoke with someone from the union, the company marked you and then fired you, and no one would defend you because that kind of behavior would also get you fired," said Balcazza. But finally, more than 60 percent of the three hundred workers opted to transform the union and get rid of the bureaucrats.

And so began "another" history. The new union would not allow the company to buy or intimidate it. It made the appropriate denouncements when illegal actions were taken, and it gained the confidence of the workers. In order to overcome difficult operational and economic difficulties, the company demanded greater productivity from the workers, which caused numerous work-related accidents. Events came to a head in 2000: An employee died in the factory due to lack of medical attention because the business, which runs twenty-four hours a day, did not have an ambulance or doctor on hand. When Daniel Ferras, age twenty-two, passed away, the workers stopped production for eights days, demanding, and finally receiving, an ambulance and a nurse. Zanon later fell behind on its wage payments (some workers went up to three months without pay) until it finally turned off the kilns in September 2001.

Management at Zanon Ceramics set out to downsize to just sixty employees, but workers saw this as a way to "clean out" the labor union. By that time, Zanon had incurred substantial debts with the provincial government, which had lent the company money so that it could pay back-wages. The workers rejected the layoffs, burnt the layoff notices in front of the Presidential Palace, erected a tent city in front of the company for five months, and, thanks to a judicial seizure of 40 percent of the company's stock, they began to sell it off to compensate for their lost salaries. Nevertheless, even though they had gone months without their salaries, a section of the ceramicists donated their pay to renovate the provincial hospital, while unemployed workers from the Neuguén's Movement of Unemployed Workers (MTD) provided the labor.

In March of 2002, 220 of the 330 workers decided to occupy the factory and began production "under worker control." At a meeting, they agreed to receive the same salary and formed commissions to focus on sales, administration, security, expenditures, production, planning, safety and hygiene, and public relations. The indigenous Mapuches, who, up to that moment had been degraded and exploited by the ceramics company, gave the workers access to their clay quarries. On April 5, 2002, the first shipment of 20,000 square meters of tiles left the factory. Three months later, they produced 120,000 square meters, half of what the company had produced under the previous owners.

The Role of the Community

From the point of view of production, worker self-management at Zanon has been successful: At the moment they are producing 300,000 square meters of tile, exceeding previous production levels, and they expect to reach 400,000 square meters in the near future. With help from the Universities of Comahue (Neuguén) and Buenos Aires, they have modernized the production process and in two years invested 300,000 dollars into the maintenance and improvement of machinery. From the 300 accidents that occurred annually under the previous ownership, there are now only 33, and there has not been a single death, whereas before approximately one worker died every month.

Under worker self-management, various new tile designs have been introduced. Previously, European and Italian medieval designs prevailed but, after the workers took control, they began utilizing Mapuche designs, created in cooperation with Mapuche communities, in the hope of celebrating a marginalized culture and to pay homage to those who had offered their clay reserves to the ceramicists.

One notable difference between Zanon and other businesses seized by workers is its relationship with the community. The factory legally changed its name to Fasinpat (short for Fábrica Sin Patrón [Factory Without Owner]), became a cooperative, and started making countless donations to hospitals, schools, nursing homes, soup kitchens, indigenous groups, disability groups, firefighters, and the Red Cross of Neuguén. Zanon workers gave thousands of square feet of ceramics to mark the help they had received and because they believe a business should return its profits to the community. The most emblematic donation was the construction of a health center for the neighborhood of Nueva España. Under the guidance of community members, including four hundred families who had run a first aid center for forty years, Fasinpat employees donated materials and built a health center for the neighborhood. Moreover, when they need to hire more employees, they seek them from organizations of the unemployed and locals. As a result, young people who had had difficulty getting jobs filled the one hundred new positions created.

But the community also supports Fasinpat. The factory is open to all who wish to visit it. Every week, students, people from across Argentina, and a large number of foreigners come to the Zanon plant to see and experience one of the few modern factories—totally automated and using some robots—in the hands of the workers. In turn, when the police attempted to remove the workers on April 8, 2003, thousands of locals surrounded the factory to stop them. Soon after, 9,000 people gathered for a rock festival inside the factory as a show of solidarity between the community and the workers.

They currently maintain a Web site, host a radio show, and distribute a monthly newspaper throughout the country.[7] They have also produced several videos documenting various aspects of their story. They have good relationships with other worker-recovered businesses and frequently take trips to tell their story and meet other workers in similar situations. In 2005, they participated in the First Latin American Gathering of Worker-Recuperated Factories, which took place in Caracas, Venezuela.

Journey to the Center of the Manufacturing Monster

In the pamphlet "Zanon Under Worker Control," Zanon workers explain their approach to work: "We want to tell you that in each ceramic tile there is a history and a reality that has made it possible for the wheel to keep turning. All processes and decisions are in the hands of the workers. We are the ones who decide what to buy, how to sell, and what and how to produce." Perhaps the major difference between Zanon-Fasinpat and other companies is the organization of the production process: "This factory is an intricate machine in which each one contributes his part, where there are no hierarchies and where the commitment to and responsibilities of work determine the quality of the product and the future of our management."

The differences between the current and previous managements are striking. As a former employee recalls, "We were not allowed to leave or go to the bathroom. The pathways were marked out with different colors. Red indicated places where there were automatic machines and you had to move with

---

7   A periodical called *Nuestra Lucha*. Its Web site is www.nuestralucha.com.ar.

caution, and blue was for places you could go. Back then, the kiln operators had to wear red clothes, electricians green, and so forth. That way, they could tell if someone from another sector was somewhere they weren't supposed to be. It was like a jail" (Lopez 2002, 178). The managers were on the upper floor, in offices with glass windows so they could keep watch, and the union organizers were nearby, who followed on the heels of all the workers, monitoring every move.

When the workers took over production, groups from each part of the production process began naming coordinators, who oversaw production and dialogued with their peers when problems arose. Coordinators rotate every few months, so that each person has had a shift as coordinator after a certain amount of time. According to those interviewed, "coordinators earn the same salary as the rest but have more responsibilities."

Carlos Saavedra, who was general coordinator of the whole factory, recognizes that the duties require more time than normal and adds, "I do not control anyone and no one controls me. We simply all report the work that we do, so it can be accounted for. The numbers are clear. Anyone can see them. Whether I am coordinator or not is a decision made by the assembly, and if I am not, then that is their decision. Everyone does what he or she is asked" (Magnani 2003, 143–44). Now, instead of control, the workers of Zanon operate through trust and shared responsibility.

The factory is divided into thirty-six sectors that work during three eight-hour shifts. Each sector has its own coordinator.

> Each Monday there is a coordinating meeting, which decides what each shift needs; it tries to resolve problems of individual sectors and if they cannot be resolved, they are brought before an assembly of all the shifts. But the final product that goes to market is everyone's responsibility, not just the person who makes it, because we all work on the same level, in conjunction with each other, from the time we start working on

the raw clay until the final ceramic piece is finished and put up for sale (Balcazza and Urbina 2005).

Once a month, the factory calls a day-long meeting in which every member participates. It is the most important meeting and treats all topics—from the type of footgear necessary for each section, to the purchases they will make, and any activist actions in which they will participate. "The social, political, and production aspects are all discussed. We have an agenda for each point and we will not adjourn the meeting until every last issue is agreed upon," recounts a worker (Balcazza and Urbina 2005). Nevertheless, they recognize that this way of functioning—democratic, participatory, and horizontal—requires a lot of work:

> It's exhausting, but productive because you find solutions to problems while debating them with everyone. What's worse is when you let time pass and people start having doubts; after all, many things aren't immediately clear. There are sectors that manage money, expenditures, sales, and administration. We assign two individuals, whom we call auditors, to manage the expenses. They produce a report every month on expenditures. This report is given to demonstrate transparency to everyone. If any money is left over, we use it to repair machinery or buy raw materials. And everything is resolved at the sectional or general assembly (Balcazza and Urbina 2005).

The assembly established some workplace ground rules. Everyone must arrive at the factory fifteen minutes before his or her shift begins and cannot leave until fifteen minutes after it technically ends, so that they can share pertinent information with the workers on the following shift. Two examples demonstrate the achievements and difficulties of this system: On one occasion, they were forced to make a painful decision and fire an employee who had been stealing, but on another "they paid for a worker with addiction problems to go

into treatment, which allowed the employee to keep working"
(Lavaca 2004).

As strange as it may seem, the time dedicated to open
debate raises the level of hourly productivity, which goes
against the current of the hegemonic business model. Perhaps because, as Carlos Saavedra notes, "hours no longer
mean what they used to. Back then, I worked twelve hours
and went home feeling exploited and exhausted. Now, if I go
home tired, it is a different kind of tiredness. Because there
is a feeling of satisfaction inside of you that is sometimes difficult to explain" (Magnani 2005, 144). Before, when the horn
sounded indicating the end of a shift, workers ran home, so
they could forget about work. "Now I stay longer even when
I don't have to," says Saavedra, suggesting that work can be
more than an obligation and actually satisfying. For his part,
an assembly-line worker named Juan sums up the feelings
of many workers: "Back then, I would pass a ceramicist on
the line, and he was just a ceramicist. Period. Now, each ceramicist that I pass on the line is like something of ours in its
rightful place, something that belongs to you" (Cafardo and
Domínguez 2003).

Today, the ex-Zanon workers hope that the Argentine
government will recognize their status and let them to continue to operate under their own control. They hope that some-
day the state, which has yet to make a purchase from them,
will become a client and contribute to the growth of a project
that demonstrates that "another world really is possible."

Chile: The Long Mapuche Resistance[8]

The Mapuche people, history, culture, and struggles have long been blanketed in silence. The few news items that come from southern Chile are usually about repression or the Chilean government's denunciations of "terrorism." The Mapuche suffer social and political isolation and have few options other than struggling to survive in the countryside or enduring unstable, poorly paid jobs in the cities. However, they still continue to resist timber and hydroelectric multinationals and fight to keep their traditions alive.

"The Chilean State considers me a criminal for defending my family and lands," writes twenty-five-year-old Waikilaj Cadim Calfunao of the Juan Paillalef community in Region IX, Araucanía, in a brief letter from the high security prison in Santiago, whose guards prevent me from entering for bureaucratic reasons. With only slight variations, other Mapuche prisoners tell the same story. José Huenchunao, one of the founders of the Arauco Malleco Coordinating Group (CAM), was sentenced to ten years in prison for his participation in the torching of logging equipment.

"Prison is the place the Chilean State and its political and judicial operators use to punish those who struggle on behalf of the Mapuche people-nation," wrote Huenchunao (2007) on March 21 from Angol prison. Héctor Llaitul, thirty-seven, another CAM leader, was detained on February 21 on the same charges as Huenchunao and began a hunger strike to denounce the political-judicial frame-up that he was facing. The

---

8   A version of this article appeared on the Web site of the Americas Program of the Center for International Policy (www.ircamericas.org), May 17, 2007.

majority of the more than twenty Mapuche prisoners have re-
sorted to hunger strikes to call attention to their situation or
demand transfer to prisons near their communities.

Like most Mapuche organizers, Llaitul highlights the
problem with the logging companies:

> The Mininco Company and one of our main adversar-
> ies, the hydroelectric company ENDESA, have changed
> their policy. They no longer use violence alone. They
> are diversifying the repression: they study the areas
> where they operate and develop plans (for publicity,
> courses, etc.) tailored to each one, often financed by the
> Inter-American Development Bank, in order to create
> a security rim around their properties. They arm small
> farmers and hunting and fishing clubs, so they can form
> vigilante groups, which are legal in Chile, to defend
> themselves against "bad neighbors." This is how they try
> to isolate the people who struggle (Llaitul 2007).

"My community has been severely repressed—every
member of my family is imprisoned—my mother, father,
brother, aunt, etc.," writes Calfunao, describing how his community's lands have been "stolen" by the logging companies
and the Public Works Ministry. The courts have abetted the
theft, as they do not respect "our common law or our legal
customs." Calfunao stands accused of unlawful seizure for
blocking a road, of causing public disorder, and of destroying
the tires on a truck that was transporting logs from the Mapuche region. Any effort that communities make to prevent
logging companies from stealing their lands falls under the
Chilean government's "antiterrorist" legislation, which it inherited from the Pinochet dictatorship.

South of the Bío-Bío
Arriving in Concepción, the landscape abruptly changes. Located 500 km south of Santiago, the narrow valley between the
Andean mountain range and the Pacific is planted with the
orchards that make Chile an important agricultural exporter.

Timber covers hill and mountain, highways turn into paths that snake upward and disappear among pine trees. Then suddenly, a dense white cloud of smoke announces a paper mill, surrounded by green farmland.

Lucio Cuenca, coordinator of the Latin American Observatory of Environmental Conflicts (OLCA), explains that the timber sector grows at an annual rate of over 6 percent. "Between 1975 and 1994 timber cultivation increased by 57 percent," he adds. The timber and logging sector accounts for more than 10 percent of exports, with half sent to countries in Asia. More than five million acres of tree farms are concentrated in Regions V and X, traditional Mapuche lands. Pine makes up 75 percent, eucalyptus 17 percent. "But almost 60 percent of planted areas are in the hands of three firms," says Cuenca.

To explain this concentration of ownership, as with anything else in today's highly privatized Chile, you must examine the seventies and the Pinochet regime. In the sixties and seventies, Christian Democratic and Socialist governments implemented a policy of agrarian reform that returned lands to the Mapuche and promoted the creation of farmer cooperatives. The government worked as actively in forestry as in other forms of industrial development.

Cuenca explains what happened under Pinochet:

> The military dictatorship managed a counter-reform, modifying ownership and land use. In the second half of the 1970s, between 1976 and 1979, the state privatized its six main companies: Celulosa Arauco, Celulosa Constitución, Forestal Arauco, Inforsa, Masisa, and Compañía Manufacturera de Papeles y Cartones, and sold all of them to private interests at 78 percent of their value.

Chile's timber industry is now in the hands of two large Chilean business groups led by Anacleto Angelini and Eleodoro Matte. In the rest of the continent, the industry is in the hands of large European or American multinationals. However, the owners' nationality is much less relevant than the degree of concentration. In Chile, small landowners only own 7.5 percent of timberland, while 66 percent belongs to large owners with at least 2,500 acres. The Angelini group alone has 1.9 million acres, and the Matte group's property exceeds 1.25 million acres.

"The areas where this lucrative business developed," Cuenca continues, "have become the poorest in the country." While Angelini is one of the six richest men in Latin America, Chile's Region VIII and IX have one of the highest poverty rates in the country. "Profits are not distributed, and nothing stays in the area, except overexploitation, pollution, loss of biological and cultural diversity, and, of course, poverty," the OLCA coordinator concludes.

For the Mapuche, the expansion of the timber industry means their death as a people. Each year the industry absorbs an additional 125,000 acres. On top of feeling literally drowned by the tree plantations, the Mapuche are beginning to experience water shortages, changes in the flora and fauna, and the rapid disappearance of native woodland. A report by Chile's Central Bank confirms that Chile will have no native forest left in twenty-five years. Yet, everything indicates that the timber industry is unstoppable.

The Corporación de la Madera [Wood Corporation] predicts that 1995 rates of timber production will double by 2018. The rapid growth has prompted complaints of environmental and social deterioration; resistance by many Mapuche communities, fishers, and farmers; and even analyses by government agencies that warn of the dangers of continued timber industry development. Further increases will be accompanied by the construction of new cellulose processing plants. Chile externalizes a range of labor and environmental costs, allowing it to produce a ton of cellulose for just $222, compared to $344 in Canada and $349 in Sweden and Finland. This is the only argument that carries any weight.

Three Centuries of Independence

It is impossible to understand the current reality of the Mapuche people without reviewing their history. Unlike the other great peoples of the continent, the Mapuche managed to remain autonomous and independent from Spanish authorities for 260 years. They were conquered only at the end of the nineteenth century—by the independent nation of Chile. Their history differs from that of other indigenous peoples in this sense.

It is estimated that there were one million Mapuche when the Spaniards arrived, concentrated in the Araucanía area (between Concepción and Valdivia). They were fishers, hunters, and gatherers and subsisted on a diet based on potatoes and beans grown in forest clearings, and seeds from the giant Araucaria or Monkey Puzzle tree that dominated the southern landscape. They were sedentary but did not found towns, and each family had territorial autonomy. The abundant resources in these very rich lands permitted the existence of "a much larger population than one which a pre-agrarian economic system could support," according to José Bengoa, the main historian of the Mapuche people (Bengoa 2000, 25).

The only permanent social institution of this society of hunter-warriors was the family or clan, grouped around chiefs, or *loncos*. This also distinguished the Mapuche from other indigenous societies the Spanish found in America. The Mapuche successfully resisted the Spaniards from 1546 to 1598. In 1554, Chief Lautaro defeated Pedro de Valdivia, a general captain of the conquest and then executed him for "having wanted to enslave us."

Despite typhus and smallpox epidemics that claimed the lives of a third of the Mapuche population, a second and a third generation of chiefs succeeded in resisting the colonizers' renewed attacks. The course of the war changed in 1598. The Mapuche's superior military troops, who became great riders and had more horses than the Spaniards, put the *conquistadores* on the defensive. They destroyed all the Spanish cities south of the Bío-Bío, among them Valdivia and Villarrica, which was only refounded 283 years after the "pacification of Araucanía."

A tense peace was installed in the "border region" for many years. On January 6, 1641, Spanish and Mapuche sat together for the first time in the "Parliament at Quilín." The

Bío-Bío River became the border between Spanish and Mapuche zones, and Mapuche independence was recognized, though the Mapuche had to return prisoners and allow missionaries to preach. In 1726, the Mapuche Negrete Parliament regulated trade, which was a source of conflict, and the Mapuche promised to defend the Spanish Crown against the Creoles.

How can we explain this Mapuche singularity? Various historians and anthropologists, among them Bengoa, agree that, "in contrast to the Incas and Aztecs, who had centralized governments and internal political divisions, the Mapuche had a non-hierarchical social structure. In the Mexican and Andean cases, the conquerors struck at the heart of political power and, by seizing it, assured the dominance of the empire. This was not possible with the Mapuche, given that subjugation would entail conquering thousands of independent families" (Bengoa 2000, 41). The continuation of this pattern helps explain why it has been so difficult for the Mapuche movement to construct unitary, representative organizations.

Toward the seventeenth century, and under the influence of Spanish colonies that had begun extensive cattle-raising, the Mapuche began adopting a mercantile, cattle-based economy. They soon came to control one of the largest territories held by an ethnic group in South America, expanding to the Argentine Pampa and what is today the Province of Buenos Aires. This new economy strengthened the role of the loncos and generated relations of subordination that the Mapuche had not known before. "The greater concentration of cattle in the hands of some loncos and the need to rely on leaders who could negotiate with colonial authorities intensified social hierarchization and the centralization of political power," according to historian Gabriel Salazar.

The mining economy of the new independent republic required the expansion of agricultural production after the crisis of 1857. In 1862, the Chilean army occupied Araucanía, and a war of extermination was unleashed that lasted until 1881, when the Mapuche were definitively defeated. After subjugation, they were confined to reservations, and their 25 million acres were reduced to 1.25 million, and the government auctioned off the rest of their lands to private interests. Thus, the Mapuche were turned into poor farmers and forced to change their customs, forms of production, and legal practices.

A New Reality

Some 100 kilometers south of Concepción, the small town of Cañete is a center point of Mapuche struggle. On Christmas in 1553, the Mapuche destroyed the Tucapel Fort built there by Pedro de Valdivia and executed him. Five years later, the Great Chief Caupolicán was executed in the town square that bears his name today. In that same square, on a rainy April morning in 2007, more than two hundred Mapuche and students congregated to demand freedom for Huenchunao, a CAM leader jailed by the government just weeks earlier during an offensive in which CAM's main leaders, including Llaitul and Llanquileo, were also imprisoned.

When the march ended, after going for five blocks surrounded by a large contingent of anti-riot police units, loncos Jorge and Fernando took me to their community. A short distance from one of the many towns in the area, in a clearing among pine trees, a handful of dilapidated houses make up the community named for Pablo Quintriqueo, "a Hispanicized indigenous man who lived in the area around 1800," explained Mari, a Mapuche social worker living in Concepción. Surprisingly to those who have visited Andean or Mayan communities, there are just seven families in the community and it was established only eight years ago. The community's small garden cannot possibly provide for more than thirty people.

Passing around maté, they tell their story. The families had left their ancestral properties, where they had been born and lived until a decade ago, and migrated to Concepción. Mari married a *huinka* (white man) and has two children and a good job. Many young people, like Llaitul, now imprisoned at Angol, graduated from the University of Concepción and later created organizations to defend their lands and communities.

When the timber companies advanced onto their lands, they returned to defend them. "In this community alone, over 4,000 acres are in dispute," they say.

Understanding Mapuche reality is not simple. Lonco Jorge, 35, one of the youngest in the group, gives a hint, saying that, "rejuvenating the Mapuche people is based on recovering our territory." From this, we can conclude that the Mapuche are living a period that other indigenous peoples on the continent experienced half a century ago, when they won control over lands that had belonged to them since the beginning of their history. Everything also indicates that the Mapuche's defeat is still very close (only a century ago), in contrast to the three or five centuries since the defeat of Túpac Amaru and the Spanish invasion, respectively. Mapuche memory of the loss of independence is still fresh, which could be the reason for a sentiment that appears repeatedly in conversation: Unlike the Aymara, Quechua, or Maya, the Mapuche see themselves as victims.

Jose Huenchunao states that the communities are facing a new period of desperation and fires off a warning that does not seem exaggerated: "If the government, if the actors in civil society, do not address our situation, we may face conflicts, which are already occurring in isolation, that may become forceful and coordinated. This could get much more serious and could ultimately cost society much more than returning a certain amount of land, which is the minimum that the communities demand" (Huenchunao 1998). It is not clear that electoral democracy has improved the lives of marginalized Chileans. According to political scientist Gomez Leyton:

> The political strategy of the Concertation, over its sixteen years in power, has been oriented toward the "minimum political and social change," as well as the spread of neoliberalism throughout society. The Concertation administration has governed the market more than the society, thus worsening the unacceptable distribution of income and turning Chilean

society into the second most unequal, after Brazil, on the Latin American continent (2006, 109–10).

However, there are clear symptoms that time is running out for the Concertation. It is also possible that Huenchunao's prediction may come true. Not only has the Mapuche people's long resistance endured, but it has also been rekindled time and again, despite repression. In recent years, south of the Bío-Bío, others besides the Mapuche have resisted the savage neoliberal model. Small fishers in Mehuin and farmers who found their water polluted have already organized several protests. At the beginning of May 2007, the Carabinero police killed a timber worker, Rodrigo Cisternas, who was participating in a strike for wage increases.

This murder may represent the beginning of the end for the Concertation. For more than forty days, workers at Bosques Arauco in the Bío-Bío region, owned by the Angelini group, held a strike that three unions representing 7,000 members also joined. The company had earned a 40 percent profit and the workers demanded a corresponding wage increase. After long and ineffective negotiations, they struck again and surrounded the plant where the company had concentrated its three shifts to break the strike. "When they saw that the Carabineros enjoyed destroying their vehicles, they defended themselves with heavy machinery, and police shot and killed one of the strikers and seriously wounded several others," according to a statement by the Asamblea del Pueblo [Assembly of the People].[9]

In recent months, Michelle Bachelet's government has opened too many fronts. On top of the conflict with the Mapuche, there are student protests against the new education law that sparked enormous demonstrations last year. At the beginning of this year, there was a battle over the restructuring of public transportation in Santiago, which underserves the poorer sectors. And now government forces killed Rodrigo Cisternas. As we see in other countries in the region, it may be that the Chilean people have begun to turn the page on savage neoliberalism.

---

9   Posted May 5, 2007 on www.piensachile.com.

Democracy Against the Mapuche

One of Pinochet's ministers boasted that "there are no indigenous people in Chile; everyone is Chilean." The dictatorship issued decrees to end legal exceptions for the Mapuche and introduce the concept of private property in their lands. However, "when the state deprived the Mapuche people of recognition, it reinforced their ethnic identity," according to Gabriel Salazar, recently awarded the National Prize for History.

At the beginning of the eighties, there was a "social explosion" among the Mapuche people in response to the 1979 decrees authorizing the breaking up of more than 1.15 million acres of indigenous lands. Salazar says: "The division did not respect areas that always had been considered communal and were fundamental for the Mapuche people's material and cultural reproduction, such as areas set aside for forests, grazing lands, and religious ceremonies. The increase in population, together with the reduction in territory, contributed to the 'emptying' of the communities of their people and culture."

As it turned out, democracy was not generous with the Mapuche people either. Whereas the dictatorship wanted to annihilate them by changing them from Indians into rural farmers, the advent of the Concertation coalition in 1990 brought new expectations.[10] President Patricio Aylwin lent his support to a law under debate in congress. But, in contrast to what happened in other countries on the continent, in 1992 the Chilean National Congress rejected the International Labor Organization's Treaty 169 on Indigenous and Tribal Peoples, and declined to make recognition of the Mapuche people part of the Constitution, which the United Nations had promoted.

Currently, "the rural indigenous world is a constituent part of structural poverty in Chile," says Salazar. In 1960, each Mapuche family owned an average of 23 acres, though the government maintained that each needed 125 acres to live

---

10 The Democratic Concertation is the coalition of the Christian Democratic Party, Party for Democracy, Radical Party, and Socialist Party that has governed in Chile since Pinochet left the presidency. The following were its presidents: Patricio Aylwin (1990–1995), Eduardo Frei Ruiz Tagle (1995–2000), Ricardo Lagos (2000–2006), and Michelle Bachelet (2006).

"with dignity." From 1979 to 1986, each family had 13 acres, which has now shrunk to only 7.5 acres per family. Under the dictatorship, the Mapuche lost 500,000 of the 750,000 acres that they still had. Timber and hydroelectric industry encroachment onto their lands causes an exponential increase in poverty and emigration.

In desperation, many communities invade lands appropriated by timber companies and are subsequently accused of "terrorism." The dictatorship's anti-terrorism law continues to be invoked against Mapuche communities that set fire to forests, block roads, or disobey Carabinero orders. Currently, many Mapuche organizations vacillate between collaboration with authorities and militant autonomy, and new urban groups continue to appear regularly, especially in Santiago, which is home to over 40 percent of the million Mapuche in Chile, according to the 1992 census.

Landless Workers Movement: The Difficult Construction of a New World

"Smashing through the fences at the large estates was not as difficult as fighting the technological packages of the transnationals," Huli recounts as he sits in his kitchen and pours hot water into the maté that we share while his son romps around the house. He says the *campesinos* of Brazil's Landless Rural Workers' Movement (MST, in the Portuguese acronym) dreamed for years of reclaiming their land, believing that it would solve all their problems, providing food for their children, a life of dignified labor on the farm, education, health, and housing. However, the reality proved much more difficult than they had imagined.

Huli Zang is part of one of the 376 families that make up the Filhos de Sepé (Sons of Sepé) settlement, a 23-square-mile municipality in Viamao, 25 miles from Porto Alegre, the capital of the southern state of Rio Grande do Sul. Established in February of 1999, the settlement has four sectors, in which the land is organized into what the landless call an *agrovila* (agricultural village): The houses are grouped together in one area rather than on each campesino's parcel of land. This arrangement ensures that the homes, built solidly out of wood or brick, have access to electricity and potable water, with the result that daily life for the campesinos is much like that of the average city-dweller. Huli's house has a gas and wood stove, a refrigerator, television, and computer. There is a route connecting the housing area to the nearest town, Viamao, as well as the individual parcels, each one an average of 17 hectares.

The settlement sits next to a 10-square-mile wildlife refuge called Bañado dos Pachecos, home to thousands of species of birds, fish, and mammals. The surrounding marshland irrigates the area, which makes it suitable only for cultivating rice, although there is enough space next to each settler's house to grow vegetables and fruit, and nearly everyone raises chickens and has one or two milk cows. This allows some degree of self-sufficiency as far as food is concerned.

Within the settlement, the MST operates one of its Training Centers, which can house 120 people with its array of bedrooms, plus communal bathrooms, meeting rooms, computer labs, and dining hall. During the month of August, some eighty activists from half a dozen countries participated in a seminar delivered annually by the Latin American Coordinating Agency of Campesino Organizations. The 1,800-person village also has a school attended by 230 children.

Land and Rice

Before moving to their current location, the landless campesinos lived for nearly four years along Brazil's highways in hovels made of black canvas, enduring extreme cold during the winter and suffocating temperatures in the summer. After negotiating with authorities, they secured access to the land upon which they now live, which is the biggest settlement in the state. A testament to the settlers' will to create a new world for themselves and not just have a strip of land to cultivate, is the fact that they decided to create an agrovila. Several settlements have built housing on each individual parcel of land, a choice that creates almost insurmountable political and social problems. Not only is it almost impossible to deliver water and electricity to all the inhabitants (due to large distances between houses), but community living is also almost out of the question, thus heightening the campesinos' individualism and blocking any attempt to create a different type of society.

Any visitor that manages to arrive at an agrovila, with its simple, picturesque homes, sown plots of land, colorful flower arrangements, and domestic animals grazing and cackling in the sun, sees a bucolic setting, where everything runs smoothly. Nothing could be further from the truth. The Filhos de Sepé settlement faces its share of problems, mostly derived from the global crisis faced by small farmers as they compete with multinational agribusinesses.

One problem emerges from the very choice to create an agrovila. Individual parcels frequently end up far away from the housing areas, sometimes as much as 6–8 miles. "This causes some families to quit farming altogether and instead lease their land to other settlements," says Huli, who doesn't shy away from questions. In order to address this problem facing the agrovila, over the last few years MST has implemented a new design for the settlements. Units consisting of fifteen to twenty families are grouped together and the land is lined up in triangles with the vertex of each coming together in a central area. This way the homes are all near each other and the parcels of land relatively close to the residential area. This of course reduces the density of the settlements from an average of one hundred families to what has been termed a "housing nucleus" that does not exceed twenty families.

But perhaps the most serious problem is their dependence on multinationals that impose a style of farming based on the heavy use of agricultural toxins. As Huli says,

> Monsanto brings us technology packages, herbicides and pesticides—poison, in other words—and then they supply the rice. Over the course of time, we went from depending on the landholding elite to depending on the multinationals that own the technology. We can only conclude that, we have not moved forward despite our efforts, that we struggled for years to be in a new state of dependence, and all the while we are poisoning our own families and the people who consume the rice we produce.

A Struggle Without End

In order to escape these constraints, the settlers have opted for agroecology. In the settlement, 1,600 hectares are farmed "conventionally" (that is, with pesticides), but after an intense internal debate, the community decided that a small group of families would cultivate organic rice. Last year, twenty families cultivated 120 hectares (almost half a square mile) without chemicals and formed the Association of Rice and Fish Producers. Because they have abundant water, they have also been able to produce fish, thereby diversifying their production. That year, they produced 6,000 bags of organic rice; they sold this to schools for the preparation of lunches in the city of Viamao, which is governed by the Workers' Party. This year, thirty-five families are participating, and they are hoping to grow 150 hectares and produce 10,000 bags.

They have discovered that growing organic rice is not only profitable, but also twice as productive as rice farmed with chemicals. They have recovered and implemented an old campesino tradition of preparing the land with ducks. "Ducks eat up all the herbs, clean the land much better than an agrochemical toxin could, and in addition they leave it fertilized with their waste. We leave the ducks there over a period of months and they do all the prep work. Later, when it is time to sow the rice, we remove them and either sell them or eat them," Huli relates with a huge smile. Farming organically gives them their own seeds and supplies, so to produce they don't depend on markets, and they are improving the health of both the producers and the consumers.

Now, however, they face the problem of certification. In Brazil, there are only three businesses that can certify organic origin, and they are all linked to multinationals. "Once more we are bumping into the same enemy," Huli continues. But what angers them most is that the "certifier" will only visit the settlement once a year, charge them thousands of dollars, and do not inspect the cultivation process, a fact that allows any "organic" producer to use chemicals while still receiving the organic label. To address this unexpected problem, the movement is exploring the possibility of creating a "community certification" team, which would allow them to bypass the multinationals.

In addition, the settlers complain that state and federal governments do not provide credits for agroecological production. In short, they face a whole series of problems, and each time they overcome one, they run into a new problem that is ultimately the same: the control of large multinationals over agricultural technologies. The development and control of new technologies by multinationals has made possible a new type of oppression. While campesinos no longer lack the means of production, control over work schedules, and labor methods, the multinationals' dominance is of an "immaterial" sort, resting upon control over knowledge and the market in order to maximize profit accumulation. Huli explains how the price of rice continues to fall, so that even 1,600 hectares of rice does not provide enough for settled campesinos to survive.

Before leaving the settlement, I ask him what sources of income the Filhos de Sepé campesinos have. There are three: family vegetable gardens, rice, and work in neighboring municipalities, where the women are employed as cleaners and the men as construction workers. "What percentage of your income comes from these types of work?" I ask. Huli cannot avoid a look of sadness: "Unfortunately, the bulk of it comes from cleaning and construction. That's the way it is."

The struggle for land turns out to be much more complicated than anyone could have imagined. Perhaps the biggest triumph of the landless is that the campesinos have remained on their settlement rather than adding themselves to the burgeoning belt of poverty seen in Brazil's big cities. However, it is more complicated than the struggle for land, since capital has shown its capacity to control the mechanisms of domination, which in this case are almost invisible. The battle will take persistent training and learning, which are indispensable tools in the struggle.

Sepé Tiraju

On February 7, 1756, Spanish and Portuguese troops killed the Guaraní Indian Sepé Tiraju in the city of Sao Gabriel (in the southern part of Rio Grande do Sul). The 1750 Treaty of Madrid, signed by the two countries, decreed that all Indians belonging to the Guaraní Reductions (seven towns laid out by Jesuits and built by indigenous people) must abandon their homes and move to the banks of the Uruguay River, a territory that today belongs to Argentina.

A Portuguese-Spanish army of 3,500 soldiers armed with cannons and the best military equipment of the day confronted the Indians armed with spears and arrows. Three days after the death of Sepé, on February 10, nearly 1,500 Indians were dead. Despite the annulment of the treaty in 1761, it had accomplished its goal: the Guaraní Reductions—described by Voltaire as "a triumph of humanity" for their successful cooperative living and artistic endeavors such as music, book publishing, and development of astronomy and meteorology—were destroyed. In 2007, the landless and other social movements commemorated the 250-year anniversary of the fall of Sepé in combat as part of a retrieval of the most significant experiences of different worlds existing on the same continent.

11

The Other Campaign, or Politics from Below

A revolutionary sets out to change things primarily from above, not from below, unlike the social rebel. The revolutionary asserts: we will make a movement, take power and change things from above. The social rebel organizes the masses and fights for change from below without having to address the question of seizing power.

Subcomandante Marcos (2001)

The long journey of the Zapatista movement reveals a dual dynamic: the daily, continuous construction of local autonomy and the national and international struggle to change the balance of power. The link between the two processes, which are interrelated and interdependent, seems be one of the most salient and compelling aspects of *Zapatismo*. I will trace this relationship from the early days of the uprising in order to show that material autonomy and political autonomy cannot be separated, and that one encourages the other. Indeed, the Other Campaign that the EZLN launched on January 1, 2006 demonstrates that there can be no political autonomy without material autonomy. Furthermore, material autonomy will discover its limits if the autonomous territories are unable to change the state of affairs prevailing in each region, in each country, and, ultimately, on the entire planet.

Thanks to the militant journalism of Gloria Muñoz Ramírez (2004; 2005), we have insight into the most important aspects of the new world being built by the Zapatistas in the municipalities and autonomous regions of Chiapas. The first anniversary of the Caracoles and the Good Government councils in August 2004 was an opportunity for the movement to give an account of how they have constructed their autonomy.

Autonomy has a long tradition among the popular sectors and indigenous peoples across the continent, and it has been a hallmark of the Zapatistas from the first day of the uprising. However, the current movement taking shape in the Good Government councils has an exact date of birth: December 8, 1994. On that day, the Zapatistas announced the end of the truce and that their troops would advance, and launched the Peace with Justice and Dignity for Indigenous Peoples' campaign—through which they created thirty autonomous municipalities in areas of EZLN influence (EZLN 1995, 170–182). Thus, a reality took shape that was already evident in incipient form some time before: The EZLN is the armed wing of the Indigenous peoples of Chiapas, at their disposal to fight when necessary. Furthermore, the guerrilla army is subordinate to the civilian communities, implementing the decisions made by them.

From that moment, the construction of autonomous spaces took a leap forward and followed a stealthy path beyond the Zapatista world, a process that Gloria Muñoz reveals in her writings and texts. Since the creation of those thirty autonomous municipalities in December 1994, the construction of material autonomy has been central to the Zapatista struggle and represents what Marcos calls "the material conditions for resistance" (Marcos 2003b).

From Autonomous Municipalities to the Good Government Councils

From the very beginning, the Zapatista autonomous municipalities had a different function from the Mexican State municipalities. The communiqué announcing their creation determined that "the civilian populations of these municipalities have appointed new authorities," while "the laws to which the new rebel municipalities must and do comply with, in their practice of leading by obeying, are: the United Mexican States Constitution of 1917; the Zapatista revolutionary laws of 1993, the local laws of the municipal committee that will be determined by the civilian population" (EZLN 1994, 181–182).

Autonomy rests upon the control of territory, though it is more than just a declaration or an ideological objective. Autonomy is linked to difference. Indigenous peoples need autonomy to protect their culture and cosmovision—their world—as something distinct from the hegemonic world. In the territories controlled by the Zapatistas, an autonomous process began to spread. And it is necessary to emphasize the "process" aspect of it, in the sense that autonomy cannot be the result of "a single act" but requires "a relatively long period, whose duration is not possible to determine beforehand" (Díaz Polanco 1997, 156–57). This is because autonomy is not a concession from the state, but rather a victory of the social sector that needs to protect and strengthen its difference in order to continue to exist as a people.

We thus arrive at a sort of triad: territory, self-government, and autonomy (or self-determination), in which each dimension is inseparable. In these self-governed areas in the Lacandon Jungle and Los Altos, the Indigenous peoples under the auspices of "leading by obeying" took a gigantic leap forward between 1994 and the birth of the Caracoles in 2003. Looking back, we can say that from the 1974 Indigenous Congress (and probably even before) the communities underwent a process of strengthening, an "internal growth," that enabled them to free themselves from their traditional ties (Zibechi 1999, 87–122). However, another stage began with the declaration of the autonomous municipalities in 1994 that represented the creation of a new world in the Zapatista territories.

This revolution in the Zapatista zone has many dimensions. First of all, there are changes in the production and reproduction of everyday life: The communities and municipal councils have taken education, health, and agricultural production into their own hands. This has led to a significant improvement in the quality of life in Zapatista communities and has been one of the crucial material foundations upon which self-government rests.

The second dimension pertains to the construction of political autonomy. While the basic nuclei of autonomy is the community with its assembly, a higher body has been created—the Municipal Council—that brings together representatives of each community making up the autonomous rebel municipality. Although the EZLN kept the organizational structure under wraps for a long time for reasons of security and self-defense (on February 9, 1995, the Mexican state launched a military offensive designed to take out the leadership of the EZLN), various studies indicate that each council consisted of a president, vice president, secretary, and treasurer, as well as commissions or committees responsible for justice, land issues, health, education, culture, and production, among others (Ornelas 2004).

In the eight and a half years between December 1994 and August 2003 (i.e., between the proclamation of the autonomous municipalities and the creation of the Caracoles in the space previously occupied by the Aguascalientes), a dense network of initiatives connected to these communities, municipalities, and autonomous regions was created.[11] During those years, the Zapatistas did more than create a new and different world, they also maintained a strong national and international presence: In 1994, they convened the National Democratic Convention, launching the first Aguascalientes center in Guadalupe Tepeyac; they participated in the San Andrés Talks in 1996, networking extensively with other indigenous peoples throughout Mexico, which gave birth to the National Indigenous Convention; they convened the Gatherings for Humanity and Against Neoliberalism (the first one was held in Chiapas in 1996); they held widespread consultations with civil society; and they organized large mobilizations, the most important of which was the March of the Color of the Earth in 2001.[12]

---

11   The Zapatistas set up meeting spaces called Aguascalientes in five key rebel communities in late 1994. They were intended as centers of interchange with national and international civil society.

12   About the National Democratic Convention, see EZLN 1994; about the San Andrés Accords, see Hernández Navarro and Vera Herrera 1998; and about the march, see EZLN 2004.

But we should focus less on the Zapatistas' familiar public activity and more on the movement's internal structure, specifically its two dimensions: the construction of power and the moral and material basis of this new world. We should remember that since the beginning of the uprising, the Zapatistas applied a set of "revolutionary laws" in the rebel-controlled area. Although the most well known is the womens' revolutionary law (which includes the rights to decide how many children to have, to be elected to military or civilian posts, and the abolition of obligatory marriage), there are a set of "laws" that in some ways provided a political framework for the world being born in the autonomous areas.

When the Zapatistas unveiled the Caracoles and the Councils of Good Government in August 2003, and decided to tell the world their own story, we learned in detail what had occurred during the previous years. *La Jornada* journalist Luis Hernández Navarro describes the enormous changes that took place in Oventic, the most well-known Zapatista town in Los Altos:

> In 1994, Oventic was only a sparsely populated rural community situated near important municipal headquarters like San Andrés. Ten years later, this place has become an urban center equipped with a high school and a hospital full of murals and cooperatives, where the Good Government Council (the Central Heart of the Zapatistas in Front of the World) sits (Hernández Navarro 2004a).

According to this analyst, the explosive growth of Oventic is due to the political role played by the locality, to which seven autonomous municipalities belong. He defines self-governed spaces like Oventic as "a laboratory for the transformation of social relations" and "a school of alternative governance and politics." He concludes that the people "have retaken control of their society and are reinventing it" in Zapatista areas. We see now—through Gloria Muñoz's book *EZLN: The Fire and the Word*, and the series of EZLN communiqués The

Thirteenth Stele—the profile of more than a thousand Zapatista communities in Chiapas, grouped in twenty-nine autonomous municipalities and five large regions covered by five Good Government Councils and home to some 200,000 people.

From a quantitative point of view, the communities have constructed two hospitals, eighteen clinics, and about 800 community health houses in the five regions, with no less than 500 health promoters trained under the criteria adopted by the Zapatistas.[13] In the area of education, there are about 300 schools and 1,000 educational "promoters" that make up the Zapatista Rebel Autonomous Education System, as well as a center for secondary education at the municipal headquarters in Oventic. The communities achieved and manage all this without any state aid.

Let's take a closer look. In the Caracol based in the community of La Realidad (named Mother of the Caracols of the Sea in Our Dreams), the hospital has surgical facilities for small and medium-sized operations. "Thousands of indigenous support bases" participated in the construction of the hospital over three years, working in shifts and overcoming enormous obstacles in the process, including the lack of doctors (Muñoz 2004, 317). The treatment patients receive is very different to what they receive in the state hospitals, where the staff humiliate the indigenous, so much so that even many indigenous supporters of the PRI prefer to go to the Zapatista health clinic. The hospital has a dental consultant and an herbalist clinic, underscoring the fact that the Zapatistas are not limited to reproducing capitalist health practices. Part of the hospital complex is also a school for female and male health promoters, where some 118 promoters were trained in 2003. The zone has three municipal clinics and more than a hundred community clinics "where free consultations are available to Zapatista support bases, and when available, free medicine" (Muñoz 2004, 318).

The Caracol also grows herbs, has a kitchen, and has proudly trained more than 300 female bone-setters, herbalists,

---

13   The figures are cited by Gloria Muñoz, but they are based on approximations with no statistical value.

and midwives. An account contained in Gloria Muñoz's work shows that the process of redeeming the tradition of healing bones and bone-setting meant overcoming many obstacles:

> This dream started when we realized that the knowledge of our elders was being lost. They know how to cure bones and sprains, they know how to use herbs, they know how to oversee the delivery of babies, but their knowledge was being lost with the use of medicines purchased in the pharmacy. So we came to an agreement and brought together all the men and women that know about traditional healing. It was not easy to bring everyone together. Many compañeros did not want to share their knowledge, saying that it was a gift that cannot be transferred because it is something carried within them. But a sense of awareness and understanding grew among the people, the health authorities held discussions, and they convinced people to change their way of thinking and to participate in the courses. They were some twenty men and women, older people from the communities, who acted as teachers of traditional health. About 350 students signed up, most of them Zapatista compañeros. Now the amount of midwives, bone-setters, and herbalists in our communities has increased (2004, 319).

I think this example shows how the Zapatistas are building a new world. They are not directly linked to national or international forces, not even their own Caracoles and Good Government Councils. This reveals something much deeper: the capacity to change the world or, as pointed out by Marcos on one occasion, to build or re-invent it.

First of all, it shows that the resources needed to solve the health-related problems lay within the people and their communities. This is a very different concept from that of the state system, which treats human beings and especially the indigenous like children. Following the example of international agencies like the World Bank, state institutions refer to the indigenous not as poor but as "disadvantaged," and thus objects of charity. It follows, then, that the disadvantaged must be considered incomplete and need to come under the state's care, which really knows what they need. In contrast, the Zapatistas emphasize the value of dignity and rebellion and, above all, consider human beings as subjects of their own lives and their own health. The opposite of this is state health care, which profits from health. Capital must turn human beings into passive patients, objects to be taken under the wing of the medical and state establishment.

Second, recovering traditional knowledge is a long process of inner discovery that creates its own problems. For instance, some in the communities have the knowledge but do not want to share because they believe this knowledge gives them special power. Or sometimes the knowledge, which is really the heritage of the whole community, is not yet afforded collective value. Overcoming such problems takes time and a lot of internal work that a power external to the community cannot carry out or impose by decree. It is a matter of conscience and, therefore, of social ties. In recuperating bone healing, as well as herbal and child-birthing practices, other kinds of connections are being made, knowledge is being democratized and socialized, powers are dispersed, and the community as a whole acquires new knowledge and powers.

Third, the Zapatistas combine traditional and allopathic medicine. In the community health centers two medical kits are used: one with herbs and the other with pharmaceuticals. This practice of combining "the two medicines" is a result of experience within the communities and is tied to the indigenous cosmology and culture that promotes the use of traditional medicines.[14]

Fourth, the health network begins in the community health clinic, the ubiquitous dispensary found in every community no matter how small and isolated it may be. This network emerged in the community, from the bottom up. Visitors to the communities in the mid-nineties would witness a small and modest house where a health activist (usually a woman)

14 On this theme, see: Acero and Dalle Rive 1989.

attended to the people's basic health needs. She would also lead courses and workshops on topics ranging from reproductive health to basic sanitary practices, like teaching the importance of boiling drinking water and personal and domestic hygiene. The state system does the opposite: It constructs a large hospital in a major town and the community members must travel long distances to get there, where they inevitably receive inhumane treatment. The construction of the municipal hospitals in the Caracoles of La Realidad and Oventic took two decades; hundreds of small community health centres, microclinics, and dispensaries were built from the bottom up.

A health network created from the bottom up that integrates different kinds of medicine and recuperates and socializes medical knowledge is part of an emancipatory process that no state can take over. New social ties are created in this process, underscoring the idea that healing is a collective and community-based process (Maldonado Alvarado 2003). Furthermore, by being an autonomous communal construction, it is part of an emancipatory process in which there is no separation between medicine and health care and the community. That separation is one of the key elements of capitalism. All aspects of capitalist society are mediated by a bureaucratic layer that manages the interests of society (health, education, state). No such bureaucracy exists in the Zapatista autonomous regions and, instead, there is a process that goes against the grain of the last five centuries of capitalist history. Capitalism appropriates traditional healing knowledge and concentrates it in the state-led medical body, whereas Zapatista communities re-appropriate their knowledge and the people are collectively recovering control over their own bodies. This is emancipation in action.

The lack of separation between health and community ultimately reflects the form in which a person engages in health. The communities choose health promoters and—provided that they agree—they are trained to attend to the people's health concerns. Control remains within the community from the beginning and this prevents the formation of a separate body to oversee medical care. Ultimately, the Good

Government councils are responsible for the maintenance of health activists (Colectivo Situaciones 2005, 67–71).

The same set of principles guided education. Before the Zapatista uprising, there were few schools in the communities and where there was one, it often lacked teachers. Beginning in 1997, the Zapatistas developed their own curricula, and there are now three generations of education promoters teaching in more than 300 schools built in communities and villages by the locals themselves.

Like the health system, the education system grows from the bottom up. Not content with simply establishing a school and installing teachers, the Zapatista system of education attempts to integrate the schools into the community and the struggle. Based on the pedagogical notion that education "springs from the peoples' own knowledge," education activists describe a process in which "the children consult the elders and, together, they go about constructing their own educational program." They do not use grades: "Those that don't know do not get a zero; instead, the whole group does not proceed until everyone is on the same level, so no one is failed. Similarly, at the end of the course the indigenous promoters organize a series of activities attended by families and parents, who are invited to note the progress of their children *without assigning any grades*" (Muñoz 2004, 351).

Communities elect the female and male activists, schools are built by the same communities, and the children bring a chicken to feed the teachers/promoters as a kind of "tuition." The Good Government councils are in charge of providing teaching materials. The schools do not receive or accept any government subsidy and teachers are not paid a salary, but are fed and clothed by the communities. The entire educational process is guided by the principles: "Nobody educates anybody else, nobody is educated alone"; "educate while producing"; and "educate while learning" (Nachman 2004). Thus, the Zapatistas have eradicated the state from their schools. This is the concept of self-education, as expressed explicitly by Zapatista education activists: "Education occurs among all of us. No one can say 'I will liberate you'; liberation comes from the will of all of us. Nobody raises the awareness of another, nobody raises their awareness alone" (Muñoz 2004, 351).

We see that Zapatista education is community self-education; the communities are taking education into their own hands and, as in health care and all aspects of their lives, they have not created a separate "specialized" or "professionalized" body of educators. The pedagogical content and educational standards emerge from communities and indigenous people; those who provide education are chosen by the communities and their work is supervised by them.

In the Ricardo Flores Magón municipality, a training center for activists has been set up, with the support of Greek sympathizers. After three years of community work involving almost all the men of the one hundred communities that make up the municipality, the center opened in August 2004. A member of the Autonomous Council, Julio, spoke of the type of education they wish to provide:

> We have to completely change education. We want an education with a different politics and that is taught differently in the classrooms. We do not want students seated in rows, looking at each other's back. We want them to be seated in circles, so that they may face each other. This is why we like the project that the Greeks presented to us, which is a school with six-sided rooms so that the benches can form a circle. The school-rooms are hexagonal, not square.... So education is different, from the shape of the classrooms on. Sitting in circles will create unity among students, increased solidarity, and greater intimacy (Muñoz 2004, 4).

During the first anniversary of the Good Government councils, Subcomandante Marcos summarized the "radical change" in health and educational practices in the Zapatistas like this: "Where once there was death, now life is beginning"

(Subcomandante Marcos 2004). In only one year, fifty schools were built and the three hundred that already existed were equipped without receiving a single peso from the state.

There have also been significant changes in production and distribution in the Zapatista zone. The indigenous people have always produced a substantial portion of their own food. The Zapatistas seek to combat the power and influence of intermediaries (the so-called "coyotes") who pay the producers miserable prices for their products. In La Realidad, the Zapatistas bought a truck to carry their products directly to the market town of Las Margaritas, where a Zapatista-run market operates. In some communities, such as Veracruz, the rebels have set up supply warehouses to supply hundreds of Zapatista and non-Zapatista community stores (Muñoz 2005, 323). In the Los Altos region, the Zapatista communities sell organic coffee through two of their own cooperatives and women embroiderers formed cooperatives to market their handicrafts and eliminate the greedy and racist intermediaries in the nearby commercial center of San Cristóbal de Las Casas.

There are cooperatives and libraries in all the Caracoles, and in some there are cobblers, bicycle workshops, cafes, and other services. Women collectively plant vegetable gardens, sew, embroider, make candles, and bake. "The autonomy of the people begins with caring for the land," they say, using bio-insecticides to control pests instead of agrochemicals. "We don't seek to eliminate pests but to drive them away." Projects are underway, such as concrete-block production, cooperative pig, hen, sheep, chicken, and cattle farms, and fruit tree plantations (Muñoz 2005, 323).

Social change correlates closely with autonomy, both individually and collectively. This is very visible in areas such as education and health. Learning involves self-learning—that is, "the people must control their own learning process." The same is true in health: "We talk of curing ourselves, of allowing our bodies to recover and to learn to heal ourselves. Given that nobody can learn to heal my own body except myself, I have to learn to heal myself; I'm in control, I am the agent. If I speak of their education and health, I am depending on the system" (Esteva 2005, 193). In short, this integrated vision of autonomy carries the principle of self-government to all aspects of life because it is a way to overcome dependencies. Autonomy is a whole; it touches all aspects of life or it is not autonomy.

Nevertheless, progress is always partial. The issue of women's emancipation is one issue where progress has been slow, according to documents released by the Zapatistas. What is certain, notes Hernández Navarro, is that "against the current, they are producing and reproducing a different society"; they are "reinventing tradition." According to this analyst, the Zapatistas are growing from the bottom up and, as we have seen, "they have been integrating the most advanced experiences in each of the different fields of action in which they are engaging. In many ways, they are a synthesis of them" (Hernández Navarro 2004b).

The Zapatista movement is also carrying out agrarian reform from below. Having displaced large landowners, as well as their intermediaries and local chieftains from their territories, they are introducing new forms of popular organization, unleashing the creativity and transformative energies of the people, communities, and villages. Likewise, they have displaced state authorities and professional politicians. The balance of forces has changed within the Zapatista territories. The decisive actor in this process was the Zapatista army—understood as the armed wing of the communities—which was able to "clear the ground" for many of the projects we have seen. In other words, the expulsion of state power and the creation of a space controlled by the communities allowed this huge number of initiatives to appear.

Let us now look at distribution of power in Zapatista territories. The implementation of the rotation of administrative duties was one of the most important achievements of the Good Government councils during their first year, and it is something that allows us to truly speak of "good governance." "We were all government, we had no leader, it was a collective government, and between us all we taught ourselves what each one knew" (Subcomandante Marcos 2004).

Moreover, three of the Caracoles issued a report at the beginning of 2005, as the Good Government councils entered into their second year of operation, expressing surprise at the number of youth involved in the tasks of government. But more surprising still is the strength of the system of rotation. The members of each council are elected by the assemblies of the communities and remain in office for three years, but,

> its members rotate every eight days, so in this way, they return to oversee the task several times. Each member travels from their municipality to the Caracol, where they remain day and night for a week and then return home to continue working the land and attending to their domestic labors and family. They receive no salary. It is a responsibility, not a privilege…. The practice of rotation, reversibility, and accountability in the good government councils and the fact that gradually everyone will go through the experience of governing and being governed will result in nothing less than the elimination of the governing class (Navarro 2005).

Achieving this was a learning experience for the people and the Zapatistas, especially for the EZLN. Much of that process is summarized in *The Thirteenth Stele* series of communiqués in which the Zapatistas announce the creation of the Caracoles and the Good Government councils and the end of the five Aguascalientes that had, in turn, been born as a response to the destruction of the Aguascalientes of Guadalupe Tepeyac after the state army's military offensive on February 9, 1995. From the point of view of constructing autonomy, it was a decisive and fundamental step. *The Thirteenth Stele* contains a summary of actions and a public self-criticism of the EZLN and, on the basis of the critique, the Zapatistas put forward alternatives and responses.

It outlines the two main problems needing resolution: the relations between autonomous authorities and national and international civil society and those between Zapatista and non-Zapatista communities. The fifth part of *The Thirteenth Stele*, entitled, "A History," details them. It argues that there has been uneven development in the various autonomous municipalities, in the communities and even within Zapatista families. The most well known or most accessible municipalities receive more projects; families that housed or had close contact with visitors receive more attention or gifts. Such things are considered natural in human relations, but, also, "this can introduce imbalances in community life if there are no counterweights" (Subcomandante Marcos 2003b). The second issue is more complex and affects the relationship between civilians and military personnel. Tradition deems that when a person is not fulfilling their responsibilities (and these traditions operated before the existence of the EZLN) that they would be replaced by another in a "natural" manner. But the presence of the Zapatista Army created some problems:

> As a political-military organization, the leadership makes the final decision here. What I mean is that the EZLN's military structure has in some way "contaminated" a tradition of democracy and self-governance. In a manner of speaking, the EZLN was one of the "undemocratic" elements in a relationship of direct community democracy (another anti-democratic element is the Church, but that's a matter for another paper) (Subcomandante Marcos 2003b).

He argues that when autonomous municipalities began operating and self-government grew from local to regional levels, the "shadow" of the military structure was alleviated from the autonomy process because the EZLN does not intervene in the affairs of the local municipalities and regions. Furthermore, "since the EZLN, due to its principles, does not fight for the seizure of power, none of the military commanders or members of the Clandestine Indigenous Revolutionary Committee may hold positions in the community or in the autonomous municipalities" (Subcomandante Marcos 2003b). Whoever wishes to do so must leave their position in the Zapatista army. The Zapatista self-critique is strongest when it addresses one of most sensitive issues: how the autonomous councils administer justice and how results have been occasionally "irregular" and sometimes problematic. On this point Marcos and the EZLN are very transparent and it is useful to reprint in detail the nature of their comments:

> If the relationship between the Autonomous Councils and the communities is full of contradictions, the relationship with non-Zapatista communities has been one of constant friction and confrontation.
>
> In the offices of non-governmental human rights defenders (and in the General Command of the EZLN), there are more than a few complaints against Zapatistas for alleged human rights violations, injustices, and arbitrary acts. When the General Command receives complaints, it turns them over to the committees in the region in order to investigate their veracity and, when they are confirmed, sets out to resolve the problem, bringing the parties together in order to come to agreement.
>
> But organizations that defend human rights are confused, because they don't know whom to address. The EZLN or to the Autonomous Councils? And they have a good point (Subcomandante Marcos, 2003b).

The text attributes these problems to the confusion between civilian and military roles. But, as Marcos points out, it also reflects the fact that it is not only Zapatistas who have constructed indigenous autonomy but also "hundreds of thousands of persons of different colors, different nationalities, different cultures, different languages, in short, of different worlds" (Subcomandante Marcos, 2003b).

Autonomy and difference go hand in hand, because autonomy implies that people have the right to govern themselves completely, "to determine their own form of government, their own sociocultural practices, and their own economic organization" (Díaz Polanco and Sánchez 2002, 45). This point is extremely important because autonomy is often reduced to the function of government—this is how the powerful often receive the peoples' demands for autonomy. In contrast, the Zapatista experience teaches us that autonomy is comprehensive and strategic—ranging from the smallest cooperative, to a school or a health center in the jungle—reflecting the form and manner in which each projects is carried out, in whom sovereignty resides, how they make decisions, and how they organize themselves.

Autonomy and heterogeneity are also related. If we are truly autonomous, each collective will do things as they decide. This enormous diversity is what the Zapatistas call "another world in which many worlds fit" and it shows us that "it is possible to act uniformly without suppressing diversity." In that sense, the Good Government councils "are an instance of unified action rather than a mechanism of uniformity, to the extent that they do not centralize powers or dictate the terms of the base" (Ornelas 2004, 10). In this way, the Zapatistas cannot help but to undermine the homogenizing and excluding practices of capital. The political left replicates these modes of capitalism by seeking the cohesion and uniformity of antisystemic forces, while, for the Zapatistas, "the multiplication of the subject of social transformation is the alternative to the mechanisms of power that characterize the capitalist system" (Ornelas 2004, 11).

The five Good Government councils, operating in as many caracoles, attempted to carry out the following tasks:

- to offset inequities among the autonomous municipalities and communities.

- to mediate disputes between autonomous municipalities and between them and state municipalities.

Territories in Resistance

- to address complaints against autonomous councils in matters of human rights violations and complaints; to oversee correction of errors and monitor compliance.

- to monitor the implementation of projects and community work in the autonomous municipalities, ensuring compliance with the schedules and standards agreed upon with communities.

- to monitor compliance with laws in the municipalities.

- to help national and international civil society visit communities, carrying out productive projects and installing peace camps in rebel communities.

- to help people from autonomous rebel Zapatista municipalities participate in activities or events outside the communities.

- to ensure in Zapatista territory that leadership leads by obeying.

The Good Government council consists of one or two delegates from the Autonomous Councils in each zone. Presently there is a clear civil-military division. The municipalities carry out tasks related to dispensing justice, education, housing, land, labor, food, information, culture, and local transport. The military side, the EZLN, "monitors the operations of the Good Government councils in order to prevent acts of corruption, intolerance, injustice, and deviation from the Zapatista principle of leading by obeying" (Subcomandante Marcos 2003b).

Thus the Zapatistas hope to resolve the problems generated by the civil-military overlap. They do this through principles that they have embraced since the January 1, 1994 uprising: without creating a body that is separate from the communities and without creating state institutions or a bureaucracy, without, as Ornelas points out, "reproducing the separation between politics, society, and economy; between public and private; between 'important' and the banal; while seeking to create relationships that tend toward the (re)unification of social life" (Ornelas 2004, 11). Ultimately, the "civil" as much as the "military" depend upon the real power in the Zapatista movement—the community assembly, the community body that commands, by leading.

The Zapatistas' ability to create a new world in their territories, and to enable people to take control of their own lives, has strengthened the movement's capacity to resist the military-state encirclement. Their capacity to resist—the strengthening of difference—is what allowed them to launch the Other Campaign. An early announcement of this initiative can be found in the 2003 text about the creation of the Caracoles; it calls for the "La Realidad-Tijuana plan" that would "link all the resistance in our country and, with it, rebuild the Mexican nation from below" (Subcomandante Marcos 2003b). The plan went into motion two years later, with the announcement of the "red alert" and the Sixth Declaration of the Lacandon Jungle.

The Other, or Plebeian Politics

The Zapatista concept of autonomy is remarkable and guides all of the movement's actions. Autonomy is not only or primarily an issue of how the rebel movement relates to the Mexican state or to other movements. It is present in every aspect of Zapatista life, from the most remote community to the region as a whole, inspiring the smallest local undertaking to major campaigns like the Other Campaign. Autonomy is a way of viewing life and, among other things, politics, but it also imposes limits on autonomous spaces that fail to expand and tend to remain isolated.

The second part of the *Sixth Declaration of the Lacandon Jungle* ("Where We Are Now") addresses the problem of limits: "By our way of thinking, and what we see in our hearts, we have reached a point where we cannot go any further, and we could possibly lose everything we have if we do nothing more to move forward" (EZLN 2005). A few lines below it adds that perhaps unity of action with other sectors that have the same shortcomings as the Zapatistas will allow them to get what they need and deserve. Hence, a new step in the struggle "is only possible if the indigenous join together with workers, peasants, students, teachers, employees…" or, in other words, if all struggles are linked.

Years ago, the Zapatistas voiced a desire to establish links with those who resisted elsewhere in the world so as to avoid remaining confined in their Chiapas "island." In his letter "The World: Seven Thoughts in May of 2003," Subcomandante Marcos emphasized once again that they had no interest in conventional statist politics, given the weakness of nation states and their subordination to global powers, and that popular movements must unite their efforts:

> Turning to the traditional political class as an ally in the struggle is an exercise in nostalgia. Turning to neo-politicians is a symptom of schizophrenia. There is nothing to do up there, other than betting that maybe something can be done.
>
> There are those who are devoted to imagining that the rudder exists and to fighting for its possession. There are those who are seeking the rudder, certain that it has been left somewhere. And there are those who make of an island, not a refuge for self-satisfaction, but a ship for finding another island and another and another (Subcomandante Marcos 2003a, 10).

According to the EZLN´s analysis, the political, which is based upon class relations but maintains some autonomy from them, drove national states. With globalization, the "society of power" now occupies a higher place, a "collective leadership body that has displaced the political class and now makes the fundamental decisions" that no longer go through national institutions (Subcomandante Marcos 2003a, 6). Therefore, it does not make sense to engage in a struggle to take control of a "rudder" that either does not exist or is pure decoration.

The only way of doing politics is to change the world from below, not in order to reach the heights of power, but to create relations with others from below. This is what *La Sexta* (*The*

Sixth Declaration) is all about. "In Mexico, what we want to do is come to an agreement with persons and organizations of the left, and not that we will tell them what to do or give them orders" (EZLN 2005). Giving orders would be to reproduce the habits of the political class. Indeed since the very beginning, the Zapatistas have advanced a new way of doing politics. It is not yet defined but is "already operational in small and large fragments of societies worldwide" (Marcos 2003a, 13). This point is important because it involves two key issues: The Zapatista movement is not "the" new way of doing politics but simply another formulation (the most coherent, in my opinion); and, on the other hand, if there are different new ways of doing politics from below, in multiple movements and spaces of resistance, it is necessary to create bridges to bring them into contact with one another. That is the Other Campaign.

> Nor are we going to tell them to be like us or to rise up in arms.
>
> What we are going to do is ask them what their lives are like, their struggle, their thoughts about our country and what we should do so they do not defeat us.
>
> What we are going to do is to heed of the thoughts of the simple and humble people, and perhaps we will find there the same love that we feel for our fatherland.
>
> And perhaps we will find agreement between those of us who are simple and humble and, together, we will organize all over the country and link our struggles, which are alone right now, separated from each other, and we will find something like a program that has what we all want, and a plan for how we are going to achieve the realization of that program, which is called the "national program of struggle" (EZLN 2005).

Following meetings with partisans and groups that endorsed *La Sexta*, Marcos began a tour of the country on January 1, 2006, with the objective of listening and "building from below and for below an alternative to neoliberal destruction, an alternative left for Mexico." This is the real novelty of the

Other Campaign, which does not call for a political apparatus and communicates directly with people like them, like
the indigenous people of Chiapas. In the first three months,
Marcos met with other indigenous from other states, workers,
women, students, sex workers, housewives, youth, and the elderly in public events involving several thousand people and
in small meetings with a half dozen Sexta. "They know where
they want to go, but they will make the roadmap with others
while on the road," wrote Adolfo Gilly (2005b).

According to participants in the Other Campaign, *Zapatismo* is playing an important role in creating a space for
the communication of rebellion, much like ten years ago,
when the EZLN uprising strengthened and expanded other
movements. A good expression of this can be found in the
message that representatives of the Mixe, Zapotec, and Chi-
nantec people of the Sierra de Oaxaca read when Marcos or
"Delegate Zero" visited. It recalls that politicians of the right
and the left never took them into account, never heard or saw
them, but "you men and women of the EZLN taught us to re-
value our roots and strengthen our sense of the future." They
believe that the Other Campaign is an opportunity "to refresh
our collective memory and history and renew our hopes and
dreams." It is an opportunity to "build a new social pact that
will radically transform the current legal, political, economic,
social, and cultural structures of this country" (Bellinghausen 2006c). Joel Aquino, from the Assembly of Chontales and
Zapotec Authorities of the Sierra Norte, asserted that the Zapatista uprising "was like a torch illuminating our path," and
Ruperto Ko Wo, an elderly Maya from Campeche, said, "We
are ready for a policy of alliances to alleviate poverty in our region" and support participation in "national dialogue" (Bellinghausen 2006b; 2006a).

But why are Marcos and the Zapatistas traveling the
length and breadth of Mexico instead of inviting the collectives
and people to visit Chiapas like they did on previous occasions? Are the risks not too high? Does it make sense to travel
thousands of miles to visit a town or neighborhood and meet
with five or ten people? This must occur because politics from

below develops in different spaces than politics from above. These are spaces far from major centers of decision-making, in which those from below feel safe because they control these spaces.[15] The Zapatistas know this and decided to do politics in those spaces, which can only be known directly, without intermediaries. These are spaces that do not shine, that are beyond the glare of the media spotlight, and are, as Marcos says, "the place where they live and struggle: their home, their factory, their barrio, their town…their neighborhood, what one would call the reality of where they live and work, which is to say, where they construct their own history" (Subcomandante Marcos 2005a).

We see that for those from below there are no special stages—well lit and with microphones and cameras for TV—waiting for them to do politics, but only the same stages upon which they live their daily lives. The problem is that this is not visible for those who do politics by looking upward. This is a central aspect of plebeian politics or the way of doing politics from below.

> As we see it, and we could be wrong, this is where those from below make their big decisions: the birthplace of each persons Ya Basta!, where anger and rebellion grows, although it is not visible until the large demonstrations, where it becomes a collective, transformative force. *La Sexta* and the Other Campaign are not seeking a place for the word, but a place for listening, where you and others have done your political work and organizing. They do not call for big meetings, conventions, fronts, associations, coalitions, and so on. We will go, yes, to the gatherings and large meetings if they invite us and we can make it. We'll go with you because we trust those like you. This is why none of the meetings, representatives, fronts, dialogues, programs, etc., have reason to fear that we would dispute spaces, names, calls, signatures at the bottom, number of invited or power of

---

15   On this topic, see Scott 2000.

persuasion. But if we have to choose, we will choose
to go to a neighborhood or a factory, a market, or a
classroom instead of going to a big gathering. It will
be said then that the EZLN is missing out on the
chance that its word could be heard by thousands,
millions. And therein lies the problem, because the
EZLN is not looking to get the many listen to its word
but, on the contrary, seeks to listen to many—not all,
but those from below who resist and struggle. Whoever does not understand that this is what the EZLN
is looking for, have understood nothing and they will
be the ones demanding statements, interviews, and
communiqués in search of yet more explanations
(Subcomandante Marcos 2005a).

We see how the Zapatistas approach politics: by building
within spaces that are invisible to the powerful, political parties, academics, and intellectuals linked to power. Starting out
from the creation of spaces for listening, they hope to create
new spaces for a new vocabulary for those from below who
are in struggle. And here another one of the Zapatistas' great
creations or discoveries is born: that not just a single word
will exist, but a multiplicity of words. The idea of a rainbow of
colors within the single color of a traditional flag (be it red, or
red and black, or whatever) expresses this idea best.

Spaces created for exchange between the different people
cannot be "synthesized" into a single, homogeneous space—it
is necessary to open spaces in which differences can be expressed. This is a way of doing anti-capitalism, because the
logic of capital is a logic of standardization. Producing merchandise in the current globalized world implies the production of millions of identical products for consumption by
people who thus lose their specific traits and become identical
before the market. In politics, what unifies them is the electoral market that synthesizes for different policies:

Before leaving, Ramona gave me this embroidery
which she made while she was recovering in Mexico

City. She gave it to someone from civil society, who re-
turned it to us in one of these preparatory meetings.
She told me: "This is what we want from the Other
Campaign." These colors, no more, but no less.

Perhaps what we need to do is understand unity like
Ramona's embroidery, where each color and form has
its place; there's no uniformity, nor hegemony.

Finally, to understand unity as the agreement along
the path (Subcomandante Marcos 2005b).

This type of unity from below unlike that offered by the
trade union or traditional political parties, is not based on the
power of a leader or prominent personality but, as Marcos said
in the same piece, on loyalty among comrades. It is on that basis
that we can walk together, each one in step with a "multiplicity
of feet and ways of walking in the Other Campaign."

This walk is gathering momentum throughout Mexico.
The Other Campaign had little impact on those who supported Andres Manuel López Obrador (of the Democratic
Revolutionary Party, PRD), but it exercised great influence
among those who resist and mobilize. Its meetings "are not
rallies to pressure government authorities" or "electoral campaign events" in which the candidates make the same promises that they make in all electoral campaigns; "they are a public
space for the memory of wrongs suffered, the ground for dialogue about shared misfortunes and aspirations" (Hernández
Navarro 2006a).

But what can come of this space of exchange? People
often lament the dispersion of the organizations, the fragmentation of struggles, the inability to find common ground
between activists of different generations, from different
sectors of labor, with different demands and problems.
However, in these spaces controlled by those from below,
due to the work done by the Other Campaign, "a common
language is being created among those who until recently
could not engage with one another" (Hernández Navarro
2006a). This may seem small or insufficient but we can be
sure that once those from below find a common language

and recover the ability to speak their truths out loud that their acts will one day, any day, bring on a rebellion. The Zapatistas know that "it is only when hidden speech is declared openly, the subordinates can recognize to what extent their demands, their dreams, their anger is shared by other subordinates with whom they have not been in direct contact" (Scott 2000, 262).

New Challenges for Autonomy

The Zapatistas did not invent autonomy nor grassroots ways of doing politics from below; both have a long tradition in Latin America. The Zapatistas have endeavored to develop and improve them, creating the conditions for the expansion, growth, and diffusion of autonomist politics within the spaces of the oppressed.

However, the *La Sexta* and the Other Campaign appear on the scene at a special moment in Mexican and Latin American political life: when the social struggle has worn out the most savage forms and radical implementation of the neoliberal model, and when the tired and old parties of the right have begun to crack apart and give way to progressive and leftist forces. This is not a new problem for the movements, but it is worse in recent decades because in a few countries the popular resistance has helped the left occupy places within the state apparatus.

According to Marcos, one should situate the beginning of the Other Campaign in the year 2001, when the political parties—the PRI, the PAN, and the PRD—rejected the law of indigenous rights and culture. Parliament considered the law following the mass mobilization around the March of the Color of the Earth, during which millions came out around the country to greet the Zapatista caravan as it passed through on its way to Mexico City, where it would to support the indigenous autonomy law. The march lasted thirty-seven days, from February 24 to April 2, 2001, traveled four thousand miles, crossed thirteen states, and held seventy-seven public events, culminating in a major rally in Mexico City's Zocalo, after which the EZLN addressed Congress. But both the right and the left in parliament united to reject the law.

"At this point we concluded that the path of dialogue with the Mexican political class was exhausted and that we had to find another path," Marcos pointed out (Bogado 2006). Nevertheless this other path represented a risk that needed to be carefully weighed by the Zapatistas, namely the possibility of a surgical strike against the leadership of the EZLN due to their isolation from the political class. The Zapatistas anticipated that a good part of the people who hitherto supported their struggle would withdraw their support "at the moment when we distance ourselves from the politicians, especially those from the so-called institutional left, the PRD" (Bogado 2006). That was exactly what happened. They chose the election period to start the Other Campaign, adds Marcos, to "make it clear that we wanted to do something else" and that it would be very different from "the politics from above"(Bogado 2006).

Many supporters of the EZLN in Mexico wagered on the electoral process and the candidacy of Andres Manuel López Obrador of the PRD. Some of these voters took the position that the electoral and non-electoral path are complementary and others that the Zapatistas were negatively impacting Obrador's chances for victory. Many PRD voters distanced themselves from the EZLN when the Zapatistas asked those who participate in elections to refrain from participating in the Other Campaign. The Zapatistas were accused of sectarianism, of "playing the game to the right," among similar criticisms. Thus it became necessary to ask: Would a left electoral victory damage the Zapatistas and the social movement as a whole?

In Mexico, there was a political shift when the PRD won the elections in the Federal District in 1997 and thus acceded in principle to governance. "This changes the relationship between the parties and the social movements, and between militants and the movement. Many of them have become functionaries and subordinate to the logic of government," reflected Jesus Ramírez (2005, 301). Since the 1997 electoral victory, an important sector of the Mexican left has become embedded in government institutions, and key leaders occupy spaces leased to them by the state apparatus. One can conclude that "the defeat of many of the movements is a consequence of the role played by their leaders" (301). But this is only a first step, as we see in the cases of Brazil and Uruguay, where the Left first took municipal governments in cities like Porto Alegre, São Paulo, and Montevideo before then entering national government.

The second step occurs when the left embraces the positions of the right. This is what happened in Mexico in 2001, when all the political parties, including the PRD, united to reject the indigenous law. From that moment, "the split from the Zapatistas and other social struggles" intensified (Ramírez 2005, 302). In other words, the left begins administering parts of the state apparatus and veers rightward, leaving social movements without reference points, since the left came to power with the promise of resolving popular demands. Alongside the ideological and political disarmament induced by this, one can add an organizational crisis, as the leaders of these left movements are obliged to carry out the right's program within the institutions.

This triple disarticulation of the social movements (ideological, political, and organizational) beheads the popular struggle while laying the foundation for the co-optation of what remains. This defeat comes not through massive repression but through the familiar authoritarian actions of the state, this time overseen by the left political parties. In other words, the politics of the left lead to the same objective that repression could not achieve: a historical defeat.

We are witnessing something like this in countries like Argentina, Ecuador, Uruguay, and Brazil, with varying degrees of intensity. The social movements that created the conditions for the rise of the governments of Nestor Kirchner, Lucio Gutiérrez, Tabaré Vázquez, and Lula are now isolated, divided, and on the defensive. Some movement leaders (like prominent personalities among the piqueteros in Argentina, the indigenous in Ecuador, or unions in Uruguay and Brazil) have been put in positions in which they must defend official government policies while still supporting important sectors of the social movement. The divisions within the movement and the difficulty of mobilizing for common objectives increases governments' freedom to pursue neoliberal policies. While neoliberalism is more subtle and less directly predatory than it was in the years of savage privatization and crushing structural adjustments, its intensity and depth has not changed in the least.

It is helpful to consider comments made by one-time government supporters in the paradigmatic cases of Brazil and Argentina. In Brazil, the general secretary of the National Conference of Bishops, Odilio Scherer, says that the current government has transformed Brazil into "a financial paradise." The Archbishop of São Paulo, Claudio Hummes, a friend of Lula, was also disappointed with his management. The Bishop of Salvador, Geraldo Majella Agnelo, was categorical: "Never has there been a government so submissive to bankers" (Lavaca 2006). These statements were made in early March 2006, during Lula's reelection campaign—the Conference of Bishops had supported him directly or indirectly for several decades. Several analysts believe that relations between the government and the church are bad but feel they can get even worse. Frei Betto, a personal friend of Lula who coordinated the Zero Hunger Plan for almost two years, resigned, arguing that the government turned its back on the movements. In the case of the frustrated demand for agrarian reform, the bishops believe that Lula wagered that agribusiness would "modernize" the agrarian sector, thereby strengthening exports and meeting the demands of the financial sector. Far from introducing agrarian reform, these policies have led to a greater concentration of property.

In the case of Argentina we cede the floor to an economist who was elected deputy for a list akin to Kirchner. Claudio Lozano, an economist at the Central de Trabajadores Argentinos (CTA), is not a radical but argues that "we are now worse off than in the 1990s," the years of Menem. He insists that the policies of the previous regime have not been changed under Kirchner—not the high concentration of wealth, the regressive pattern of income distribution, the role of the state or even the country's international integration. On the contrary, there is "a greater exploitation of the workforce and further impoverishment of society." Despite the significant economic growth registered in the last three years, "in 2004 and 2005 inequality was exacerbated." Lozano points out that Kirchner's economic model focuses externally "toward placement of cheap natural products on the world market" and is also "a model from the top, in the sense of meeting the demands of the most affluent sectors of the population. This model organically maintains a more regressive distribution" (Lavaca 2006).

In both cases the continuation of neoliberalism is accompanied by policies targeted to address extreme poverty. But these policies do not address fundamental universal rights and instead attend to certain sectors that the state has deemed a priority based on its own criteria. This is because, as noted by Lozano, "universality puts into question a very good part of the political system," which functions on the basis of clientelism. The popularity enjoyed by Lula and Kirchner is due to this crucial factor of clientelism, allowing them to keep winning elections. In parallel, both manage to weaken and isolate the social movements by means of explicit politics aimed at creating "reasonable" movements—that is, those with whom they can negotiate and bargain with—while considering other movements as "radical," destabilizing forces that should be suppressed. In Argentina this is very clear in relation to the piquetero movement; in Brazil the government is privileging and building bridges with rural movements who are less combative than the landless movement (MST), with whom they tend to establish more fluid ties.

The Zapatistas understand this "progressivism" as a serious threat and compare the current situation with that of 1994, announcing a new *Ya Basta!* When Marcos said that the Zapatistas would fare very badly under López Obrador, he was saying the same thing that could be said today for the piquetero movement, the landless movement in Brazil, and the indigenous people in Ecuador. It should be understood that this is not a question of the intrinsic evil of the project of the left, nor of any particular animosity of their leaders toward the social movements. The point is that progressive and left governments are the best ones to implement the development and poverty reduction policies promoted by international financial institutions.

These policies have devastated the movements where they have been implemented without obstacles, such as those that occurred in regions of Ecuador. International programs were introduced into the country under the guise of seeking to strengthen social organizations and were overseen by local non-governmental organizations (NGOs) on the ground. However far from strengthening the social movements, these programs increase their level of internal bureaucracy, intensify their link with the state, aid in the creation of a specialized leadership separate from the base, and finally, facilitate the overall co-optation of the movements.[16] Over time, leaders begin to change their profile within the movement, assuming a more technocratic character, specializing in dealing with external funding agencies and procedures in the realm of public administration.

The divorce between the electoral left and social movements has no solution. First of all there are too many material interests and complicity with the state apparatus to think there could be a shift, except that those from below become strong enough that those above cannot ignore them. The electoral left is not the enemy of the movements, but their access to state power can do them irreparable harm if the movements have not established sufficient material and political autonomy. During his tour of Mexico, Subcomandante Marcos returned to the subject several times:

> The future history not only of Mexico but of all Latin America will be constructed from below. The rest, in any case, are steps. Maybe false steps, maybe firm ones, that is yet to be seen. But fundamentally, it will be the people from below that will be able to take charge of it, organizing themselves in another way. The old recipes or the old parameters should serve as a reference of what has been done, but not as something that should be re-adopted to do something new (Bogado 2006).

16   On this theme, consult Bretón Solo 2001b.

At this political juncture so filled with hope and yet so difficult for the movements, the EZLN have launched the challenge of the Other Campaign, with their determination to build spaces of inter-communication between those from below, showing that they can create other forms of doing politics outside of established political institutions. The success of this campaign could be the necessary encouragement for all of us who continue to struggle around this continent without looking to those above for solutions. We know that the struggle for autonomy—an endless struggle—is linked to emancipation and only those from below, with others from below, from their own spaces, can do it.

12
Colombia: Militarism and Social Movement

"Half of the country is in the hands of the *paras*," Paula says by the candlelight in a bar in La Candelaria, the historic old town of Bogotá that has been declared a World Heritage Site. "Wherever they establish their domain, they impose strict rules on daily life and customs: the haircuts of the young people, the closing times of the bars and clubs, and above all, they control and harass the women." Paula works for an environmental organization and she cannot hide her anguish over a country that she and many other Colombians feel is slipping out of their hands. Daniel, a university professor, calmly adds, "There was a war here and the paramilitaries won. The paramilitaries are not only auxiliaries of the state, but they are also the embodiment of a societal project that hopes to wipe out the social advances and conquests of more than a century."

Both assertions, at first glance, appear exaggerated. On Friday night, La Candelaria is full of young students from the private universities that abound in the area; they flock to the many bars that dot this beautiful neighborhood of narrow, cobblestone streets and old colonial houses. The night seems peaceful, with nothing suggesting that the country is at war or, as my hosts claim, controlled by armed forces. However, upon leaving the bar, we see uniformed patrols entering the nightspots, asking for documentation or simply observing the clientele. Back at the hotel, we turn on the television to a program about the Colombian armed forces, with beautiful young women extolling the virtues of the military's social work.

As the days pass, my initial doubts about militarization disappear. Bogotá is a city bristling with olive-green uniforms.

The military presence is an unavoidable part of daily life. At the main entrance of the National University, for example, several armored vehicles remind students that the soldiers may enter at any moment to restore "order." This kind of supervision is a form systematic control over the very pores of social life. And with it, according to all reports, fear becomes a way of life, with no end in sight.

If the military presence is suffocating in the big city, it is even stronger in the rural areas and, above all, more indiscriminate. The war and violence in Colombia revolve upon a singular axis: land. It is the reason for a conflict that has already lasted half a century. It began in 1948, when liberal leader and popular mayor Jorge Eliécer Gaitán was assassinated. The Colombian oligarchy, one of the most unyielding in the world, detested him. With time and global changes, the fight for land as a means of production has been supplanted by the defense of territory as a space to nurture identities, people's histories, and natural riches. Colombia is also now an essential piece of the regional, geopolitical chess game, given its ports on the Pacific and the Caribbean, its proximity to Panama and the world's most important maritime route, and for the long border it shares with Venezuela, a country that is in the sights of the White House.

Winning the War

Álvaro Uribe was elected president of the war. A half century of civil violence (starting with the Bogotazo of 1948, a spontaneous popular insurrection following the assassination of Gaitán) and twenty years of failed peace processes have generated deep skepticism in a population that is tired of politicians and their promises.

War is destroying the social fabric of the country: There have been almost three million displaced persons, 8,000 homicides annually for socio-political reasons, 3,500 detentions a year, and hundreds of forced disappearances. These are the tragic results of a conflict that appears interminable. In all, Colombia has one of the highest crime rates in the world, with some 27,000 homicides a year. The state appears incapable of providing law and order as its institutions deteriorate. This panorama explains why the population is afraid and chose security in 2002, electing Álvaro Uribe, who was promoted by the paramilitary sector, on a hard-line platform of ending the war. The ruinous situation dates back decades. In 1978, then-President Turbay Ayala (1978–1982) expanded the Statute of Security, which gave the armed forces judicial powers and opened the doors to the systematic violation of human rights. The Constitution of 1991 eliminated the state of siege with which the country had been governed for a century, but instituted a state of shock.

Colombia is torn between the drive to construct a democratic order and the impulse to construct an authoritarian one, although the wide-ranging violence and election of Uribe tipped the balance toward the latter. The neoliberal model, generator of exclusion and social marginalization, and the policies of the government of U.S. President George W. Bush—among them the "Plan Colombia," do nothing more than strengthen authoritarianism. The present Colombian administration decided to cut social spending in order to finance the war. Uribe's methods clearly indicate a totalitarian impulse: creating a net of civilian informers—up to one million people—to help the armed forces; security installations in neighborhoods and businesses; a network of taxi and other drivers dedicated to ensuring security on streets and highways; and a Day of Reward that pays citizens who have helped authorities stop acts of terrorism and capture those responsible. Moreover, the government has increased the personnel of the armed forces by 30,000 and of the police force by 10,000. It has also created 120,000 "peasant soldiers" and set up Zones of Rehabilitation and Consolidation under the military direction, in which civil liberties, such as the right of assembly and mobilization, are restricted.

This promotes the dismantling of the public apparatus while generating situations of legal informality that favor indiscretion in the use of force. It encourages the reorganization of society around a military model. Analyst María Teresa Uribe maintains that it is an attempt to "model society along

the lines of a militia and convert the citizen into a soldier."
With this vigilante society, "trust between neighbors, old loy-
alties and the threads of cordiality break, dissolve, atomize;
and in this context of mutual suspicion, collective action, public deliberation, and social organization decline. It ends with
silence prevailing and individuals retreating into the private
sphere" (Uribe 2004).

Guerrillas, Paramilitaries, Drug Trafficking

Although the previous description is correct, it does not capture the entirety of the problem. The war happens on stages
determined by geography and history's idiosyncrasies. Three
branches of the Andean mountain range divide Colombia's
fragmented territory. Jungles and mountains, foggy forests,
deep valleys, and inaccessible regions crisscross it. The Colombian state, which was formed by the gradual integration
of territories, populations, and social groups, has never been
able to control all of this territory. It never was a modern state,
and today the principal economic and social problem of the
country is the concentration of land, which has generated an
unresolved agrarian problem. In sum, there never was a true
state in Colombia or anything like agrarian reform or a redistribution of the land, which makes Colombia different from
many other South American countries.

The enormous power of the national and regional elites,
woven over a stratified social base and the marginalization
of the majority of farmers, fragmented the state's presence
by weakening the mechanisms of social regulation. "Excess"
farmers were also pushed toward the agricultural margins
and, more recently, toward the periphery of the big cities. "In
these zones, the organization of social life is left to the free
play of the people and social groups, due to the absence of
state regulation and the lack of relations with the national
society" (Gonzalez 2004).

The guerrilla was born in these areas. It is the continuation—certainly amplified and more systematic—of a duality
of powers inherited from colonial times. Marginalized groups
populated the isolated territories—mestizos reluctant to bow

to the clergy's control, whites without land, blacks and mulatos fleeing from the mines, and so on. These regions are the exact opposite of the elitist cities, which are governed as the feudal territory by the dominant groups. Daniel Pécaut, one of the most knowledgeable analysts of Colombia, maintains that the state conserves its own oligarchic and exclusive features. For that matter, so does the culture of the Colombian elites.

FARC (The Revolutionary Armed Forces of Colombia, in Spanish *Fuerzas Armadas Revolucionarias de Colombia*) was created in 1966, emerging from groups of farmers armed to defend the liberal communities that emerged during *La Violencia.*[17] Rather than organizing around ideological affinities, they organized around territorial bonds. The guerrillas consolidated themselves in zones where the peasants needed to protect themselves from the state and the landowners and where the geography offered a natural refuge. After the cultural changes of the seventies, the criminalization of peasant protest, the birth of dynamic urban movements (among workers and students), and the radicalization of the middle class contributed to the birth of the ELN (National Liberation Army, in Spanish *Ejército de Liberación Nacional*) and other rebel groups. Currently, FARC has approximately 20,000 combatants and the ELN has some 4,000. The other groups disarmed in the nineties.

The paramilitary groups (10,000 to 20,000 members) were born out of the "self-defense" groups, which the army created in the late sixties to assist in counterinsurgency operations. Amnesty International and Americas Watch have documented the close relationship between the paramilitaries and state security forces, as have the United Nations and the Organization of American States. They all attribute the immense majority of human rights violations in Colombia to the paramilitary groups and argue that they impose terror in the zones that they control.

---

17 Roughly 200,000 people died during *La Violencia*, a period of wars between liberals and conservatives. Persecuted ferociously by the state, liberals and communists took refuge in remote, inaccessible regions and resisted for more than a decade until some of them regrouped in what later would be the communist-oriented FARC.

The paramilitaries are closely tied to the large landowners (their "social cradle") and drug traffickers. While the army gave weapons to the paramilitary forces, the coffee plantation and cattle farm owners organized them, choosing to confront the FARC with groups of drug-addicted peasants. They not only targeted guerrillas, but also union leaders, professors, journalists, defenders of human rights, and left-wing politicians. However, the rise of drug trafficking has changed the situation over time. The Americas Watch 1990 report states that the drug traffickers have become big landowners and, as such, have begun to share the right-wing politics of the traditional landowners and leaders of some of the most notorious paramilitary groups (Americas Watch 1991, 22).

Various "private armies" came together to form the United Self-Defense of Colombia (AUC) in the nineties. Economically and militarily powerful, they helped elect Uribe, whom they considered a loyal friend, in addition to the numerous legislators who backed them. On July 15, 2003 the government and the AUC signed a demobilization agreement and the AUC announced a ceasefire, although in 2004 it was responsible for the death or disappearance of 1,300 people, more than 70 percent of all of the politically motivated homicides in the country not related to combat (Amnesty International 2004). Demobilization talks continue in Santa Fé de Ralito. While the government defends the demobilization of AUC and says it is following the law, the paramilitaries have rejected this possibility. One of the greatest difficulties is that many of the paramilitary leaders can be extradited to the United States, where they would be judged for drug trafficking.

Three Phases of Plan Colombia

Plan Colombia has helped militarize the country, but also, in a striking way, consolidated paramilitarism as a social and political alternative. Some analysts identify three phases in its consolidation and expansion, based on the declarations of the paramilitary leaders themselves. An important reference is the experience of Magdalena Medio, one of the strategic zones of the country where the ultra-right was able to uproot enclaves of guerillas and the union movement (as it has in the oil city of Barrancabermeja).

In the first phase, they used war and terror to "liberate" "large zones of subversives and their popular bases of support; imposing land concentration; modernizing roads, services, and infrastructure; and developing of capital and the new hierarchical structure in the social and political organization of the region." During the second phase, they focused on "bringing wealth to the region" by handing over land and by generating jobs, productive projects, technical aid, and credit. This looks good on paper, but "the new inhabitants who occupy the old liberated zones are not those who were uprooted by violence; it is a new population (of poor people brought from other regions), loyal to the 'boss' who rapidly organized them and formed their base groups. This is the paramilitary self-defense" (Sarmiento 1996, 33). There was consolidation in the third phase, when the conditions were ripe for the expansion of multinational capitalism and the modernizing state.

The goals of Plan Colombia are visible in each of the three stages: Although 80 percent of the federal budget goes to war and the military apparatus, important parts are dedicated to improving infrastructure, health, education, and alternative development. In this sense, it is important to conceive of Plan Colombia as an integral, long-range project to "open" the entire region to multinational and American control. Indeed, analysts frequently point out that Plan Colombia is a way of "preparing the turf" for the imposition of the Free Trade Area of the Americas (FTAA) (Salgado 2004).

In fact, in regions such as Magdelena Medio, some Plan Colombia resources fell into the hands of the paramilitaries' non-governmental organizations that managed the plan's social funds. At the same time, the imposition of strict control over daily life allowed "the revival of the paternalism of the old landlords without the minimum social obligations of the past" (Loingsigh 2002, 104). In Barrancabermeja, a paramilitary town, "they prohibited kids from wearing long hair, earrings, and bracelets. They closed the gay bars, and beauty parlors owned by homosexual men were transferred to women. They killed a homosexual man, and then cut off his penis and put it in the mouth of the dead body." Also, they instituted a curfew for minors and obligatory schooling until age seventeen. They limited the hours for public establishments and imposed sanctions and punishments on those who disobey. The report from various human rights organizations about the Magdalena Medio notes, "On a side street in any of the neighborhoods of Barrancabermeja and Puerto Wilches, one can see boys with machete in hand, cleaning the public areas as part of their punishment. In other cases, they are forced to wear signs that say that they are thieves, prostitutes, etc." (2002, 24). Reaching the end of the report, I can see that the anguish of my hosts in Bogotá, Paula and Daniel, is more than justified.

The Difficult Task of the Social Movements

How can one create a social movement in a militarized society, one in which the spaces for public action are closed, and where the activists and leaders are systematically killed and kidnapped? And how can civil society avoid reproducing militarism in the process? For those seeking demilitarization, there is no question that all actors in the conflict violate human rights, including the guerillas. In Colombia, Pécaut points out, "Violence is not only a series of happenings, it is the eruption of a new modality of politics" (Pecaut 1987, 523). In other words, politics since 1948 or even earlier represent violence. The depths of the violence in Colombia are such that not only does it impregnate all manifestations of the political and social, but it also constitutes them.

Nevertheless, it is possible to escape the polarization through the creation of demilitarized zones that are off limits to the different actors in the conflict: the guerillas, paramilitaries, and army. This is not simple, as groups will break in to murder, kidnap, and torture. Furthermore, all the actors in the conflict have at one time or another considered these zones as home to real or potential "enemies." And there is a temptation to respond to the violence with violence or to simply abandon the land. Luis Angel Saavedra, director of Inredh, a human rights organization in Quito, maintains that "Plan Colombia is a part of a greater strategy to control the social movements of Latin America, and the resources of this part of the world" (Saavedra 2003). He argues that similar plans for military control have been deployed in all of the countries of the Andean region under the pretext of coca eradication (in sites where the peace movements are most active).

The second problem is the absence of a national social movement capable of providing an alternative to the conflict. Many pacifistic initiatives are local, with the notable exception of those led by indigenous peoples, who make up only 2 percent of the Colombian population but have an influence over broad geographic areas.

The Regional Indigenous Council of the Cauca (CRIC) is a member of the National Indigenous Organization of Colombia (ONIC), which unites all the ethnicities of the country. After hundreds of years of resistance, the indigenous peoples obtained recognition of territories called "indigenous havens." There are 712 in the country and they occupy 30 percent of the Colombian territory. The Constitution of 1991 recognizes collective rights and the Indian people's territories, although they now face the threat of a "new invasion." The pressure is on to eliminate Article 329 of the Constitution, which recognizes the inalienable character of indigenous territories in order to implement the FTAA.

The indigenous peoples of the Cauca resist the war by not participating in the conflict. They do it as a community and collectively, based on their cosmology, in an unarmed, nonviolent way. They believe that the forces of global capital have launched a new invasion and seek to defend their territory against cultural, social, and economic threats. They are trying to maintain diversity in the means of production, rescuing and strengthening traditional ways of cultivating the earth, conserving seeds to prevent the disappearance of crops—everything contrary to the intentions of the FTAA. They believe that their territorial organization is "a perfectly viable way for the general population to resist the war" (Caldon 2004).

They resist being uprooted and hold onto their land. They preserve their own languages as a way to defy cultural homogenization. They value and fortify traditional knowledge of healing. Their communities have organized "Indian guards"—unarmed commune members carrying ancestral canes of authority or *chontas*, who protect residents. The guard "depends exclusively on the community, which in big assemblies decided to reorganize it, establishing the boundaries of its power and requisites for its members"(Acosta 2004). Guards do not perform police functions, and all commune members have to take their turns at being guards. They have set up meeting places for inhabitants to gather when an armed conflict breaks out between the guerrillas and the paramilitaries or the army. They sound alarms for the community at times of danger. Without resorting to violence, the guards have rescued people kidnapped by armed groups. They argue that other sectors of the population can use this system of guards to resist the war, too.

In additional to the indigenous communities in Colombia, other groups around the country, especially in rural areas, have declared their territory war-free, demanding that the armed groups leave. San José de Apartadó, in the north of the country, is the first of these communities of peace. Created in 1997, it maintains its stance despite the aggressions of armed groups from the left and the right. In only seven years, the small community suffered more than 360 human rights violations and more than 144 assassinations in the conflict.

Nevertheless, San José de Apartadó persists. In August, they opened the Peasant University of the Resistance, receiving support from fifteen additional communities. In December 2004, the community held the Second Meeting of Communities of Civil Resistance, "celebrating life and solidarity in reply to the Colombian state's wages of death." It is true that the communities of peace movement is small, but it has survived and even expanded in the seven years since it was founded—the most violent years of the war—and that is reason for hope.

In addition to the urban mobilizations against the war, Plan Colombia, and the FTAA, the outstanding indigenous "Minga for Life, Autonomy, Liberty, Justice, and Happiness" occurred on September 13, 2004. During *la minga* (the indigenous word for a collective project), 60,000 Indians of the Cauca (south) convened in Cali for three days, supported by all 84 indigenous groups in Colombia.

Organized by the CRIC, la minga did not focus on the government and featured no platform of demands. Rather it was directed toward the people, who were called upon to defend life against the war and oppose the free trade agreement between Colombia and the United States. The large mobilization created a demilitarized zone for three days. It opened with the rescue of the Indian mayor of Toribío, kidnapped by the FARC. The members of the indigenous guard arrived en masse, overwhelmed the armed group holding him, and liberated the mayor together with his delegation.

The indigenous people showed that it is possible to force open cracks in a militarized society if you don't try to fight war with more war. As the indigenous women of the south say, "In the logics of life, there is no other, but just a constant flow that does not eliminate but creates." They denounce the logic of destruction, saying that it only serves the oppressors and that "ends and means cannot be separated" (Unidad Indigena 2004). They believe that the transformations are made from the bottom up and from the inside out, from the local to the global and from the singular to the universal. That's what helped them break the barriers of militarism and indifference. Daniel, the professor from Bogotá, was in Cali that Wednesday in September, 2004 when thousands of Indians crossed the elegant commercial streets in the second-largest city in Colombia. "It was exciting," he confessed, "to see the rest of the population's reception of the Indians. The people were applauding and others were crying. This is the other Colombia, the one of hope."

Where the Asphalt Ends: School and Community in Bogotá's Peripheries

At the southern end of Bogotá, Colombia, in the cold, wind-eroded mountains, millions of people displaced by sixty years of war try to build the world of their dreams despite threats from armed groups and abuse from landowners.

"People have come here from different regions due to various conflicts—the ones in the forties, in the sixties, the seventies, the eighties," says Mauricio, director of the community schooling project Cerros del Sur, built on the highest point of the Potosí-La Isla hill, which splits the south from the north of the city. We arrive in a taxi that leaves us on the street that divides Potosí from the poorer and less organized neighboring hill, Caracoli, where the paramilitaries' word is law. With difficulty we climb the hill's dirt paths to the door of the school, situated three thousand meters above sea level.

The sprawling and immense suburb of Ciudad Bolivar sits one hour from central Bogotá; with a population of one million, it is the most populated of the city's twenty "localities." Almost all of the dwellings bear traces of the do-it-yourself construction that is the norm in this zone. Arriving in the Jerusalén area, where a belt of hills marks the city limits, the houses get poorer and poorer although almost all are made of bricks. Public services seem more precarious here: Only the main streets—the avenues—are asphalted; shops and public transport are scarce; flat land gives way to steep hills. We are coming to the outskirts of the outskirts.

First surprise: The school has no bars, neither at the main entrance nor on the windows. This would be unthinkable in Bogotá, especially in its poorer neighborhoods. Mauricio says that this was the wish of the handful of Salesian teachers and students who started the project in 1983 as a popular educational project: "We don't know if the school is part of the community or the community part of the school, but they have grown together and into each other" (Sanabria 2007).

Thanks to more than twenty years of communitarian work in which the Cerros del Sur school has played a pivotal role, the neighborhood is one of the few to have all the public services: paved streets, water and electricity, gas lines, transport, schools, nurseries, and parks. "Other neighborhoods that started at the same time have not gotten this far. To achieve what you see here, you need people who are great at working together," points out Pedro Vargas, an old resident (Corporación Taliber 1998, 33).

With some 15,000 inhabitants, Potosí is one of the ten sections of the Jerusalén neighborhood (population 150,000), itself one of the 320 neighborhoods that form Ciudad Bolívar, one of the twenty localities that make up the city's total of around seven million people. The capital is growing at a dizzying rate, mostly due to the arrival of migrants displaced by the war. Since 1985, violence has created three million displaced people, of whom 23 percent came to Bogotá, almost all living in very poor neighborhoods at the southern or south-eastern edge of the city, where more than half of inhabitants are direct or indirect victims of six decades of wars against the peasantry.

Twenty Years Building a Neighborhood

The slopes of Potosí were bare until the start of the eighties. The Jerusalén area housed barely 8,000 people, who had no water, electricity, sewers, telephones, transportation, or schools. Further on from the hills, there were M-19 guerrilla camps and some FARC and ELN presence.[18] In a few short years, families populated it who had arrived from the countryside or who were unable to keep paying rent in central Bogotá.

They had to walk five kilometers with pots and buckets to get water. They bought their plots of land from "pirate

18   M-19 was a nationalist guerrilla group.

developers," who took all their savings as well as televisions, irons, and other appliances. Because the sales were illegal, the police came at night and burned the cardboard and asphalt sheet settlements, considering it a land invasion. Whereas families illegally occupy land in the majority of Latin American and Colombian cities, they buy illegal lots in Bogotá and then build their own houses.

According to one resident, the construction of these neighborhoods is "the prolongation of a struggle for land that has stretched across the countryside for decades and is now expressed in the urban sphere in the form of struggles for homes." In this way, "thousands of rural and urban immigrants who lived through expulsion, exodus, and misery, trawling the streets and sidewalks in search of land and a roof, found something of what we were looking for in Potosí-La Isla" (Corporación Taliber 1998, 9).

In March 1984, the Cerros del Sur school was inaugurated, founded by Evaristo Bernate. Three hundred children attended classes at the school, which a group of self-taught instructors led in three prefabricated stalls of just forty meters. Many of the children sat on the floor or on bricks and wrote on wooden blocks that served as desks. Formally, it is a private institution but the parents don't pay because the Ministry of Education grants them scholarships.

The goal of the project was not just to educate, but also to organize the life of the neighborhood; each teacher took charge of a specific sector to "create community organization with the neighborhood leaders and find solutions to the difficulties faced." From the start, the neighborhood's Communal Action Committee was run by people looking for "a place for social climbing and personal benefit," allying themselves with the city's traditional politicians. Those were the very politicians who had sold and resold illegal lands in poor neighborhoods with the protection of the authorities.

Conflicts began as the community organized itself alongside the school. In 1986, the "communitarian mothers" group was formed. Most children typically stayed at home while their parents went out to work, as there were fires and some accidents. A group of women decided to begin taking care of the children collectively in their own houses, without official help. They themselves built a place for sixty children, including a bathroom and kitchen, and in 1987 they occupied the offices of the Family Wellness Institute to win the funds to pay salaries.

They achieved all of this through direct action: first the Jardín Alegría kindergarten, then the school, and later secondary education in Cerros del Sur. They began to displace traditional politicians, who reacted—as is often the case in Colombia—by accusing the teachers and neighborhood activists of being "communists" and "guerrilla fighters." There were dozens of police raids but, in the following years, thanks to the application of concerted pressure and the occupation of dozens of state and municipal businesses, the neighborhood got electricity and water.

But the government built very little. The residents had to do most of the construction. A group of young people organized parties to raise money for the park and later helped build it. The highway was important insofar as it enabled public transportation to reach the area. In late 1987, more than 200 residents went out with picks and spades every Sunday for three weeks to make the main road. At every step of the way they were met by new obstacles. There were violent conflicts as businesses fought to monopolize the neighborhood's transportation, but now one single bus route goes there from the center of town and is not in the hands of a monopoly.

The group later built a communal shop to keep essentials cheap and accessible within the neighborhood. They created the Medical Attention Center in the early nineties and then the community radio and the young people's dance and sport groups. Potosí quickly became the most organized area and encouraged the rest to come together in JERUCOM, an umbrella group for all the neighborhood committees in Jerusalén. On May 11, 1991, the director of the Cerros del Sur, Evaristo, was assassinated, like so many local activists. It seems that the murderers felt displaced by the community work that he represented. His murderers have never been captured.

Creating Community

Evaristo's death provoked a crisis, but the residents confronted it head on. The community school became "the center all flocked to, not just looking for education but also for a discussion of the community's problems; it became an axis of initiatives benefitting everyone. It is the principal meeting place for discussion and planning of community activities" (Corporación Taliber 1998, 75).

They conceived of pedagogy in a new way. They saw it as touching on all aspects of life, not just what goes on in the classroom. "This is also part of the pedagogic project: how people take school, how they appropriate it for themselves, how they make it feel their own, how they make it part of their own lives." The goal is that "the students attain self-determination, which leads them to transform themselves and their community" (Corporación Taliber 1998, 69).

This concept of education is very similar to the one that sustains Brazil's landless people's movement: "In this way," wrote Evaristo, "school is more than the classroom or building. It is the neighborhood as a whole. We should learn through varied social practices: in the classroom, but also through the construction of houses, the management of water, the occupation of public service buildings, street openings, etc."

In the nineties, there was a great deal of community organizing in Ciudad Bolivar. Although some services had been won, more elevated neighborhoods still suffered great shortages (80 percent were without public drains and sewage), and lack of education (some 90,000 places short) and health care. With the implementation of the neoliberal model, a new problem arose: violence. Some 300 young people were murdered every year as part of "social cleansing"—petty criminals, drug addicts, and gang members, but also social and political activists—in a place that had about 600,000 inhabitants in 1993. But parallel to this, there was a cultural reawakening with meetings, workshops, talks, and performances.

The Civic Unit was created, consisting of sixty-five Ciudad Bolivar organizations, and it called a strike for October 11, 1993. The strike was a success; the municipality accepted nearly all its demands and created commissions to ensure the completion of the terms of the signed agreements, overseen in part by community organizations. This is Mauricio's evaluation:

> The first civic strike in 1993 forced the administration to negotiate with the Ciudad Bolivar committees. From this moment on, a lot of money began to arrive, with high levels of corruption, which spoiled things somewhat. When that money came, so did the NGOs that live off misery; there was atomization, the whole organization ruptured, and many of its leaders were murdered. The organizational net ripped (Sanabria 2007).

Even so, things kept moving forward in Potosi. A Community Council replaced the Communal Action Committee in 1998, with the aim of raising participation levels. In the traditional committee a steering group of seven members was chosen but the council added various representatives from its seventeen work areas. It thus grew from a seven-person directive body to an open assembly of more than fifty people. Now, "the group makes all decisions—it is not the whims of the president or any one person that prevail, but the wishes of the majority" (Corporación Taliber 1998, 104).

Although they feel isolated due to the crisis of the social organizations in the area, relations with the authorities have greatly improved since Luis Garzón of the Polo Democrático party became Bogotá's mayor in 2004. The community work has been deepening and now they embrace productive projects called "food security." Mauricio mentions the creation of a community diner that sells very cheap lunches to four hundred people and breakfasts to children.

There is a working organic garden in the school that is part of the food security project and it has been expanded to private plots, where families are beginning to grow small quantities of organic produce, and to other school spaces and wastelands in the neighborhood. The urban agriculture began just five years ago and now a market area is being installed to avoid intermediaries so that the farmers can sell their products straight to locals. This project will rely on the support of the municipal program, Bogotá Sin Hambre.

Slow Change

With the help of Cerros del Sur teachers, students, and alumni, the community organization develops. Every issue it works on implies coordinated, block-by-block organization and weekend meetings in the community school. One of the latest successes was getting building materials to improve and redesign five hundred homes with the support of architects. The most important issues they work on are human rights, sports, community child-rearing, education for people with special needs, culture, street paving, and housing.

"South American champions have come out of this neighborhood, which shows that it's possible for the kids in these neighborhoods, the ones seen as delinquents or drug addicts, to have bright careers," Mauricio says proudly. Kids from neighborhoods like Potosí often fall victim to paramilitary groups, who have killed between 200 and 300 young people in this neighborhood alone since the beginning of the nineties.

Asked about the most important changes in his neighborhood, Mauricio explains,

> I arrived here in 1987. There has been a clear improvement since then in living conditions. Now there are public services, there is almost full enrollment in primary school, and nearly full enrollment in the secondary school. But the most noticeable change is cultural. Before problems were resolved with machetes, but it's not like that anymore. People have had the chance to finish high school and even go to college, reducing drug addiction, domestic violence, and robberies. There has been an obvious improvement in community organization. There is more autonomy.

He cites the neighborhood next door, Caracoli, as an example. We climb to the school's basketball courts to observe it in the distance. The differences are noticeable. The streets are not paved, the housing is much less secure, mostly just one floor and built with salvaged materials. As stated in an article published by *Semana* magazine, a winner of the Rey de España journalism prize, "Caracoli is a pile of sad and unfinished houses" and lacks basic services.

In Caracoli, barely 200 meters from Potosí, the paramilitaries are in charge. "They tried to get their groups involved here but the people rejected it," Mauricio says. "The paramilitaries base their work and resolve their drug and robbery issues through violence. You leave or they kill you. That is their style in every case. If you're a store owner, you need to pay them protection money."

One of the biggest changes relates to domestic violence, which is very common in Colombia. "Women can now go out and study, but this is just one side of the story, because although now women are in other spaces, this has provoked ruptures in the family and there are many single women. Machismo has been reduced a lot; there are many young single mothers. You can see twelve- and thirteen-year-old girls pregnant, although in our school there are many less than in other neighborhoods. Our sexual education program still needs development," Mauricio concludes.

Before we return to the avenue where the taxi left us, we walk through part of the neighborhood: the playground, the diner, and the community mothers' house. Mauricio explains other projects that are newly up and running. One of these sells clothes, toys, and shoes and gives the money earned toward special needs education. A group of young mothers has created the Potosí Cultural Corporation, in whose dance hall they hold art classes with young and elderly people together to "rescue, value, and feed our culture and offer them a possibility of a different life."

It is impossible to hide the poverty in Potosí, just like in La Victoria (Chile) and Villa El Salvador (Peru). But community organization has given life some dignity and helped provide not just public services but also a high level of collective and personal autonomy to Potosí's residents. It's no small achievement, when you consider that they've done it themselves.

Ecuador:
A Prolonged Instability[19]

Ten years ago, political and social instability came to Ecuador as a strong indigenous movement emerged as a new actor. It actively opposed the entrenched elites who have long refused to give up their control over the state. While President Rafael Correa scored an overwhelming victory in the referendum held April 15, 2007, in which more than 80 percent of the electorate voted in favor of his proposal to convene a constituent assembly, and the referendum paves the way for elections to choose delegates amid extreme polarization between the administration and the right, there is no guarantee that this will lead to changes in state control or that Ecuador will become more stable.

Correa's first months in office were marked by his inability to overcome the institutional instability that has racked the country for more than ten years. Since 1996, no president has served a full term in office due to the recurrent insurrections and social protests that have convulsed the country. It will be hard for Correa to succeed where others failed. The population, especially the indigenous, seems unwilling to tolerate continued rule by the white elites who plunged a nation rich in natural resources—including oil—into poverty. On the other hand, the elites are averse to losing their privileges. This is the source of today's climate of confrontation.

Correa owes his surprising victory in the November 26, 2006, runoff to an organized civil society that has vocally rejected neoliberal plans. Despite being an independent with no

19 Originally published in *Programa de las Américas del International Relations Center* (www.ircamericas.org), April 2007.

party and no fellow party candidates running for Congress, the new president has the backing of a significant portion of Ecuadorians. He now faces the difficult task of dismantling a colonial state created by the elites. His main weapon, which has provoked the tenacious resistance of the privileged class, is a constituent assembly to create a new foundation for the country and to give it a state that truly represents those who have been excluded for five centuries.

A Long History

The last president to serve a complete term in office was the conservative Sixto Durán Ballén (1992–1996). His eight successors have governed in the context of nearly constant social upheaval, but instability grew worse in June 1990, when a powerful indigenous uprising spearheaded by the Federation of Indigenous Nationalities of Ecuador (CONAIE) set off a political and social cataclysm and placed the indigenous population center stage in Ecuadorian politics. Since then, they have been the force other actors must either negotiate with or confront. They are no longer willing to play a secondary role.

Abdalá Bucaram, a right-winger, won the 1996 elections. He remained in power for only six months before Congress ousted him, citing his "mental incapacity to govern." Bucaram's tempestuous term in office was plagued by irregularities and sparked massive protests. Bucaram was succeeded for a few hours by vice president Rosalía Arteaga, but Congress instead named its president, Fabián Alarcón, to serve as interim president. In the August 1998 elections, Jamil Mahuad defeated billionaire Álvaro Noboa in the second round.

Mahuad governed from August 10, 1998, until January 22, 2000, when a broad-based indigenous uprising backed by a group of rebel colonels, most prominently Lucio Gutiérrez, forced him to resign. Vice President Gustavo Noboa took over. All of this occurred amid a financial collapse that led the authorities to freeze bank deposits and replace the Ecuadorian sucre with the dollar.

In the 2002 elections, Gutiérrez came to power riding a wave of indigenous support. He promised to carry out sweeping changes, declared himself to be a "nationalist, progressive, and revolutionary," and proposed a "second independence" for Ecuador. Gutiérrez's cabinet ministers included prominent indigenous leaders, such as Nina Pacari, who became the first indigenous woman on the continent to serve as minister of foreign affairs.

However, Gutiérrez quickly betrayed his allies, signing an agreement with the International Monetary Fund (IMF), introducing a structural adjustment program and turning to the right-wing Social Christian Party (PSC) for support. CONAIE sank into a deep crisis from which it has still not fully recovered. Its leaders distanced themselves from their base, many taking government posts. Gutiérrez also used government funds to divide and co-opt the movement, even resorting to selective repression against dissidents. Finally, in July 2003, six months into the term of a government that had raised enormous expectations, CONAIE withdrew its militants from the cabinet.

As the unpopularity of Gutiérrez's government spread, so did the protests. The agreements with international financial institutions led to the privatization of the state-owned electricity and telecommunications companies and to the suspension of subsidies on domestic gas use. On April 20, 2005, Congress ousted Gutiérrez amid a massive urban protest led by middle-class citizens and young people in Quito known as the "forajidos," or outlaws (as Gutiérrez referred to his critics).

Alfredo Palacio succeeded Gutiérrez. He distanced himself from his predecessor's pro-American stance and made economist Rafael Correa minister of the economy. This marked a turning point in the country's recent history. Correa had negotiated the sale of $500 (U.S.) million in foreign-debt bonds to Venezuelan president Hugo Chávez and decided that a portion of oil exports would be reserved for social expenditures rather than paying down the foreign debt. But pressure from Washington, the IMF, and the World Bank forced Correa to resign, as Palacio veered to the right and prepared to sign a free trade agreement with the United States.

As the pendulum swung rightward, the indigenous population took the initiative once again. The most recent, major indigenous uprising (of a total of more than ten since 1990) took place in March 2006. The government respond-ed to the demonstrations, the roadblocks, and the paralysis of the country by decreeing a state of emergency in half of the nation's twenty-two provinces. Grassroots activists, ral-lying around the slogan "We do not want to be a colony of the United States," scored a resounding victory when it forced Palacio's government to back down on May 15. Bowing to so-cial movement pressure, it expelled Occidental Petroleum and confiscated its assets as a way to ease tension. The proposed free trade agreement was put on hold, as the White House said that it would not sign it under existing conditions. It was in this climate that Correa was elected.

The Recent History

In the run-up to the October 15, 2006, elections, Rafael Correa founded Alianza País [Country Alliance], an umbrella organi-zation of progressive groups. The traditional left ran its can-didates, as it has always done, and the indigenous movement backed Luis Macas, president of CONAIE. Neither of these two sectors fared well at the polls or came close to defeating the right, which had rallied around banana magnate Álvaro Noboa. Amid complaints of fraud—never proven or ruled out—Noboa won the first round while Correa placed second. A vast social movement supported Correa's candidacy dur-ing the second round. It was made up of the Pachakutik (pro-indigenous) Party, the Democratic Popular Movement, the socialist and democratic left parties, and, most importantly, more than two hundred civil society organizations.

This broad-based movement dashed the hopes of the right, which had seemed poised to win. Correa stated that he opposed the Free Trade Agreement with the United States; re-jected the Bush administration's labeling of the FARC as a "ter-rorist" organization; said that he would not renew the contract for the U.S. airbase at Manta; and endorsed Hugo Chávez's regional integration project, the Bolivarian Alternative for the Americas. On the crucial topic of oil he was categorical: "We cannot permit the multinationals to take four of each five barrels produced and leave us only one. We are going to revise the state's participation in these contracts" (Lemoine 2007).

Although Correa defended his friendship with Chávez, he rejected the claim that he was a "Chávista." He stated, "We are stakeholders in a twenty-first century socialism that seeks social justice, national sovereignty, defense of natural resources, and regional integration based on a logic of coordination, cooperation, and complementarity" (Lemoine 2007). With this orientation and the support it garnered, he won the second round on the run off on November 26, with 57 percent of the vote. Correa's victory came as a surprise outside the country. He won overwhelmingly in the Andean Sierra, inhabited by Quechuas, garnering 75 percent of the votes in the province of Cotopaxi, and received more than 60 percent of votes cast in nearly all of the jungle provinces. But he lost in three coastal provinces—the stronghold of the financial and banana oligarchy—despite making a strong showing in several; in Guayas, the home of Guayaquil, the country's second most important city, he received 43 percent of the vote.[20]

Wasting no time, Correa quickly called for a constituent assembly. Congress immediately objected, arguing that its one hundred members would continue in session even if an assembly met. Nevertheless, Correa intended to give the constituent assembly power to annul the parliament and dismiss all its elected officials. On March 1, 2007, the Supreme Electoral Tribunal (TSE) called Ecuadorians to an April 15 referendum to decide whether or not to convene a constituent assembly. The executive branch cannot directly call for a constituent assembly. Moreover, since Correa did not run candidates for Congress and thus lacked allies there, a majority of congressional representatives—57 of 100—rejected the call for the referendum. Therefore, it was necessary for the TSE to call the referendum.

In early March, a majority in Congress voted to dismiss the president of the TSE for calling the referendum, even though Congress had appointed him. The TSE retaliated by dismissing the fifty-seven deputies who had voted to fire the

---

20 Figures from the Supreme Electoral Tribunal, November 28, www.hoy.com.ec.

president of the TSE, on the grounds that the law requires the removal of officials who obstruct an electoral process (Lucas 2007). This power struggle shut Congress down for a month.

The administration ratified the TSE's ruling and installed a police guard around the Congress building to prevent the dismissed legislators from entering and holding session. When Congress reconvened on April 10, a majority of its representatives were alternate deputies who had officially replaced those fired by the TSE. This new Congress was a recognition of the validity of the dismissal of the fifty-seven deputies. Correa had prevailed: He weathered the crisis without violating the law and finally gained approval for the referendum on a constituent assembly. Moreover, the appointment of alternate deputies gave him a majority in Congress.

Clearly, Correa could not have gained the upper hand in this confrontation were it not for his strong popular support (70 percent according to polls) and the enormous disdain that most Ecuadorians feel for the "partocracy," a term they use to describe the political system, alluding to the widespread perception of the corruption of politicians. The next step for Correa would be the election of the 130 delegates to the constituent assembly in October and November, 2007. One hundred delegates would be chosen in provincial districts, twenty-four in national districts, and six by emigrants in Europe and the United States.

A New Social Movement

Right-wing parties have had a stranglehold on political life and government machinery for twenty-five years in Ecuador. Even the former managing director of the IMF, Michel Camdessus, once noted the "incestuous relation between bankers, political-financial pressure groups, and corrupt government officials" in Ecuador (quoted in Burbach 2007). Those "corrupt officials" are in reality the politicians of Álvaro Noboa's Institutional Renewal Party of National Action (PRIAN), Lucio Gutiérrez's Patriotic Society Party (PSP), the Social Christian Party, and the Christian Democratic Union, which have long divvied up government posts and monies. Because of this collusion, only 5 percent of the population trusts Congress and other politicians. This allowed Correa to win the election, particularly because he did not run with any candidates for Congress (Tamayo 2007).

The country's seventeen largest economic groups own 563 companies with $5 billion (U.S.) in revenue or 14 percent of Ecuador's gross domestic product. However, their 2005 income tax statements claim only 6 percent of their total revenue (Tamayo 2007). Grupo Noboa, owned by Álvaro Noboa, alone controlled 144 companies with $575 million in revenue in 2005 and $3.9 million in profits. But the group's income tax statement declared only $978,000 (Tamayo 2007). These figures provide just a glimpse of the conduct of the economic groups that dominate the country, which are the right's constituency and which oversee the appointment of corrupt officials who allow them to evade taxes. These groups fear that a transparent government would put an end to their fabulous profits.

The "citizens' movement" that has emerged in the last decade to oppose this state of affairs brought Correa to power. Economist Pablo Dávalos argues that three important actors have emerged in recent decades: workers, whose strength was undermined by the neoliberal model; indigenous peoples, who, despite their impact, have been weakened by various internal dynamics; and the new citizens' movement, which represents a broad-based and heterogeneous range of interests and whose main objective is "political reform" (Dávalos 2007a; 2007b).

This is not a traditional movement, nor one with a clear political identity. It represents the deep moral outrage of the citizenry. "It proposes the moralization of the liberal political system, by neutralizing political parties' influence over oversight agencies, elections, and justice, and by bringing about procedural changes in the selection of representatives and in the exercise of power. Among other measures, these changes would allow for the removal of elected officials, anti-corruption mechanisms, and greater scrutiny of the political system" (Dávalos 2007a; 2007b). The "moralization" of politics might not seem like much from the perspective of the old left, but in

Ecuador it would be revolutionary. What is undeniable is that this diffuse movement is changing the country: First it threw out Gutiérrez and now it has put Correa in the presidential palace.

Unlike previous movements, the current citizens' movement is made up of urban middle classes, who indulged themselves in consumerism under neoliberalism and now demand a working democracy. These sectors have benefited from dollarization and especially from the remittances sent by emigrants. Between 2000 and 2005, two million Ecuadorians—out of a population of twelve million—left the country. In 2006, they sent home $3 billion (U.S.), a fabulous sum that rivals the annual $3.6 billion from oil sales, Ecuador's largest export. That money arrives directly to families and lubricates mall-based consumption. For Dávalos, "the middle-class sectors want the political system to work with the same transparency with which they believe the market works" (2007).

President Correa's challenge is to make the political system transparent and efficient—that is, to overhaul it. First, he must overcome the elite and government resistance. Second, he must solve the conundrum of dollarization, which has turned the country into a colony of the United States. Moreover, he must maintain his positions on the defense of national sovereignty and resisting the renewal of the Manta airbase contract. If Ecuador readopts the sucre, the middle classes will feel cheated since it will reduce their buying power. But if it fails to do so, millions of campesinos and poor urban dwellers, mostly indigenous persons whose livelihoods were destroyed by dollarization, will be further impoverished. Sooner or later, Correa will have to choose between dollarization's winners and its losers. A difficult choice, but one he will not be able to avoid.

III

The Peripheries of
Latin America:
Territories of Hope

The Urban Peripheries:
Counter-Powers from Below?

When the proletariat was rebellious and self-active,
it was described as a monster, a many-headed hydra.
Peter Linebaugh and Marcus Rediker
The Many-Headed Hydra

If a specter is haunting the Latin American elites at the beginning of the twenty-first century, it is for sure living in the peripheries of large cities. The main challenges to the dominant system in the last two decades have emerged from the heart of the poor urban peripheries. In between the Caracazo of 1989 and the Oaxaca Commune of 2006, there have been popular uprisings in Asunción in March 1999, Quito in February 1997 and January 2000, Lima and Cochabamba in April 2000, Buenos Aires in December 2001, Arequipa in June 2002, Caracas in April 2002, La Paz in February 2003, and El Alto in October 2003, to mention just the most relevant.

In the following pages, I will briefly and selectively tour some of the past half century's urban movements in an effort to grasp the long-term itineraries and hidden agendas of the urban poor. The poor of the cities do not usually formulate explicit agendas, with key strategies and tactics laid out, nor political programs or demands, but, as is often the case in the history of the oppressed, they make the road by walking. One can only *a posteriori* reconstruct the coherence of a journey that always seems to pass by or amend the initial intentions of the subjects. Before reviewing the new strategies being developed by the imperial right to address the challenges posed by the peripheries of large cities, I will offer a set of theses that challenge those who doubt that the marginalized can be considered political subjects.

Militarization and the State of Exception

Control of the urban poor is the most important goal for governments, global financial institutions, and the armed forces of the most powerful countries. Estimates indicate that one billion people live in the suburbs of third-world cities and that the number of poor in cities around the world has risen to two billion—one third of humanity. These numbers will double in the next fifteen to twenty years, and 95 percent of this growth will occur on the peripheries of southern cities (Davis 2006b). The situation is even more serious than the numbers suggest: Urbanization, as Davis explains, has become disconnected and autonomous from industrialization as well as from economic development, which implies the "structural and permanent disconnection of many city dwellers from the formal world economy" (2006b), while the current modes of accumulation continue to force people out of the countryside.

Many large Latin American cities seem to be on the edge of social explosion and several have been exploding in the last two decades. Fearful, the powerful embrace a two-fold strategy for dealing with the crisis: try to stall or block the explosion and also prevent the consolidation of those "black holes" outside of state control, the spaces where those from below, as noted by James Scott (2000), "rehearse" their challenges to the state before they become full rebellions.

Therefore, throughout the continent governments have been directing economic subsidies (known as "social plans") and other material benefits toward the populations of urban peripheries, seeking to implement new forms of social control and discipline and, through research, to develop a better understanding of those areas. Meanwhile, military and financial publications have addressed the challenges presented by Mara Salvatrucha and street gangs in recent years, discussing the problems created by the urban war.[1] The

---

1   See, for example Boraz and Bruneau 2006; Brevé 2007; Chiarelli 2005; Brown 2007; Blanco 2005; Diaz 2007; Banco Interamericano de Desarrollo 2006.

concepts of "asymmetrical war" and "fourth generation war" are responses to problems identical to those created by Third World urban peripheries: the birth of a new type of warfare against non-state enemies, in which military superiority does not play a decisive role. From this point of view, social plans and the militarization of the urban peripheries are two sides of the same attempt to control populations outside the reach of the state.[2]

William S. Lind, director of the Center for Cultural Conservatism of the Free Congress Foundation, asserts that the state has lost its monopoly on war and elites feel that "dangers" are multiplying. "Almost everywhere, the state is losing" (Lind 2005). Despite supporting a quick pullout from Iraq, Lind defends "total war," which engages enemies on all fronts: the economic, cultural, social, political, and also military. He believes that dangers for US hegemony lie in all aspects of daily life or, if you prefer, in life itself. He asserts that "in Fourth Generation War, invasion by immigrants can be just as dangerous as invasion by a state army." New problems rooted in the "universal crisis of the legitimacy of the state" place "non-state enemies" at the center. This leads him to warn military leaders that no state military has succeeded against a non-state enemy, and that the underlying problem is that the armed forces of a state were designed to fight against the armed forces of another state. This paradox is at the heart of new military paradigms, which must be completely reformulated to face challenges emerging from areas that used to be designated as "civilian."

Military commanders deployed in Iraq seem to be aware of the problems they face. Based on his recent experience on the outskirts of Baghdad in Sadr City, Cavalry Division Commander General Peter W. Chiarelli, writes,

> The conduct of war in the way we are used to has changed. The demographic progression of large urban areas, together with the local government's inability

---

2   I have addressed social plans as a way to control and discipline the poor in Zibechi 2006a.

to keep pace with basic services, creates ideal conditions for fundamentalist ideologues to take advantage of the marginalized elements of the population. To use our economic strength with an instrument of national power balances the process of achieving sustainable success in the long term" (Chiarelli 2005, 15).

"Executing traditionally focused combat operations... works, but only for the short term. In the long term, doing so hinders true progress and, in reality, promotes the growth of insurgent forces working against campaign objectives" (Chiarelli 2005, 14). This implies that the two traditional goals of armed forces of operation—combat and the training of local security forces—are insufficient.

Therefore, three "non-traditional" lines of operation should be undertaken: Essential services must be provided to the population, a legitimate government must be built, and a market economy instituted. Infrastructure improves circumstances for the poorest sector of the population, creates employment opportunities, and sends visible signs of progress. In the second place, creating a "democratic" regime is an essential point for legitimizing the whole process. For US commanders in Iraq, the "point of penetration" of their troops occurred with the January 30, 2005 elections. This reduced democracy to producing a vote, which is not contradictory and is actually functional in a state of siege (Agamben 2003). Finally, insurgents' recruitment capacity can be reduced through the expansion of the market and "by 'gentrifying' city centers and creating business parks" that dynamically stimulate the rest of society (*Military Review* 2005, 12). This is how "democracy"— the expansion of services and the market economy—becomes a mechanism that strengthens power and domination. Today's armed forces of the chief global power see it as a way to get "long-term security." In the future, the poor urban peripheries will be, in military jargon, "the center of strategic and operational gravity." In countries with weak states and high concentrations of urban poor, biopolitical mechanisms are enrolled as part of the militarization of society. Meanwhile, the armed forces occupy the place of the sovereign for a time, rebuilding the state and implementing—in a vertical and authoritarian manner—biopolitical mechanisms that ensure the continuity of domination. Disciplinary control mechanisms and the biopolitical are intertwined and in extreme cases such as in Iraq, the favelas of Rio Janeiro, and the slums of Port au Prince in Haiti form an essential part of the military plan.

Since the September 11, 2001, attacks, U.S. policy has been consistent with the concept of a "permanent state of exception" as defined by Agamben, while consolidating a trend that had already been in place. It is applied to very different situations and for very different reasons, from internal problems to external political threats, from economic emergency to natural disaster. The state of exception was used in response to financial and economic crisis in Argentina, December 2001 (which gave rise to a broad social movement); to the aftermath of Hurricane Katrina in New Orleans; and to the rebellion of the poor immigrant suburbs of French cities, and so on. The common factor is that in all cases it was a means to contain the urban poor: blacks, immigrants, and the unemployed, etc. For Agamben, totalitarianism can be defined as "the establishment of, through the state of exception, a *legal civil war*, which allows not only the *physical elimination* of political adversaries, but of entire categories of citizens who for whatever reason are not integrated into the political system" (Agamben 2003, 25). These citizens are mainly residents of poor neighborhoods who are structurally disconnected from the formal economy.

In the eighth thesis of his "On the Concept of History," Walter Benjamin states that "the tradition of the oppressed teaches us that the state of exception in which we live is the rule." Acknowledging that the statement is based on the reality of everyday life of those from below means addressing the second part of the same thesis, which holds that "we must arrive at a concept of history that corresponds to this situation." It does not seem sufficient to challenge the Western idea of progress; the crux of the problem lies in the so-called rule of law. Violence ("mythical violence," according to Benjamin) is the foundation of law and guarantees its conservation. If indeed "the law is the submission of a part of life to power" (Mate 2006, 147), then that portion of life is that which corresponds to a part of society existing in a lawless space.

This domination of life by violence is what Agamben registers in the concentration camp, the space where the state of exception becomes the dominant mode of governance (Agamben 1998). But the *bare life* to which human existence has been reduced in the camp (or on the urban periphery) implies a challenge to how politics have been done in the West since the French Revolution. In Agamben's terms, "from the concentration camps there is no possible return to classic politics," to the extent that there is now no possible distinction between "city and house," between "our biological body and our body politic"(Agamben 1998, 238).

Is there no way out? Is the totalitarian state here to stay and we have no choice but to become inhabitants of camps like Guantánamo? Agamben claims that exodus is not a practicable option largely because, at least in the First World, there is no outside to migrate to, since capital and the state have colonized the very pores of life. What is certain is that there is no alternative outside of or away from spaces where the state of exception prevails, in the camps/peripheries where people live on a dollar a day, because that is where the true "original structure of statehood" is manifested in all its harshness (Agamben 1998, 22).

The Return of the Dangerous Classes

The crisis of liberalism and the crisis of the nation-state is the foundation of this situation. The world revolution of 1968 was the turning point that showed the ruling classes that it could not maintain the welfare state—or extend it to the entire world—without affecting the process of capital accumulation. The formula of the liberal state—universal suffrage plus welfare state—"worked marvelously well" as a means "to counter democratic aspirations" and "contain the dangerous classes" (Wallerstein 2004, 424).[3] In the core countries, this system

---

3   A more detailed analysis can be found in Wallerstein 1996.

could be maintained on the basis of the exploitation of the South grounded in racism. But the revolution of 1968 convinced the dominant classes of the need for a change of direction. This was the beginning of a long-term systemic change. Hereinafter "the southern countries could not expect substantial economic development," but nevertheless the pressure to democratize—that is, "an egalitarian and anti-authoritarian attitude"—continues to grow. The welfare state ceased to function, those from below again fought for a better world, and the result was that "the dangerous classes became that once more" (Wallerstein 2004, 424).

A many-faceted chaos replaced the welfare state and industrial society. Wallerstein outlines five factors that gave rise to this: the weakness of the U.S., escalating wars and violent conflicts due to the ineffectiveness of the interstate system, the rise of a multitude of defensive groups, the increase in local, national and regional crises, and the spread of new diseases (Wallerstein 2004, 425–427). Urban peripheries are one of the important fractures in a system that tends toward chaos. States have only a minimal presence within them, and conflict and violence—resulting from the disintegration of society— are part of everyday life, where youth gangs are so strong that they sometimes take control of neighborhoods and, ultimately, these are zones where disease spreads exponentially. Put in Wallerstein's terms, some of the most important fractures in capitalism occur in the suburbs: race, class, ethnicity, and gender. These are territories of almost complete dispossession— and conversely, hope, as Mike Davis points out.

But there is another important dimension. Wallerstein has detected eight major differences between the previous phase of capitalist expansion—which he situates from 1945 to 1967–73—and the current phase expected to last until 2025 or so. Briefly, these differences include the existence of a bipolar world (understanding that the *entente* between the USA and USSR formed an unipolar world); that there will be no investments in the South; strong migratory pressure toward the north; a crisis of the middle strata of the north; ecological limits on economic growth, deruralization, and urbanization;

middle classes and poor people tending to unite in the South; and the rise of democratization and the decline of liberalism (Wallerstein 2004, 418–424). The crisis of the middle strata and their possible unity with the poor would make the system unsustainable and, according to this analysis, would eventually rupture its legitimacy.

During the years of prosperity, "the middle tier became an important pillar for the stability of political systems and constituted in fact a very strong pillar" (Wallerstein 2004, 420). Today, even in the North, new forms of accumulation are based on production processes that significantly reduce the size of the middle classes as well as state budgets. Damaged by the wave of labor militancy during the sixties, capital took these decisions as a way to relaunch the process of accumulation. Now there are other factors to be included, such as the existence of multiple poles of growth confronting each other. Fierce competition within different capitalist centers leads to an intense struggle to cut costs, thus weakening the middle class.

Meanwhile, the weakening of the middle class intensifies the crisis of the legitimacy of states. The appropriation of surplus value "takes place so that there are not two, but three participants in the process of exploitation," as there is a "mid-level which participates in exploiting the lower tier but is also exploited by the higher" (Wallerstein 2004, 293). In the factory—the core of capitalist production—there are many mid-level operatives: foremen and their assistants, controllers, supervisors, administrators, and so on. Even in Third World countries, this layer represents between 15 and 20 percent of the total factory workforce.[4] This is a crucial political issue:

> Such a three-tiered format is essentially stabilizing in effect, whereas a two-tiered format is essentially disintegrating. We are not saying that three tiers exist at all moments. We are saying that those on top always seek

---

4   I have shown that the defeat of the Uruguayan working class was linked, among other causes, to capitalists' ability to isolate them and cede power to the middle classes (Zibechi 2006c).

to ensure the existence of three tiers in order the better
to preserve their privilege, whereas those on the bottom
conversely seek to reduce the three to two, the better to
destroy this same privilege. This fight over the existence
of a middle tier goes on continually, both in political
terms and in terms of basic ideological constructs (those
that are pluralist versus those that are manicheist.) This
is the core issue around which the class struggle is
centered (Wallerstein 1975, 368).

We can apply this trimodal (center, semi-periphery, periphery) model to the planet and also to cities (districts for the
rich, the middle strata, and the poor). The problem facing the
rulers in many Latin American countries is that the middle
class is in decline, like the industrial working class, while the
poor in the slums—the so-called marginalized or excluded—
are growing. This is why they generate so much fear and why
there are so many attempts to control them.

The urban peripheries are disconnected from the formal
economy and territories beyond the control of the powerful.
Through the increased militarization of these spaces, elites
try to solve this "anomaly," and simultaneously, in order to
obtain long-term security, implement biopolitical methods
of governance.

The Latin American peculiarity is that progressive governments implement biopolitical techniques by means of
their "social plans," but also through military forces. In Brazil,
to give just one example, the state applies different forms of
control simultaneously: The "Zero Hunger" government plan
goes hand in hand with the militarization of the *favelas*. The
Latin American left regard the poor peripheries as pockets of
crime, drug trafficking, and violence; spaces where chaos and
the law of the jungle reign. Distrust takes the place of understanding. There is not the slightest difference in perspective
between left and right on this issue.

Mike Davis has a different view of the urban peripheries and summarizes the difficulties in one insightful sentence: "The suburbs of the cities of the Third World have become the new decisive geopolitical scenario" (2007). Davis's work focuses on the how and why these peripheries have become such "decisive scenarios" in Latin America. His work also explores how and why these spaces have become something akin to a popular counter-power and from which the lower classes have launched formidable challenges to the capitalist system.

Can the Marginalized Be Subjects?

Few social scientists or academics understand the reality of urban peripheries in Latin America. Class categories, a blind faith in progress, and the application of concepts coined for different contexts distort readings of those places where the popular sectors oscillate between rebellion, dependence on local bosses, and the search for state patronage. Such thinking insists on seeing the slums as an anomaly, almost always a problem, and rarely a place of emancipatory potential. We will briefly explore some of these ideas here.

During a polemic against Proudhon in *The Housing Question*, Frederick Engels emphasizes that property—land or housing—is an obstacle from the past that prevents the proletarian struggle for a new world. Marx and Engels believed that complete dispossession would allow workers to fight for a new world and thus, as property owners, the peasantry would never be a revolutionary class. By contrast, Proudhon argued that Paleolithic man, who has his cave, and the Indian, who owns his own home, were in a better condition than modern workers who remained "virtually in the air." Engels's answer lays bare the difficulties of Marxism, linked as it is to a linear conception of history, so it is worth citing it despite its length:

> In order to create the modern revolutionary class of the proletariat it was absolutely necessary to cut the umbilical cord which still bound the worker of the past to the land. The hand weaver who had his little house, garden and field along with his loom, was a quiet, contented

man—in all godliness and respectability—despite all misery and despite all political pressure; he doffed his cap to the rich, to the priests and to the officials of the state; and inwardly was altogether a slave. It is precisely modern large-scale industry, which has turned the worker, formerly chained to the land, into a completely property-less proletarian, liberated from all traditional fetters and free as a bird.... The driving of the workers from every hearth and home...was the very first condition of his spiritual emancipation.

The English proletariat of 1872 is on an infinitely higher level than the rural weaver of 1772, who had his "house and hearth." And will the troglodyte with his cave and the Indian with his own home ever accomplish a Paris Commune (Engels 1976, 30–31)?

Proudhon argues that workers improve their status in society by owning property, which Engels rightly criticizes, but it is not true that property is, abstractly, a brake on the constitution of a subject. Latin American social struggles reveal the opposite. Popular sectors have been able to resist the system by maintaining or re-creating spaces under their own control and possession. Seizing the land, housing, and factories strengthens their struggles. Likewise, the poor have launched formidable challenges to the states and elites from their conquered territories. Engels and other Marxists have not recognized that capitalism, far from being an improvement, was a significant setback for the poor of the land. They did not value, particularly, the loss of autonomy represented by the loss of their plots, homes, and means of production, which stopped them from being stripped totally bare by capitalism.

The peasant and indigenous movements gained strength as they fought to defend their land and recover territories stolen by landowners. The landless movement in Brazil has taken over 22 million hectares in twenty-seven years, an area the size of several European countries. And using this land as a base, they continue to struggle for agrarian reform without any expectation of winning state power. In Latin America, the poor are making land reform from below. The indigenous are recovering their ancestral territories, from which they resist the multinationals; within these territories they are teaching alternative ways. As we shall see later, the urban poor are following similar paths.

In the field of Marxism, the French urbanist Henri Lefebvre moves away from the economic and deals with urban issues with an open mind, starting from the assumption that capital accumulation has a geographic footprint that survives by occupying and producing space. He recognizes that the "production of space" clashes with private ownership of urban land. He relates the European experience, in which the ruling classes use space to "disperse the working class, to distribute them in places allocated for them—to organize the various flows, subordinated to the institutional rules—consequently, to subordinate space to power," with the objective of preserving capitalist relations of production (1976, 140).

Lefebvre asks whether it is possible to take the instrument of space from the ruling classes. He is skeptical, because the experience of the European working class has not led to the creation of spaces beyond the control of dominant classes. He adds that the possibility of doing so should be in a function of "new realities and not as a function of the problems of industrial production for more than a century" (1976, 141). He clearly perceives the limits of the classical theory to which he subscribes. He has a vision of reality that leads to the conclusion that the working class is constrained in space and capital flows and the division of labor. He is aware that "industrial production and capitalism have taken over the cities." He goes one step further: He shows convincingly that business enterprise is no longer the center of capital accumulation but the whole of society, including "the interstitial urban tissue" involved in production. But the limits of his thinking are closely connected to social struggles. Lefebvre's conclusion is clear: "In 1968, the French working class was almost at the extreme of its objective and subjective possibilities" (1976, 157).

Here is the point where even as fine a sensibility as Lefebvre's could not get past: that space is a product of social struggles. He was unable to see how those from below are capable of creating their own spaces and converting them into territories, which they can do, at least in Latin America. In his polemic against the dismissal of space in the *Communist Manifesto*, the geographer David Harvey says that the bourgeoisie has won by mobilizing domination over space as a producing force peculiar in itself. From this, he concludes that the working class must learn to neutralize the bourgeoisie's capability to dominate and produce space. And so long as the working class "does not learn to deal with the bourgeois capacity to master space and produce it, to shape a new geography of production and social relations, it will always be in a position of weakness rather than strength" (Harvey 2003, 65).

However, this is not occurring in the First World today. Agamben's pessimism about finding alternatives to the expansion of totalitarianism could be correct. He believes that the main difficulty is that "a truly heterogeneous way of life does not exist, at least in the advanced capitalist countries" (Agamben 1998, 20). Lefebvre asserts that the remnants of the old society disappeared after the Second World War in Europe, alongside the remains of artisan and peasant production. In its place, the "consumption-led bureaucratic society" has been able to impose a distinct division and composition of everyday life, and even a "programmed everyday life in *an urban setting* suited for that purpose" (1972, 85). The consumption-led bureaucratic society produces a homogenous life that is subordinate to capital; it occupies all the interstices of life, and thus prevents the creation of territories of flows beyond its control.

The sociologist Loïc Wacquant is one of the leading scholars of urban poverty in the central countries. His sympathies lie with the "urban outcasts." He denounces the criminalization of poverty, the stigmatization of the ghetto, and the "criminal state," arguing that the only way to respond to the "challenge posed to democratic society by advanced marginality" is to rebuild the welfare state (2007a, 186). He recognizes that a portion of workers have become redundant in the current period of capitalism and will not return to work, which complements the growing precariousness of employment in general. He notes with concern the changes in the urban context: He says that we have gone beyond a situation in which poverty (although he uses the term "marginality") was "residual" and could be absorbed by the periods of market expansion to one in which the poor "seems to have been decoupled from the cyclical fluctuations of the national economy" (2007a, 173). Many analysts share this conclusion.

Wacquant finds six differences between the "new regime of marginality" and the Fordist period that ended in the sixties and seventies. The two most important, from our Latin American perspective, are related to how wage labor has become a source of fragmentation and social precarity rather than homogeneity, solidarity, and security, as happened under the welfare state (2007b, 271). I commented on the second difference above: the disconnection of poverty from the cyclical fluctuations of the economy. However, he recognizes an additional difference based on his empirical studies. In the city of Chicago, where he lived for several years, "the financial situation of 80 percent of the inhabitants of the ghetto showed signs of deterioration *after four years of economic growth* sustained under the presidency of Ronald Reagan" (2007b, 274). Economic growth and job creation not only did not solve the problem of urban poverty but exacerbated it. In a similar manner, the economic "development" we can expect in Latin America in this period of capitalism concentrates wealth and poverty at opposite poles, and cannot stop doing so.

Throughout his work, Wacquant, like other scholars, emphasizes the problems of violence and drug trafficking in the periphery. For many academics, the ghettos are "a menacing urban hydra personified in the defiant and aggressive youth gang" (2007b, 36). In my opinion, it is important to recognize that the ghettos of the First World, particularly in the United States no longer have the race riots of the sixties but rather the "silent or slow upheavals" of today. Grasping this allows us make a serious attempt to understand the logic that leads the young, black, and poor ghetto inhabitants into violence and drug trafficking. In part, this is because urban black poverty today is more intense and concentrated than during the sixties and because the gap between rich and poor is widening. As Wacquant notes:

> The openly racial uprisings in African-American communities of the northern cities in defiant rebellion against white authority gave way to the "slow upheaval" of black on black crime, massive rejection of school, drug trafficking and internal social decay. During the evening news broadcast, scenes of white police officers unleashing state violence against peaceful black protesters demanding the mere recognition of their basic constitutional rights have been replaced by reports of drive-by shootings, homelessness and teenage pregnancy (2007b, 35–36).

Wacquant's account is interesting in so much as it fails to capture a defiant attitude to the established order in these images of self-destruction—a defiance that is very different than that of the sixties but no less important. Nevertheless, even analysts committed to the First World poor are unable to see the peripheries as anything but a problem, defined always in negative terms such as "suburbs of despair" or as a "museum of horrors" (Eckstein in Wacquant 2007b, 282; Durán 1996, 148). When inhabitants are not stigmatized, they are seen as "survivors of a huge collective disaster" (Bourdieu 1999, 11). The inhabitants are never regarded as subjects, but just objects for study by researchers who are responsible, as Bourdieu says, for shaping a discourse that they themselves, the "precarious," could never produce because they "have not yet acceded to the status of a 'class object'" and are required to "form their subjectivity from their objectification by others" (Wacquant 2007b, 285).

Like Bourdieu and Wacquant, Manuell Castells emphasizes the state's role as a generator of urban marginality. "The world of marginality is, in fact, built by the state in a process of social integration and political mobilization, in exchange for goods and services that only it can procure" (1986, 266). In his extensive survey of the slums of Latin American cities, to which we will return later, he argues that the relationship between the state and the settlers is organized around the delivery of services as a means of political control, and thus a populist relationship. He dismisses the idea that inhabitants of the neighborhoods can act as subjects and insists that the most common trend in Latin America is for squatter settlement movements to become "an instrument of social integration and subordination to the existing political order rather than an agent of social change" (1986, 274). According to Castells, their material and social status prevents them from overcoming dependence on the political system.

Coming from another theoretical position, Antonio Negri agrees that the rebellious youth of the peripheries are not subjects to the extent that "they know what they do not want but they do not know what they want" (2006, 2). He asserts that urban youth of the peripheries have a "completely negative" identity and that the concentration camp in which they live is their only commonality. He agrees with the analysis outlined above: The inhabitants of the peripheries cannot escape their situation. Hope is only to be found in the new models of governance embodied by Lula in Brazil and Kirchner in Argentina, who, engaged with social movements, are negotiating the "radicalization of democracy" (2006, 2). However, I would argue that young people from the Brazilian favelas do not feel like they are reconstructing their country under Lula so much as suffering the rigors of everyday state repression.

Had proponents of the (erroneously named) "theory of marginality" constructed in the sixties in Latin America witnessed the socio-political activism of the urban settlers in the eighties, largely caused by the effects of globalization, they might have been more likely to see the urban poor as social and political subjects. However, I think these theorists have established one significant point: Dependent capitalism creates a "marginal pole" in society, which means breaking with the Eurocentric analysis emphasizing the differences and particularities present within South America (Quijano 1977). This systemic approach to "marginality" helps us place imperialism and the political and social problems it represents in the center of the analysis, which many European and North American intellectuals fail to do. On the other hand, it is useful to return to these theorists' reflections on the differences between the concepts of "marginality" and the "reserve industrial army." Three decades later, these differences have become extenuated to such an extent that some traditional concepts seem to have outlived their usefulness.[5]

In conclusion, I would like to mention two further analyses published during the same period as the aforementioned. Larissa Lomnitz discusses the bonds shared by the poor inhabitants of a Mexico City slum in a work that seeks to understand the reality "from below" and therefore "from within" (1975). The second study, by Peruvian José Matos Mar, concerns the capability of the people who have settled in the slums of Lima to "overflow from below" and, in the process, change the face of Peru (1989 and 2004).

Lomnitz's work marks a turning point in studies about urban poverty and marginality (Svampa 2004). Social networks of reciprocal exchange, according to the author, are "the most significant element of the social structure in the barrio" (Lomnitz 1975, 219) and are what enable the marginalized to migrate from the countryside, settle in the city, organize in movements, get a roof over their heads, and survive. Lomnitz's emphasis on networks, familial relations, solidarity, and reciprocity paints a picture of a world where trust and reciprocal exchange are the key elements in social relationships. This meticulous work had the insight to place the emphasis on the internal resources of the "marginal" world. In other words, the analysis focused on the internal potentialities nesting within the population of the peripheries, which are the secret of their survival, their existence, and their daily lives.

Matos Mar goes a step further and places this "marginal" sector at the center of his research, at a time when its capacity to "overflow" the established order is undisputed. He argues

---

5   See the introduction to Quijano 1977 and Nun 1969.

that there are in reality "two Perus," two parallel societies: the official and the marginal. The first consists of the state, political parties, businesses, the armed forces, and trade unions, and it has adopted a foreign culture. The second is plural and multiform, has its own economy (which he calls an "oppositional economy" rather than an informal one), system of justice and authorities, religion, culture, and community; and it possesses a communitarian Andean heart (2004, 47). A process that began with the invasion of urban plots of land in the fifties that resulted in an overflow and expansion consistent with Matos Mar's idea of the "other" Peru—a submerged Andean Peru reemerging to be reinvented in the cities, especially Lima.

According to Matos Mar, confrontation is inevitable, but it will not be a traditional clash between opposites, but a circumstance in which "millions of participants from the 'other society,'" attempt to "impose their own terms by means of mass force" (2004, 101). Sometimes he seems to present a situation in which the other society asserts itself in a capillary manner, while at other moments he describes a process in which "the masses generate semi-autonomous pockets of power, based on asymmetric patterns of rural reciprocity adapted to the urban situation. They oppose the state and the state ignores them" (2004, 105). When evaluating the path followed by the "overflow" in the last two decades, Matos Mar argues that "the oppositional style of overflow used by these masses since the early fifties keeps advancing their conquest and possession of new physical, cultural, social, economic and political territories, once reserved for the wealthy, upper and middle class urbanites" (2004, 130). He employs the concept of "overflow" to describe a social change that challenges the concepts of integration, reform, and revolution; it operates as a sort of Andean stain that spreads in physical as well as cultural, economic, social, and political space. Meanwhile, as this occurs, the institutional world grows increasingly isolated, broken, and incapable of governing this "other" world.

More urban rebellions have occurred since the publication of this work. In analyzing them, it is important to take a long-term perspective, because otherwise it is difficult to understand their ebbs and flows and to decipher the trajectories and processes that form their backdrop. These rebellions do not follow programs or established objectives—there is no well-beaten path—but we can attempt to identify the broader tendencies where they exist.

Social Movements, or Societies in Movement

The concept of social movements is an additional obstacle in understanding the reality of the urban peripheries. When analyzing social movements, analysts often emphasize the more formal aspects, like organizational forms, cycles of mobilization, the movement's identity and cultural contexts, and so on. And they usually classify them according to goals, membership, and the timing and reasons for their emergence. There are entire libraries written on the subject, although very little fieldwork on the quite distinct, Latin American terrain and its unique bases. In the arduous task of decolonizing critical thinking, a discussion of theories of social movements is of primary importance.

One of the most complete and comprehensive analyses of the Bolivian movements, coordinated by Álvaro García Linera, relies uncritically on European and American paradigms. The various Bolivian movements are defined as "a kind of collective action intentionally seeking to change established social systems or defend some material interest, for which they organize and cooperate with the purpose of initiating public actions based on these goals or demands" (2004, 21). All social movements share three features: a structure for mobilizing or a decision-making system, a collective identity or cultural characteristics, and codes of mobilization or methods of struggle. However, this kind of analytical framework is applicable to only a few movements: the institutionalized, those with a visible structure that is separate from everyday life, and those who elect leaders and have a definite program and set of goals.

But the bulk of social movements do not work in this way. For example, poor women in urban peripheries generally do not participate in social movements in the way described by the theory above, even though they play a very important role as a force of social change. Women's movements generally have, beyond a small nucleus of women organized in a stable manner, a capillary form. This kind of organization, although not institutionalized or stable, can still be huge and capable of changing the world from the ground up. García Linera's study touches upon some of these themes while addressing the Unique Confederation of Rural Laborers of Bolivia (CSTUB), a peasant organization of the Altiplano Aymara:

> Strictly speaking, the CSUTCB is a kind of social movement that sets in movement not just a part of society, but a different society: a set of social relations with non-capitalist forms of labor and modes of organization, meaning, representation, and political authority that are different from the dominant society. Hence, Luis Tapia's notion of a societal movement is relevant in this case (2004, 130).

The concept of a "societal movement" helps us understand the different social relations that exist in Latin America. They are not "remnants" from the past, but social relations that grow alongside and are distinct from the dominant forms. This theory attempts to conceptualize the movement "as a society in itself, or a complete system of social relations" and identify the movement as "a part of society that is within the other" (Tapia 2002, 60–61). Tapia observes the existence of "several societies" within the one society, or at least the articulation of two distinct sets of social relations. In a similar vein, I have argued for conceiving of these movements as "societies in movement" (Zibechi 2003a). What is compelling is how these ideas can grasp that social relations existing in rural areas among the indigenous and landless are now appearing in urban areas. In cities like Caracas, Buenos Aires, and Oaxaca these territorialized social relations have become visible in social struggles during the last fifteen to twenty years, with El Alto in Bolivia being the best example of the trend.[6]

---

6   See my analysis of the urban "communities" of El Alto in Zibechi 2010.

The central aspect of this debate is whether a system of social relations can exist in a given territory. In the analysis of movements, this implies focusing less on forms of organization and codes of mobilization and more on social relations and territories—to look at the flow and circulation, not the structures. This brings new concepts like autonomy, culture, and community into focus. Carlos Walter Porto Gonçalves argued this point: He analyzed the rubber tappers working with Chico Mendes in Brazil for many years. "In the battle for the decolonization of thought, the recuperation of the concept of territory would perhaps be a contribution" (2006, 161).

In effect, the indigenous, landless, and—increasingly— urban dweller movements in Latin America are territorialized. The social relations within them and the subjects who form them are what make up the territories (Porto Gonçalves 2001). This means returning to Lefebvre's assertion that the production of space is the production of differentiated space: Those who produce space embody differentiated social relations rooted in territories. This is not limited to the possession (or ownership) of land, but is rather about the organization of a territory that has different social relations and that embodies the subject. It is the subject's need to give shape to counter-hegemonic social relations that create the new territorialities.

Place and space have been privileged concepts in the theoretical analysis of social movements and should be applied to territories in Latin America, including its cities. In his excellent work, Porto Gonçalves says that the "new subjects suggest the introduction of new territorialities" (2001, 208). He reaches this conclusion after studying the rubber tappers, who had constantly moved around before building a movement, leading Porto Gonçalves to the conclusion that their force "had emanated from their domestic-and-productive-space" (2001, 203). It was this disengagement, the moving away from their original and inherited place (in society), that allowed them to form anew as a movement.

Classes are not things but rather human relations, as indicated by E.P. Thompson (1989). These relations are not given, but rather are constructed in the midst of struggle and confrontation. This construction of class as a relation includes the notion of space. Thompson postulates that social classes are constituted in and by the struggles of the protagonists locked in concrete situations. In this way, the protagonists not only occupy the space, but also constitute it. Thus, "social movement is, rigorously, a changing of social place," a point that intersects at the crossroads of sociology and geography (Porto Gonçalves 2001, 197–198). Based on this, we come to a different definition of social movements than that found in sociology, which always focuses on organizational aspects, structures, and political goals:

> Every social movement begins from the starting point of people breaking the inertia and moving, i.e. chang- ing place, rejecting the place historically assigned for them within a given social organization, and their desire to increase opportunities for expression, an action that, as Michel Foucault warned, has strong implications for the political order (2001, 81).

This potent image emphasizes the character of a social movement as a moving-of-itself, as a capacity to flow and shift, or to circulate. A movement is always shifting spaces and moving away from inherited identities (Espinosa 1999). When that movement/shift takes root in a territory or when the subjects who undertake this moving-of-themselves are rooted in a physical space, they constitute territories defined by their difference from territories of capital or the state. This implies that land/space is no longer understood as a means of production and becomes, instead, a political and cultural cre- ation. Territory becomes the place where counter-hegemonic social relations are deployed and where groups and collectives can practice different ways of living. This is one of the ma- jor contributions made by the indigenous movements of our continent to the fight for emancipation.

By introducing concepts such as territory, autonomy, self-determination, and self-government—all of which be- long to the same problematic—indigenous movements are producing a theoretical and political revolution, as noted by Díaz Polanco (1997). At some point in their centuries-long struggle for land, indigenous communities started to expand local and communal self-government into wider spaces as part of their construction as national subjects and peoples. During the First Continental Gathering of Indigenous Peoples in 1990, this very process was deliberated upon, leading to the Declaration of Quito.

Until then, all existing territory was a property of the state, both materially and symbolically. The idea of territory could not be separated from that of the nation-state. For Weber, "the state is that human community within a particular territory—the concept of 'territory' is essential in this definition—that claims for itself (successfully) the monopoly of legitimate physical coercion" (2002, 1056). With the emergence of the Indian movement during the last two decades, since the mid- to late eighties, the concept of territory changed due to the impact of indigenous struggles. The Declaration of Quito says that "the right to territory is a fundamental demand of indigenous peoples" and concludes that "without Indian self-government and without control of our territories, there can be no autonomy" (Declaration of Quito 1990, 107).

This theoretical and political revolution suggests a new distribution of power. Important questions arise, like how did the indigenous movements move from the struggle for land to constructing territories, from demanding rights to demanding autonomy and self-government? That is, how did the transition from resistance against domination to the affirmation of difference occur? How this was achieved is of particular importance to the formation of urban communities taking root in self-constructed urban spaces.

The Formation of Popular Neighborhoods

The night of October 29, 1957, a group from Zanjón de la Aguada—a 5-kilometer by 100-meter belt of poverty in the center of Santiago with a population of 35,000—prepared to carry out the first organized mass seizure of urban land. At 8:00 p.m., they began to dismantle their shacks, tied strips of cloth over their horses' hooves to prevent them making noise, and gathered "the three sticks and the flag" with which to create the new settlement. Around 2:30 a.m., they arrived at the chosen site: a state-owned property in the southern part of the city.[7] It is worth dwelling on this story, in the form of an account given by a participant, which may have been the first organized mass land seizure in Latin America:

> At eight o'clock in the evening, the most determined ones began to gather at the agreed spot: with the three poles and a flag, and some utensils and blankets, the convoy took shape.... The column kept advancing and people joined it...quietly we were reaching our goal. Under the lights of Los Cerrillos airport during this dark, moonless night, we felt like Jews escaping from the Nazis: the darkness meant we could only advance step by step. With the first lights of dawn, everyone began to clear a piece of brush, build a hut, and raise the flag" (Garcés 2002a, 130).

Some twelve hundred families from various rural towns converged on the chosen site of about fifty-five hectares. The "encampment" withstood police eviction actions, and families began to build the settlement. They defined the terms of the experience from the outset: The construction of the settlement, which they called "La Victoria" [victory], was "an enormous exercise in self-organization by the settlers," who had to "work together and innovate, drawing on every bit of knowledge and all of their skills." The government did not throw them out, but did not assist in the construction of the settlement either (Garcés 2002a, 138).

The premise of self-organization distinguished the action from previous struggles. On the first night, the settlers convened a large meeting and created committees to attend to security, food, and health care, among other necessities. From then on, all important decisions were made through

---

7   The first land occupation in Chile is documented by Mario Garcés (2002a) and the Grupo Identidad de Memoria Popular (2007).

collective debate. The second distinguishing aspect was its self-construction. They constructed the first public buildings, the school, and the health clinic collectively. Each settler had to contribute fifteen adobe bricks for the school; women brought the straw, young people made the bricks, and teachers stacked them one on top of another. Within a few months of the camp's establishment, the school began to function, although the teachers worked without a salary. The health clinic began attending to residents under a tent while its building was constructed collectively, like the school. Within two years, La Victoria had 18,000 inhabitants and more than 3,000 dwellings. It was a city built and governed by the poorest, based on a "rich and extensive community network" (Garcés 2002a, 142).

The "seizure" of La Victoria followed a pattern of social action to be repeated throughout the following decades up to today, not only in Chile but also throughout Latin America. There is collective organization prior to the occupation, careful selection of a suitable space, and then a sudden action—preferably at night—accompanied by outreach to churches or political parties, attempting to legitimize the illegal action. If the occupiers withstand the initial eviction efforts by security forces, it is very likely that the occupants will be able to remain.

Interestingly, this pattern of social action began in Santiago and Lima during the fifties but only spread to Buenos Aires and Montevideo, the most "European" of Latin American cities due to their homogeneity, in the eighties. This pattern is very different from individual families joining shantytowns—"favelas," "callampas," or "villas miseria." The fact that they occurred decades apart is not significant; what is really important here is the adoption of a similar pattern of collective action.

Let us look at La Victoria in more detail, which will shed light on the new processes at work. Land seizure "entails a radical break with institutional logic and with the fundamental principle of liberal democracies: property" (Grupo Identidad 2007, 14). Legitimacy takes the place of legality, and the land's use value prevails over its exchange value. With a seizure, an invisible group becomes a socio-political subject. In La Victoria, something more happens: Residents appropriate space by constructing homes and a neighborhood, and, when they subsequently inhabit them, the "we" becomes the basis of the area's self-government.

Thus, the pattern of direct action modifies the relation between people and the state embedded in the dominant culture and also a relation that the Left and the labor movement have adopted—the logic of class/union/party rooted in representing the interests of a sector within the state apparatus. In this new kind of movement, self-construction and self-determination take the place of demands and representation. This change is still very much in its infancy, but a different course is now slowly being charted by the popular sectors. It parallels what we have seen in indigenous movements since the eighties. They place the question of territory at the center of their activities, in addition to a series of theoretical and political concepts that belong to this genealogy: autonomy, self-government (Díaz Polanco 1997, 14).

Accounts from the people involved go even further. They reveal a number of issues that we will see repeatedly in struggles the length and breadth of the urban peripheries in Latin America.

- The capacity to *self-organize* and, on that basis, self-construction and self-determination of life. Not only did the inhabitants of La Victoria construct their own homes, streets, water system, and electricity system, they also erected a health clinic and a school, the latter reflecting participatory values, in that it is a circular building. They governed their own lives throughout area, establishing forms of popular power or counterpower.
- Women played a prominent role, to the extent that many left their husbands to participate in the land seizure or did not inform them of the crucial step they were about to take in their lives. "I went alone with my seven-month-old daughter, since my husband didn't go with me," recounts Luisa, who was eighteen at the time of the seizure (Grupo Identidad 2007, 58). Zulema, age forty-two,

remembers, "Several women secretly came with their children, hiding from their husbands, like I did" (Grupo Identidad 2007, 58). Even in the mid-fifties, popular sector women—strictly speaking, we would have to say mothers, or the women and their children—had a surprising level of autonomy. The women took the lead during the occupation and in resistance to evictions, facing down security forces with their children:

> One time the soldiers threatened to shoot us all, so all the women went to leave the children with our mothers and then we returned to fight. All day long we were waiting for the soldiers to arrive and they didn't arrive but the police came in kicking down flags and tents and threatened to kill us. And there we were, fighting against eviction and shouting "You will only get us out of here dead!" (Grupo Identidad 2007, 60).

Chilean historian Gabriel Salazar states that prior to 1950, poor women had learned by necessity to organize tenement house assemblies, tenant strikes, land seizures, health care groups, resistance to police evictions, and other forms of opposition. In order to become "home owners," they had to become activists and promote land seizures. As a result, female settlers began to develop "a certain type of popular, local power" that amounted to the ability to create free territories in which they "directly exercised sovereignty" in truly autonomous communes (Salazar y Pinto 2002a, 251). Further on, we shall see that women have always played a prominent role in Latin American movements, imbuing the movements with a cosmovision that is different from the dominant world view of the nation-state and organizations like political parties and unions. It was the women who led the wave of land seizures that swept the continent in the years ahead.

- La Victoria was built as a *community* of sentiments and feelings, where pain and death played a role in bringing the people together. It is important to emphasize how identity is not anchored in the physical place, but in affections and shared life experiences. As the comments from participants affirm, in the early days everyone called each other "compañero," partly because everyone shared responsibilities. However, it was not so much an ideological comradeship but something far more sobering: The November rains caused the death of twenty-one infants one year. "These things unite us. With a neighbor by our side, we did these things together. When one lacked something, the other would help. She had three girls and one died…" (Grupo Identidad 2007, 36). The death of a child is something profound for the whole community. In Brazil, when the landless occupy a property, they raise a large wooden cross. Each time a child from the camp dies, they drape a piece of white cloth on the cross and leave it there: It is a sacred thing. In La Victoria, when a child died, or sometimes an adult, a long caravan walked through the streets of the neighborhood before heading to the cemetery.

Women play such a decisive role in organizing the barrio/community because they are the most affected. Angela Roman, who was twenty-seven when the occupation took place, says,

> We came together in group meetings organized by block. I still participate to this day. If a neighbor dies, I'm the first one out with a basket to collect money, at whatever hour, because this is what we learned to do when the children died and there was no money for burial. In block meetings, we discuss things we need to take care of, like when were we going to have water, etc. We discussed what we needed; this is how we organized (Grupo Identidad 2007, 37).

Thus the community form becomes a form of struggle. For instance, during resistance to evictions, a pattern emerged that will be repeated again and again across the continent: "The children in front, the women behind, and the men last; this is why they could never kick us out, because people were very united" (Grupo Identidad 2007, 53).

- The seized land, the housing, and the self-constructed neighborhood are experienced and felt as a *use value* in a society that prioritizes exchange value. Many neighbors insist they will not sell their house at "any price." On October 30 of each year, the whole community celebrates the anniversary of the land seizure and decorates the entire barrio. "Every year I participate in the remembrance celebration.… We decorate floats, with the children riding on them, and recall how important the land seizure was in our life," says Rosa Lagos, who was sixteen in 1957 (Grupo Identidad 2007, 74).

The prevalence of use value, or rather, the deconstruction of exchange value in exchange for use value is closely linked to the "self," as in self-determination and also the role of women. A domestic logic began to expand—the production of use value was confined to the domestic space for a long time—into the public space and, from there, throughout the whole social fabric, particularly at critical times for communities.

- They established relationships with the state, political parties, and the church, but due to the community's reliance on self-organization and self-government, these were instrumental in nature. Communist and Christian organizations predominated in La Victoria but, despite their presence, the population made its own decisions in its own decision-making bodies. The same autonomy was evident in relation to the state. Such instrumental relationships indicate that the people do not wish to be represented by such institutions and desire to be autonomous. While this type of relationship can be construed as "clientelist," they are in reality instrumental relations, since they represent the way two different and opposing worlds relate.

Over the years, the occupation and construction of La Victoria represented a watershed. The state attempted to organize and contain the settlers, but the inhabitants circumvented the state's policies and implemented "their own housing policy: the extended occupation of the city through 'land seizures'" (Garcés 2002a, 337). Up until to 1973, popular sectors were the main creators of urban space in the city. In late 1972, during the government of Salvador Allende, there were 400,000 people living in settlements in Santiago alone (Castells 1986, 281). Analysts from various traditions agree that the movement was very important. Castells argues that "the movement of settlers in Chile was potentially a decisive element in the revolutionary transformation of society" (1986, 291). Garcés points out that by September 1970, the capital was in full transformation due to the encampments, which were "the most influential social force in the urban community of greater Santiago"(Garcés 2002a, 416).

This pressure from below transformed the course of social struggles and the cities. In the Chilean case, Garcés notes that "in the revolutionary discourse emerging in 1970, even more important than the struggle for state power, radical leaders had to prioritize forms of sociability within the 'camps'"(Garcés 2002a, 423). The changes of "place" involved a third of the population of Santiago:

> At the end of the sixties, the people who had "occupied places" in the city were also simultaneously occupying a new "place" in Chilean society. Specifically, the most radical change that we see in this was the movement of the *callampas* into the general population....[8] What people brought into play in the sixties was not only a new territorial position but also a new social and political positioning (Garcés 2002a, 423–424).

Pinochet's coup sought to reverse the almost hegemonic position attained by the popular sectors. That third of

---

8   *Callampas* are the settlers in popular encampments, who get their name from the callampa mushroom, which grows overnight.

Santiago's population—those who had built their own barrios, houses, schools, and health clinics, and pushed for basic services—was a threat to the capital's authorities. The military regime attempted to override this by displacing the entire population to suburbs built by the state or the market.

Between 1973 and today, there has been a profound reversal in city housing, a true urban counterrevolution. Between 1980 and 2000, 202,000 "social housing units" were constructed in Santiago, in order to move a million people—one-fifth of the capital's population—from self-constructed areas to segregated housing complexes far from the city center (Rodriguez and Sugranyes 2005). It is useful to take a closer look at this process to see how the state and capital tries to halt and reverse the "taking of positions" of the popular sectors in the cities. Sixty-five percent of people in these complexes want to leave because of overcrowding in small houses, compounded by the isolation of being confined to the outskirts of the city. The dictatorship's policies, continued and intensified in the post-dictatorship era since 1990, have resulted in regressive changes embodied in "the uniformity of social housing as compared to the spatial complexity of the popular settlements"; "organization to fragmentation" and "the land seizures representing an act of integration into the city, compared to social housing as an expulsion from the city as perceived by the *villa* inhabitants"(Rodriguez and Sugranyes 2002, 17).[9]

The operation's objective was to destroy a popular territorial power as embodied in the settlements; the dictatorship initiated it and the democratic government post-1990 continued it. A huge mass of low-standard housing was built for the poor throughout the country; it was constructed in a manner that explicitly sought to eradicate the settlements. At the beginning of the plan, the production of subsidized housing during the eighties "was applied almost exclusively in programs for the eradication of 'settlements,' particularly in the regions of Santiago and Las Condes" (Rodriguez and

---

9   In Chile, an illegal occupation of a property is called a *toma*, an irregular settlement is called a *campamento*, and all housing built by the state is called *villa*.

Sugranyes 2005, 30). First, they "cleaned up" wealthy neighborhoods. There were two goals here: to end the distortions in
land value created by the settlements in wealthy districts and
to consolidate the spatial segregation of social classes for the
purposes of security.

Between 1979 and 1983, some 120,000 people were forcibly transferred from settlements they had occupied in the
sixties and seventies into the periphery. Chilean urban analysts consider the dictatorship's eradication of the poor from
the consolidated city as "a radical measure, singular on the
continent" (Rodriguez and Sugranyes 2005, 31).[10]

Re-settlements occurred in thirteen of the twenty-four
districts of Santiago. The eradicated lost their jobs, faced an
increase in transportation costs, and continued to have major
problems in accessing education, health care, and social benefits. Above all, the forcible transfer contributed "to uprooting
the informal network of help and support among the population and a strong decrease in participation of residents in
community organizations" (Rodriguez and Sugranyes 2005,
31). That was precisely the aim of the transfer. The transplant-
ed family tends to remain confined inside their house and social bonds are broken. Over the years, a new housing pattern
was established: large urban areas containing intentionally
separated concentrations of rich and poor.

And from the point of view of capital and the state, one
has to wonder, was the continuity of the settlements and
popular neighborhoods so terrible? Apparently so. The wave
of mobilizations in 1983 in these neighborhoods—after ten
years of fierce repression and the social restructuring—put
the dictatorship on the defensive and convinced the elites to
expedite their efforts to eradicate popular settlements. Land
seizures started in 1980 threatened to spread during the protests of 1983. This new generation of land seizures occurred
because the residents refused to be part of the new state housing policies that "would have inevitably meant leaving their

---

10 The dictatorships in Argentina and Uruguay tried to eliminate "slums" in
Buenos Aires and Montevideo by relocating inhabitants to the periphery, but
they were not as successful or aggressive as the Pinochet dictatorship.

communities and moving to the outskirts of the city" (Garcés 2002b, 30).

Elites saw the existence of settlements and barrios constructed and governed by the popular sectors as a direct threat to their privileged social position—hence, as the Corporation of Social Studies and Education has pointed out, they created a policy of forcefully resettling people on the periphery, causing the new inhabitants to be uprooted and in debt. But it also marks the change of one form of society to another:

> [T]hey go from a state of relative autonomy, to a clientelist dependency, leaving behind a society that recognizes use value as its fundamental axis to one dominated by the commodification of social relations. Moreover, the daily violence endured by the inhabitants of these social housing projects subsidizes political peace in the rest of the country (Skewes 2005, 101).

This could not be achieved without imposing spatial discipline, a careful but violent reconstruction of the panopticon deconstructed by residents. In short, social control was achieved in Chile via a reconstruction of public space and forced incorporation into the market economy. This dual strategy successfully eradicated the relatively autonomous spaces created by the population. Let's take a close look at this world that had to be destroyed. The researcher Juan Carlos Skewes lived in a "settlement" for a year and then accompanied an uprooted family to a housing project, which allowed him to observe the changes in lifestyle between the two places.

Skewes argues that there is a "popular design" in the settlement that is different from the official, hegemonic world. Since there were no plans or preconceived ideas about how to organize the space, the design reflects the day-to-day practice of those who, in order "to live, create a livable space" (Skewes 2005, 106). He notes eight characteristics of the spatial design: labyrinthine structure, porosity of the boundaries, invisibility inside the settlement, interconnection of housing, irregularity of internal boundaries, use of markers to rank spaces, the existence of focal points, and, finally, lookout posts.

There is a logic to the settlement's form of internal interconnectedness, and this determines the flows, corridors, and passages. It is a structure that ensures autonomy, in part due to the internal invisibility and self-regulation that mark the limit of the settlement. This delineation of an inside and an outside represents a macro limit that cannot be reproduced inside the camp where boundaries are porous because use value determines it so. The design protects residents from the outside, but "facilitates social control through acoustic, visual, and olfactory means, contributing to the formation of a porous environment that reinforces the fusion of individual lives" (Skewes 2005, 114).

When moved to public housing, inhabitants lose their self-sufficiency. With its panoptic design and straight lines, residents are fragmented and isolated, while being stripped of a sense of community protection. A living space focused on people is converted into a space centered on objects, housing, and what Skewes describes as "the transition from a female domain into a masculine world, and from local control to external control" (Skewes 2005, 120). The networks of mutual support and sense of neighborhood community are all destroyed, and the inhabitants are left in a state of debt and dependency, coping with a high level of daily, localized crime. In sum, the state attempts to destroy a social sector through relocation because the urban settlers threaten the hegemonic order. Ultimately, it comes down to destroying or corralling popular sectors by means of criminalizing poverty.

But the events in Santiago were not unique in the continent. In 1970, 50 percent of the population of Recife and 30 percent of those of Rio de Janeiro lived in popular settlements, which was also true of 60 percent of the population in Bogotá; 49 percent of Guayaquil, 40 percent of Caracas, and 40 percent of Lima in 1969 (Castells 1986, 249–250). Another study shows the percentages of residents living in self-constructed homes: 60 percent of the population of Mexico City in 1990, 61 percent of Caracas, and 31 percent in Bogotá of 1985 (Gilbert 1997, 104).

Millions of people have created their own spaces and means of survival beyond the market. There was talk of the existence of two societies long before the actual disengagement of a sizable portion of the population from the formal economy, of "different conceptions of the world and life, so diverse that they seemed irreconcilable" (Romero 2001, 364). If these two worlds had something in common, it was, as Romero put it, a "revolution of expectations." But neoliberal globalization erased that point in common.

Of course, not all self-constructed neighborhoods and cities follow the same trajectory, and in some cases they seem to be very far from constituting forms of popular power or local self-government. But there is no doubt that undiscovered potentialities for social change are nesting in these spaces.

To conclude the first part of this essay, I would like to quickly address the experience of the city of Lima, where the occupation of urban space takes a slightly different form than in Santiago: Here the settlements and popular neighborhoods are "islands," which arise in the interstices of the traditional city. The number of settlements/islands in Lima has risen from 56 to 408 between 1957 and 1981, grouped into three large cones (south, north, and east) by 2004.

These urban cones are huge "blotches" that appear to imprison the traditional city. This is a quantitatively and qualitative dual phenomenon. If in Santiago the settlements included about 30 percent of the city dwellers in 1973, in Lima the urban periphery population increased from 9.5 percent in 1957 to 59 percent in 2004 (Matos Mar 2004, 149, 153). The difference is that the settlements were established in areas adjacent to the city in the vast, empty sand flats that surround Lima and are relatively continuous and homogeneous territories, forming real "blotches" populated by urban migrants from the highlands.

From the point of view of the forms of land occupation, there are no major differences here compared to the case of La

Victoria in Santiago. These are invasions by organized groups of poor people who illegally occupy land, hoist Peruvian flags, resist the security forces, set up their residents' associations, and start building their shacks with straw mats; the whole neighborhood then acts as one community, nestled in the hillsides and the sand. The first neighborhood formed in this manner was San Cosme, established in May 1946. The practice of seizing lands and forming shantytowns grew slowly in the fifties and reached a peak during the seventies. Villa El Salvador was a part of this process; for a time, it was considered a model of neighborhood self-management.

In the late eighties, Matos Mar estimated nine million people lived in 2,100 settlements across the country (1989, 120). He believes that because of the enormity of the process, the country faces what he calls an "overflow from below" that is changing the face of the cities and particularly the capital. He argues that urban land invasions are part of a process begun by Juan Velasco Alvarado's military government (1968–1975); it forced peasants to move from the sierra when it advanced a program of agrarian reform, attempting to break up the traditional haciendas of the landowners. By 1984, 80 percent of the population of Lima lived in popular settlements: 37 percent in shantytowns, 23 percent in popular urban peripheries, and 20 percent in alleyways and yards (Matos Mar 2004, 69). The remaining 20 percent lived in middle-class and wealthy residential neighborhoods.

Migrants continued taking over land until the mid-eighties without the presence of state institutions, which marks a crucial difference from the occupations in Chile. The Andean migrant installed in Lima had to adjust not only to the challenging physical aspect of the city but also its patterns of sociability and everyday culture.

Some architectural features of the constructed homes—gabled roofs and fences—are derived more from the mountains than European influences; a growing common practice is to employ indigenous systems of reciprocity such as the *minka*. The new housing is christened with the Andean *tinka*—a cross of flowers crowning the highest point. To protect the house from evil and thieves, talismans and amulets—especially vegetables—have become a standard part of popular urban religion (Matos Mar 2004, 80).

This migrant population has developed an oppositional economy, according to Matos Mar, which is distinct from the "informal" economy because it reflects a reality that bears an antagonistic relation to the official. To call it "informal" suggests ceding a central place to the established economy, hegemonized by the ruling classes. Instead, they have a survival economy and one organized around resistance—the economy cannot be separated from the set of social relations at work in the settlements. The popular sectors have created a different city with its own means of communication, its own religious and cultural practices (like *la chicha* music), its own means of transport (the microbus), and even its own "autonomous neighborhood surveillance systems and, for extreme cases, people's courts and summary executions" (Matos Mar 2004, 188). The popular economy sits within this overall context, while maintaining ties with the economy of the ruling classes.

These considerable achievements rest upon the reinvention of the Andean community and kinship and reciprocity networks at work in the new urban space. The urban community creates public spaces through cooperation between the inhabitants: streets, sidewalks, lighting, water supply, schools, and health facilities are all constructed collectively. Family networks constructed the homes: 500,000 homes in shantytowns have been built in the traditional stages method. Two out of every three homes in Lima have been built in this collective way. It's another way of making a city, a different city, where living spaces are often places of work and shops simultaneously. This other city belongs to the *other* Peru, which has a more dynamic economy. According to data from the Peruvian Chamber of Construction, 70 percent of housing construction is done in the shantytowns by families working informally with master builders and small businesses, a form of direct self-construction (Tokeshi 2006).

Matos Mar's work points to the existence of two countries, "the official Peru of the institutions" and "the marginalized

Peru, plural and multiform" (2004, 97). Supporting this view-point, sociologist Carlos Franco observes three distinctive characteristics in Villa El Salvador: a mode of organization and distribution of space, the organizational form of the population, and a project of economic and social development (Tokeshi 2006). It is not a separate country that is a subsidiary or dependent on the other; there are two autonomous, self-sufficient worlds that relate to one another as such. The main difference is that one is in decline and the other ascendent.

In effect, the Peru-from-below went from seizing land and properties in the fifties to invading "the official culture in its economic, educational, legal, and religious forms through new styles introduced by the constantly overflowing and expanding masses" (Matos Mar 2004, 101). Furthermore, the masses became uncontrollable and established "semi-autonomous pockets of power" based on Andean communitarian traditions of reciprocity (Matos Mar 2004, 105). The official and the autonomous countries relate, confront, and interpenetrate, according to Matos Mar, but the dominant sectors are slowly losing hold of their traditional physical and symbolic spaces. This kind of spontaneous social change is expressed in the Andean concept of *Pachakutik*.[11]

Popular sectors have been able to veto Creole politicians (for example, blocking Mario Vargas Llosa's election attempts in the late eighties), but they have not established stable alliances with political parties and leaders. Instead they establish "relations in terms of costs and benefits that serve a calculated processes of negotiation" (Degregori and Grompone 1991, 46). This does not indicate populism or patronage but, as Carlos Franco notes, that the "urban plebs" are moving from "delegated representation to political self-representation" (Degregori and Grompone 1991, 46). What we see happening here, much like what occurred later in Bolivia, is that the population does not feel the need to be represented in the hegemonic world and is creating a separate or "other" world. At this point, the traditional concepts coined to describe and analyze

---

11 *Pachakutik* is a Quechua word that signifies change, rebirth, transformation, and the coming of a new era.

the social struggles in *a* society are no longer useful because here we encounter two worlds in conflict and alliance over wide range of issues. And so, from an academic point of view, it becomes necessary to write a new narrative.

So far we have looked at two groups of popular urban sectors that have followed different paths, although they share points in common. Pinochet's dictatorship (1973–1990) and the Fujimori regime (1990–2000) marked the end of one epoch for the urban, popular sector movement. It was a new movement, and, notwithstanding its heterogeneity, I think we can identify some of its common features:

- It is a movement of *rural migrants* arriving in cities that are the centers of power for the dominant classes. The mass influx of rural population into the cities changes social, economic, and cultural relations; popular sectors create multiple islands in urban spaces in the midst of traditional cities, which are sometimes interconnected. This is a form of resistance to elite power and an affirmation of the popular world.
- The spaces they construct (settlements, shantytowns, popular neighborhoods) are *different* from the traditional city of the middle and upper classes. They have been constructed differently (that is, collectively) and urban space is occupied and distributed differently within them (based on solidarity, reciprocity, and egalitarianism).
- Explicit or implicit forms of popular power are born in these self-constructed spaces, impacting the entire range of social relations—from the direct control of space (who inhabits it and how) to the regulation of relations between people. State logic appears to be subordinate to popular/community logic in these spaces.
- Economic initiatives for survival arise in the popular territories that often take the form of *a different, counter-hegemonic economy.*
- Control of these territories enables the urban popular sectors to resist, stay put, and survive even as the powers that be seek to break them, whether by disguising their

differences, through co-optation, or by neutralizing initiatives.

Recent Experiences

Urban popular sectors began a new era during the February 1989 Caracazo. From the spaces they controlled, they launched profound challenges to the system, creating counter-powers based in their barrio/territories. The overflow from below that occurred in Lima became insurrectional in other cities and marked the beginning of a new political era of survival and resistance to the hegemonic society. This is a product of neoliberalism, which led to a re-colonization of the continent and an attack on popular sectors' lifeways. The testing ground for the implementation of the neoliberal experiment was, with particular vehemence, in Pinochet's Chile.

Beginning in 1983, settlements in Santiago created by popular sectors after the occupation of La Victoria played a decisive role in resistance to the dictatorship. The self-constructed, self-governed neighborhoods replaced factories as the epicenter of popular action. After ten years of dictatorship, popular sectors defied the regimen in the streets by staging eleven "national protests" between May 11, 1983, and October 30, 1984 (some analysts argue that there were twenty-two protests between 1983 and 1987) (Salazar and Pinto 2002b, 242). The enormity and potency of these protests put the dictatorship on the defensive. The leaders were primarily young people who used barricades and bonfires to demarcate their territory and attack the closest symbols of order such as municipal buildings, traffic lights, and so on.

From the early eighties, women and young people began to assume leadership roles in the movement via their pro-survival and socio-cultural organizations, taking action against the dictatorship's attempts to dismantle the popular sector. The appropriation of territories during protests, where street barricades physically limit the state presence, represents the rejection of an external authority within the self-controlled spaces. "They shall not pass" was a popular slogan at the barricades. This effectively "closed off the population" and represented the "affirmation of the popular community as an alternative to state authority and rejection of the proposed totality of the dictatorship" (Revilla 1991, 63).

The state response was brutal. At least 75 were killed, more than 1,000 wounded, and 6,000 arrested within a year. In a single protest on August 11–12, 1983, 1,000 were arrested and 29 killed; 18,000 soldiers participated in the repression, in addition to civilians and national police. This underscores the intensity of the protests. Despite the repression, there was no defeat. Community identity was restored, and the ability to mount such protests and launch repeated and sustained challenges to the system for a year and a half following a decade of repression, torture, and disappearances, was in itself a tremendous success.

The protests show new social actors in action, at a time when the working class could no longer play a central role. The new actors—basically women and young settlers—are different from the working class in important ways. The first, discussed previously, consists of the territorial roots of the protest and therefore of the subjects who carry them out. This change is a long-term shift that modifies the character, form, and trajectory of the movements of those from below (Zibechi 2003b). The historian Gabriel Salazar notes that "autonomy, agency, and identity creation is synthesized as the country's poor gradually rose up" (1999, 127).

However, it is not the territorialization of popular power that gives the struggle its potency, but the social relations nesting in these "other" territories. In contrast to the first epoch of the movement, popular sectors, particularly lower-class women, developed new capabilities—principally, the capacity to produce and re-produce their lives without relying on the market. Salazar and Pinto captured the depth of this difference:

If women's experience in the 60s had been profound, that of the 80s and 90s was deeper still, causing an even more vigorous and comprehensive social response. After 1973, the people's movement did not decline. On the contrary: it reached its peak.

The settlers of the 80s organized not only to seize
a site, build a camp, and await a state legitimation, or
to "associate" with the populist state according to the
terms they proposed. They organized among themselves (and with other settlers) to produce (bread-
making collectives, laundries, weaving centers, etc.),
to subsist (community kitchens, family gardens, joint
purchases), to educate themselves (women's collectives, cultural groups), and also to resist (militancy,
health groups). All this was carried out not only without the state, but also against the state (Salazar and
Pinto 2002a, 261).

It was this movement that forced the dictatorship to
withdraw. It was also, as Salazar observed, the longest and
most vigorous resistance movement in Chilean history, one
that even brutal repression could not be defeat. Poor women
in the most difficult conditions drew from the memory of
the struggles of the fifties and earlier. Women's strength—
and this is a characteristic of current movements across the
continent—rests on something as simple as coming together,
supporting one another, and resolving problems "their" way,
using the infallible logic of doing things as they do them at
home. They transferred the style of a private space to a collective space and utilized the spontaneous community attitude
seen in movements like Argentina's Mothers of the Plaza de
Mayo (Zibechi 2003a).

These women have modified our understanding of the
term "social movement." They did not create bureaucratic
structures or ceremonies with the usual pomp and circumstance inherent in those institutions, which are necessarily
separated from their base. But they acted, and did they ever!
Under the dictatorship, Chilean women settlers became

little ants that crisscrossed between and among area
houses, meeting and chatting with all the neighbors,
dealing with professionals from the NGOs or social
vicarages (and later with professionals and politicians

from the municipalities), attending workshops and training courses and regional and national coordinator meetings. Their mobility allowed them to weave "neighborhood nets" and even community networks that made formal neighborhood board meetings unnecessary, such as the neighborhood councils and mothers' centers (Salazar and Pinto 2002a, 267).

This is a social movement that prioritizes the movement as a moving-of-itself, displacing organizational structures, as we have seen before. The description of poor women moving about in the neighborhoods as they weave local networks—that are, as Salazar points out, "community cells"—is the best image of a non-institutionalized movement and the creation of non-state powers, which are not hierarchical or separated from the rest. Thus was born a new way of doing politics in the hands of new subjects, with whom state institutions do not know how to interact.

For these women, the transition from dictatorship to democracy was a disaster. After the restoration of constitutional democracy in 1990, they suffered an unimaginable defeat. In other words, "The dictatorship did not vanquish the settler movement on the battlefield the settlers chose, but on the field of compromise chosen by their supposed allies: middle class professionals and left-of-center politicians" (Salazar and Pinto 2002a, 263). It is difficult to describe the transition from dictatorship to democracy in better terms. The population had created the Commando of United Residents and the Settler Women's Movement (CUP and MOMUPO). They were invited to participate in multi-sectoral bodies such as the Civility Assembly, where professional and middle-class militants advocated for a transition "from within the popular movement," which led firstly to the marginalization and later the disintegration of popular organizations (2002a, 262–263).

From this experience, we can deduct several relevant lessons. The first is that the movements—which I will call "communitarian" for lack of anything better (that is, they act as a coherent, territorially bound social actor)—cannot be defeated by repression, however brutal it may be, excepting the mass slaughter of its members. The second is that emancipatory forces can suffer defeat when at the mercy of what is generally called "the left"—that set of professionals, NGOs, and political parties who are responsible for overseeing the softening and fragmenting of the movement. To do this—and this is the third lesson—it is necessary to co-opt or break key individuals or collectives within the movement. This is what happened in Chile in the crucial year of 1986, when the rules of the transition were defined, and later in much of the continent.

Young people, the other key players in protests from 1983 onward, followed a similar course. During the early years of the dictatorship, thousands of "cultural" groups were created, operating as shelters from an exterminating regime. Under the protection of Catholic parishes, theater groups, youth clubs, discussion groups, and workshops, various forms of popular education were set up, "forging a youth culture quite different from the '68 generation: this one more rooted in the present than in the past, the collective more than the individual, more artisan than professional, and more participatory than scenic" (Salazar and Pinto 2002b, 237). The various youth groups comprised a large, diverse, and spontaneous network. At the same time, but uniting with the activities of women settlers, the youth began to organize outdoor "cultural" events that eventually attracted thousands of people.

In those safe spaces beyond the control of the dictatorship (Scott 2000), young people tested out their rejection of the regime and then, around 1983, moved onto the streets. The period of retreat, from 1976 to 1982, Salazar defined as "a communitarian cycle centered in cultural construction" with a rotating and informal leadership. In this period and in these spaces, a powerful youth culture was born that continues to have a presence even today:

> Perhaps the most striking legacy of this cycle was to demonstrate that the articulation of open groups with free participation could be a militant and democratic force, socially more transparent than the functional

and hierarchical structure of political parties (Salazar and Pinto 2002b, 241).

This new horizontal youth culture had to not only confront the military dictatorship but also sections of the militant left who sought to instrumentalize the youth initially for the insurgency and later for electoral participation. Broadly speaking, it can be described like a clamp on the new youth cultures: the dictatorship on one side and the old left on the other. Later on, when the electoral system was restored, the clamp on the youth was represented by neoliberal policies or the market on one side, and the institutions, governed by the right or left, on the other. NGOs are very often part of the second side of the clamp.

The rejection of political parties and electoral abstentionism is common among oppositional young people in Latin America. Across the continent, where there were dictatorships and also constitutional democracies, a clear separation existed between base activists and the leadership, the latter always willing to negotiate "solutions" with the military, elites, and/or traditional parties. In the eighties and early nineties, popular sectors (again, basically women and youth) suffered serious reverses that were not inflicted by authoritarian regimes or the right in power. Just as left-wing professionals and trade unions played a role in reinstalling constitutional democracies with restricted freedoms in the southern Cone, some armed leftist groups contributed to weakening popular forces, particularly the urban poor.[12]

Chilean youth, like most youth in Latin America, withdrew from the militant stage and from formal politics in order to temporarily retreat to spaces where they felt more secure, away from the control of the system. The "re-grouping of youth 'from below' occurs in various forms, in the subcutaneous tissue of institutions, on the edges of the regulatory system, or in the intersubjective intricacies and burrows of private space" (Salazar and Pinto 2002b, 265). And something happened in those spaces during the nineties: After that

---

12   I am thinking of the Shining Path in Peru.

period of retreat, the youth reappeared as a force in the streets. Hundreds of thousands of high-school students—the "Penguins"—protested the neoliberal educational policies in 2006, and fiercely challenging the government of Michelle Bachelet and the Chilean elite.

The mobilization of the youth came as a big surprise. The Chilean ruling coalition had brought the popular sectors off the streets and into the political arena, not as actors but as objects of targeted government policies seeking to control and neutralize movements. And this begs the question—how long will they be able to neutralize movements through directed policies?

We do not know, but past experience has left its mark. The young people, according to Salazar, now "know" that things have gone wrong with both the right and the left and that they have to do things for themselves after the huge disappointment with formal politics and electoral democracy. Perhaps that's why organizations that survived the transition to democracy are different from those of previous periods. The new community organizations are more autonomous and focus on various campaigns: to recuperate the memory of struggle and neighborhood identity, to solve community health problems, and to try to "access economic alternatives for themselves and their families" (ECO 2001). In other words, they seek to produce and reproduce their lives beyond the control of any institution, state, or party.

The land seizure in Peñalolén, Santiago, in March 1997 greatly resembled the taking of La Victoria forty years earlier. And, as with other popular organizations during this period, the relationship between the settlers with the state remains strictly instrumental and rigorously external. For this reason, no political party has a significant influence in Peñalolén. At the Pedro Mariqueo Cultural Center in La Victoria, during preparations for the twelfth anniversary celebration of the founding of the Primero de Mayo radio station, I personally witnessed the high degree of autonomy among the new local organizations. One slogan made an impression on me: "Our problem began with the return to democracy." This was not an ideological affirmation, just a common sense sentiment shared by the approximately thirty people, mostly youth and women, present.

In fact, governments throughout Latin America employed the same "model" of transition, which was very similar to the Spanish transition after the death of Franco. But popular sectors are boiling over, to such an extent that the Chilean state has to intervene in urban spaces under the pretext of drugs and crime through the Safe Neighborhoods Program. The Interior Ministry launched this program in 2001 with funds from the Inter-American Development Bank, leading to police and social intervention in "marginal" and "conflicted" neighborhoods. The first area affected was La Legua and the second was La Victoria, followed by up to nine more neighborhoods during the first four years. The plan's objectives are not clear and all that authorities will say is that its purpose is "to combat illegal street vendors and delinquency in downtown Santiago."[13]

The state tries to involve local social organizations in its program, particularly the neighborhood councils, which divides the neighborhood and its organizational nuclei. Members of the Esteban Gumucio de Yungay Cultural Center, one of the communities taken over by the Ministry of the Interior, claim that the "government bulldozer" is an attempt to dismantle "self-governing territorial organizations" (Perro Muerto 2006, 12). In this neighborhood, autonomous collectives seized a public space and constructed a cultural center and a community kitchen in which residents make bread and pies. Police, with the support of the local neighborhood council, have subjected the community to a virtual state of siege.

The blatant manipulation of the community resulted in the installation of street lights, paving, and speed bumps, all with the approval of neighborhood councils—one of which consists almost entirely of municipal officials and represents, in practice, the eyes, ears, and voice of the municipality—even though the steps of the housing blocks are falling apart and the application to build a social headquarters for popular

---

13 See www.gobiernodechile.cl.   ·

organizations was dismissed with an abrupt "the municipality opposes the headquarters" (Perro Muerto 2006, 13).

The state continually tries to stifle any autonomous activity among the poor, whether political, economic, or cultural. Therefore, in order to isolate the autonomous collectives it is necessary to co-opt local organizations or social leaders, since repression produced the opposite effects of those sought. "Democratic" legislation is also part of this low intensity war against the popular sectors. In December 2003, a bill entered Parliament to "modernize" the free outdoor flea markets that are "residual spaces of popular sovereignty" for the people (Páez 2004). The flea markets are areas where popular producers and buyers form horizontal links, and this kind of trade is often an "economic and political weapon with which the popular classes can exercise their rights as citizens" (2004). Both the rulers and the ruled know that it is from these microspaces of everyday life that the beginnings of insurrections can take hold and occasionally pour out onto the great avenues of social control.

Collective social action by poor women is particularly inspiring in the city of Lima. In 1994, there were 15,000 popular organizations in the city: 7,630 Glass of Milk Committees, 2,575 mothers clubs, 2,273 popular soup kitchens, and 1,871 neighborhood councils, according to official sources.[14] Many of the organizations have links to political parties; for example, some mothers clubs have had connections to Peru's American Popular Revolutionary Alliance (APRA) since 1985 or were co-opted by them. Designed to provide breakfast to children under the age of six and to pregnant and nursing mothers, the Glass of Milk Committee originated under leftist mayor Alfonso Barrantes in 1984, when pressure from poor women convinced the city to implement the Glass of Milk Program.

By the mid-nineties, mothers clubs, Glass of Milk Committees, and popular soup kitchens benefited four million

---

14 See www.inei.gob.pe.

people throughout the country and were run almost exclusively by women. But the female role is not fully appreciated. Often this kind of activity is seen as a type of charitable activity or a substitute for the state's role, but I would argue that these initiatives have little to do with charity or clientelism. Below, I will look closely at Lima's soup kitchens, a network of organizations born "from below" that have been functioning for almost forty years.

A nun/nurse named Maria Van der Linde created the first collective popular kitchen in the late seventies in Comas, north Lima (Blondet and Trivelli 2004, 39). The goal was to collectively prepare food rations for families and individuals, using donated or subsidized food. The idea of neighborhood collective kitchens spread quickly during the economic crisis: In 1982 there were 200 peoples' kitchens in Lima; in 1988, at the time of the stabilization program under APRA President Alan Garcia, the number had risen to 2,000; and during Fujimori's structural adjustment programs in the nineties, there were 7,000 kitchens. A survey in 2003 counted 5,000 soup kitchens in Lima alone, with more than 100,000 active (female) members (Blondet and Trivelli 2004, 20).

The kitchens, supported by pastoral communities influenced by liberation theology,

> promoted self-help and the self-provision of services, seeking to emphasize the autonomy of the poor vis-à-vis the state and charitable institutions, in contrast to the dependency too easily engendered by other programs. This is why personal effort and popular initiative were so important in the emergence of these kitchens, and why there was resistance to coordinating with government programs and articulating their demands in relation to the state (Blondet and Trivelli 2004, 39).

These kitchens are considered "self-managed" or "self-sustaining," while those of the state are called "administered" or "subsidized." The latter are more sympathetic to the state and political parties, but over time the differences seem minor. The evolution of the kitchens had various stages: In 1988, the First Meeting of Self-Managed Kitchens was held and the National Commission of Kitchens was created, during a period when women activists came into prominence and the government was prepared to offer a lot of help. After the economic crisis in 1988, the kitchens multiplied in number and people had to learn new ways to survive (through small "businesses" and the expansion of food loans), leading to significant popular mobilizations for government support. During the nineties, many kitchens had to close due to Shining Path harassment, while others worked from behind closed doors (Blondet and Trivelli 2004, 42–43).

Each kitchen has an average of twenty-two active women members in each neighborhood organization, according to the 2003 survey. Ninety percent of the members have received some training and has had some management responsibility. Only 20 percent of the kitchen's presidents have finished high school. In 2003, 2,775 kitchens in Lima were self-managed and 1,930 were subsidized; the latter formed in the second half of the eighties and the former in the nineties.

Each kitchen produces an average of a hundred meals daily, almost half a million each day in Lima. It is interesting to note who receives the meals: 60 percent go to members and their families; 12 percent to the members who cook as payment for their labor (there is no other pay); and 8 percent is donated to poor people in the neighborhood ("social cases"). Only 18 percent of the meals are sold, half to people in the community— usually the same individuals everyday—and the other half to people who happen to be in the area, such as service people and others. Members can buy at a lower price than non-members.

Clearly the kitchens were set up to attend to the needs of members and their families, not to make profits. The kitchens do not have savings or distribute benefits to members, and "it is most likely that the members themselves are subsidizing the kitchen directly (donating ingredients, providing labor, etc.) beyond the normal cooking duties" (Blondet and Trivelli 2004, 32). Although I will return to this later, women who work in the kitchens operate with the logic of economic solidarity, not the logic of the market, and are not guided by commercial criteria. Only 9 percent of their work is dedicated to producing goods for sale. In fact, what they receive from the state goes almost entirely to rations given to the poorest.

Most of the kitchens organize parties and raffles to generate further income, since state-provided rations barely cover 20 percent of the cost of a meal. A 2006 study by the Federation of Women Organized in Committees of Self-Sustaining Kitchens (FEMOCCPAAL), representing some 1,800 kitchens, states that "kitchens are no longer a supplement to a salary, because that salary no longer exists, and for many families, they are the only means to access food."[15] This is happening in a period of strong economic growth. A detailed study by that organization quantified the cost of each meal as follows: The state contributes 19 percent, kitchen organizations provide 81 percent; members buy food that accounts for 33 percent, free labor is another 32 percent, and the remaining 16 percent is administrative costs, transportation to pick up state-donated food, and other services compensated by work or meals.

The magnitude of the efforts of Lima's poor women shows their capacity to intervene in the political life from their own place. In the popular kitchens, the women have moved what they do in their homes into the public sphere. The same is true of other social organizations. It is the logic of family care extended and multiplied in times of crisis. However, in November 1988, during one of the most critical moments in the history of Peru, women participated not only in local organizations such as the popular kitchens, but also directly on the national political scene. During that month, a rumor spread in the barrios claiming that strangers (gringo doctors accompanied by thugs) had been abducting children to extract their eyes. Between November 29 and 30, thousands of mothers, almost all from the poor barrios, panicked and went en masse to the schools to collect their children because they believed they were in jeopardy from the *sacaojos* [eye-snatchers]. Residents set up patrols in many neighborhoods and were on the verge of lynching several people suspected of being sacaojos.

---

15   See www.femoccpaal.org.

A detailed investigation shed light on the reasons for such strange collective behavior (Portocarrero and Soraya 1991). While at first it was seen as an unusual rumor associated with myths of the colonial period, the investigation shows how the sacaojos rumor flourished around the same time as a worsening of economic conditions, government paralysis, a wave of strikes, the collapse of public services, and an increase in the attacks by the Shining Path guerrilla group. The city of Lima was semi-paralyzed and people were very afraid. In September of that year there had been a *paquetazo* [a readjustment of prices to reduce inflation] that posed a serious reduction in workers' purchasing power. Markets were empty and housewives had to wait in long queues to buy the few goods available.

President Alan Garcia's popularity had plummeted. The Prime Minister made dramatic statements in early November (he said "rivers of blood will flow," if the right returns). Around November 7, there were so many workers on strike that it looked like public services might completely collapse, especially the urban transport system, due to a bus drivers' strike. Lima was a city in chaos, with crowded bus stops, thousands of people on foot, and passengers perched on top of trucks and vans. On November 22, Sendero Luminoso blew up thirty-two electrical towers, causing a massive power outage and three weeks of power constraints. Traffic lights were not working, there was no bread in the bakeries, and the same day, the Minister of Economy announced commodity price increases from 100 to 200 percent. Many businesses shut down, but in the urban peripheries, people worked with the police to force them to open.

The level of tension was very high. Many imagined that there would be looting and a huge social explosion, followed by the inevitable repression leading to thousands of deaths. Fear and despair gripped popular sectors. The workers' syndicate called a twenty-four-hour strike that was a complete failure. And then things took a different turn:

> In the days following the *paquetazo*, there was no strike
> in Lima or looting. However, the *sacaojos* episode

occurred. The hypothesis we propose is that the rumor and panic increased the general level of stress. The *sacaojos* episode was a functional equivalent of riots or strikes. It allowed people to release tension, to collectively express the fear and despair generated by the situation, and even try to defend themselves from it. The sensation was that something had to happen in order for the fear to be dissipated (Portocarrero and Soraya 1991, 29).

The hypothesis is that the classic popular "response" (looting, strikes, and insurrection) to crisis was not worth it in the eyes of the main protagonists because of the inevitable human costs involved. But the poor, and particularly the women and mothers, were neither demobilized nor disorganized. At various points throughout the city, crowds of up to one thousand mothers demanded answers and the intervention of authorities to solve the problem of the eye-snatchers. They formed neighborhood patrols and committees to capture the culprits and, although a guilty party was never found, in several cases the people arrested "suspects" who were always doctors or foreigners.

The truth is that women and mothers were the protagonists in all of this and "not the popular leaders (which is the case in a strike) or young people (which is the case in riots and looting)," and through the eye-snatchers rumor and panic, a greater evil was prevented: "So the fear and anxiety was converted into a feeling of panic and violence within young people, especially in the private world of the poor family. These feelings were not politicized, as intended by the proposed strike. It also did not lead to looting and anomic behavior; something else occurred" (Portocarrero and Soraya 1991, 33).

At that time, the main protagonists were not trade unions or the rural farmers' groups but rather the women and mothers organized in their districts to ensure the maintenance of everyday life. When the "formal" economy of the country became paralyzed, thousands of popular kitchens, Glass of Milk Committees, and mothers' clubs held together the daily life for families. Secondly, women and mothers intervened in the country's political life at the height of its troubles, but not as expected. Why? Clearly they did not trust the trade union movement or the political parties, in which their husbands or male relatives were active. But there is even more to the story.

I lived in Lima at that time and saw for myself the impossibility of changing the course of policies of those "from above" during those months. The popular movement did not have the force or legitimacy to compel the government or elites to change their policies. It was also unable to stop Shining Path terror. The women and mothers sensed it or knew it. What was the point of a strike or rioting in this situation? The first was a gesture without consequence and the second involved running too high a risk. And therefore the women and mothers intervened decisively at this critical juncture, to protect their children, their neighborhoods, and their families just as they had been doing in the thousands of locally run organizations.

If we maintain an enlightened gaze from above—male, white, and intellectual—we will continue to underestimate actions arising and carried out by those from below, such as the massive intervention of poor women in 1988. The poor women were engaging in a different form of doing politics, neither better nor worse than men in their formal and masculine organizations, but coming from another place. We should be open to other interpretations of the political conjuncture coming "from below"—in this case, poor women—for it can help strengthen the positive features that already exist in the movement and put a stop to those that merely reproduce hegemonic modes. As we know, the popular sectors played a decisive role in the electoral tsunami that prevented the election of rightist Mario Vargas Llosa and defeated the Shining Path. And has the huge role played by women and mothers in both cases been fully recognized?

In Venezuela, there are more than six thousand urban land committees and two thousand technical water boards through which millions of people are taking control of their own lives. Although they really took shape during the government of Hugo Chávez, both organizations are part of the popular urban struggle over the last two decades. In Caracas, 50 percent of the population lives in settlements without legal rights to the land and with poor drinking water facilities (Antillano 2005). Like other parts of the continent, these barrios emerged in the fifties and sixties as a result of inequalities in oil revenue distribution.

In 1991, the Assembly of Barrios of Caracas was formed from the residents' board during the First International Gathering for the Rehabilitation of the Barrios. The assembly brought together people from over two hundred barrios in the capital and formulated a series of key demands that were later taken up by the Venezuelan government: These included co-management of the drinking water facilities, regulation of the land occupied by the settlers, and local self-government. This was the result of three decades of popular organization and mobilization in the urban peripheries.

The emergence of these barrios was the result of intense struggles to resist evictions and win basic services. In the seventies and early eighties, barrio inhabitants gained a stronger sense of common identity through cultural activities and the construction of new subjectivities. There were church groups, theater groups, literacy campaigns, children's projects, and local newspapers. "There was an invisible but powerful accumulation of forces" (Antillano 2006). Local campaigns around this time, the first stage in the development of the barrio, often focused on rising transportation costs or demands for improvements in street infrastructure. Neoliberal reforms precipitated the second stage of development due to the divestiture of state housing, allowing neighborhoods to fall into disrepair, the impoverishment of the population, the dismantling and privatization of public services, and "the weakening and collapse of intermediary agencies that had worked through a mechanism of cooptation and redistribution via political parties and neighborhood councils" (Antillano 2005, 208).

The citizens' uprising of 1989 in Caracas—known as the Caracazo—was a product of this process. Urban popular sectors took the initiative from the very beginning of this insurrection and have retained it up to this day. The intense popular mobilizations in the early nineties caused the collapse of the corrupt traditional parties, leading to a crisis in the model of domination, thus facilitating the conquest of government power by a new breed of leaders including Hugo Chávez. These same popular sectors were instrumental in halting and reversing the coup d'état against Chávez in April 2002 and in the defeat of the oil strike launched by elites shortly afterward. The urban poor in the slums of Caracas neutralized the various rightwing offenses as large sections of the middle class rallied to support the ruling class. As with other popular mobilizations around the continent, these were decisive actions undertaken without a unified coordination or centralized leadership.

The fourth stage—the present—began in 2002 with the decree for the regularization of land tenure and the rehabilitation of barrios, promoting the formation of Urban Land Committees (CTU). This process is intimately related to the nature and spirit of the Bolivarian process under the Venezuelan government, which is distinctly different from other governments on the continent. The approximately one thousand CTUs in the city of Caracas consist of about two hundred families each and are informally interconnected.

> The most relevant part of the decree is this recognition and inclusion of the barrios, in so much as it leaves participation, mobilization, and organization to the neighborhood residents themselves, so the communities themselves become agents of transformation. Thus, the urban land committees, a new form of social organization legalized by the decree, execute technical, political, and even "judicial" tasks. Thus, a precedent is set for the implementation of social policies for this government: social inclusion through the mobilization of the excluded (Antillano 2005, 210).

The technical water boards are similar. They form part of a "territorial revolution," according to Antillano (a social leader from a popular neighborhood). These are autonomous organizations, elected by barrio residents, and are flexible; they also do not require the presence of intermediaries and respond to people's immediate needs. These committees tend to become local powers; local ownership of the land is not family-based but rather "an association consisting of all the families in the neighborhood, which among other things, is responsible for regulating the use of space (common and familiar), authorizing sales or leases, and ensuring standards of living, mediating disputes and actions of collective responsibility, etc." (Antillano 2005, 214). This passage describes the distance between the organizations and the state, reflecting what I have designated as "non-state powers" (Zibechi 2006b), although in this case these organizations have been created at the behest of the Venezuelan government.

The territories of the urban poor tend to become multi-faceted community spaces; thus, popular organizations dealing with health, water, land, cooperatives, culture, and now community councils have sprung up in the hills of Caracas. In terms of production, the neighborhood becomes like one large factory or *maquila*. As in other poor parts of the continent, the people do not invent something new here without first fixing or improving what already exists, and this includes the always complicated relationship with the market or state. The productive forces—like recuperated factories in other parts of Latin America—are already located in the barrios of Caracas, thereby avoiding dependencies on external exploiters.

> Antímano is a neighborhood of 150,000 residents with a lot of *maquilas*. It operates like a very efficient factory: a ball of cotton goes in on one side and out of the other comes a shirt. There are ladies who knit, some cut, others sew, etc. The same thing happens throughout Latin America and the third world.... Here the middlemen who keep the profits are cut out, and people produce cooperatively, much as they do everything else in the

territory. One has to think of the issue from this perspective—the contribution the territory can make to
production (Antillano 2006).

In Bolivia, there have been remarkable experiences in
urban peripheries that reveal the capacity of the indigenous
grassroots to construct a genuine "other" society. One is the
city of El Alto, which has been analyzed in several works
(Gomez 2004; Mamani 2005; Zibechi 2006b). Here I examine a notable experience of regional and community water
management based on a non-state model. There are over
one hundred water committees in the city of Cochabamba
responsible for overseeing the provision of water, which the
state is unable to provide.

With the implementation of the neoliberal model in Bolivia in 1985, mine closures and migration to the cities changed
the map of the country. The city of Cochabamba's population
grew to over one million inhabitants by 2001, filled with people uprooted from rural communities and workplaces. The
state water company, Semapa, served only 50 percent of the
city's population, neglecting vast areas such as the southern
peripheries. In the early nineties, neighborhood groups organized to bring the water to their homes. They formed associations and cooperatives and without state assistance dug wells,
repaired water mains, constructed elevated tanks or bought
water in cisterns, and even built drainage and sewers.

The Association for the Management and Production of
Water and Sanitation (ASICA) was formed in March 1990 in
Villa Sebastián Pagador and was probably the first local initiative for organizing drinking water (ASICA-Sur 2003). Some
140 water committees were formed in the south of the city in
1990, comprising an average of 300 to 1000 families in each
one. They had to overcome many difficulties, including the
struggle for reductions in the price of electricity, which is necessary for extracting water from wells. Some wells dried up
and in others the water quality was too poor for domestic use.

If a well could not be found, the committee would have to buy water commercially and transport it to the affected neighborhood. Some committees have bought their own water tankers, which made several delivery trips daily (Grandidyer 2005).

Urban water committees played a key role in the Water War of April 2000. The state handed control of Semapa to a multinational company, which began threatening to expropriate the water obtained by residents through so much sacrifice. Ultimately, residents' resistance reversed the water privatization and opened a cycle of protests that undermined the neoliberal model and led to the election of Evo Morales. The expulsion of the multinational allowed people to elect their own representatives to control the state-owned water company, and so began a new era in which installing water services in the peripheries became a priority.

In August 2004, the water committees created the Association of Community Water Systems in the South and elected its first board. At this stage they were discussing how to deal with the state company, as it was clear that there was no guarantee that they would provide quality water. Clearly there was a need to co-manage water services with the state company, but the question arose as how to do so without losing autonomy, which was the only guarantee of their ability to continue monitoring the supply:

> Today we are at another crossroads. What will become of our water committees when Semapa receives the right to serve our districts? Will our organization be terminated? Will we be able to influence Semapa's decisions? Will we become individual and anonymous users for the municipal company? Or can we keep our organizations, our decision-making capacity, and the self-managed forms that we used for years (ASIC-South 2003, 1)?

The Water War and a long decade of autonomous struggle were not in vain. The residents fought and won their autonomy and did not want to lose it. For this reason, they decided to allow Semapa to provide water "wholesale" to the committees, who would distribute it to residents, thereby retaining control of service management. While the model of using water wells proved to be an alternative to centralized and hierarchical state control, the large number of wells drilled damaged the water table around the valley, causing wells to dry up or to lose water quality. So the committees opted for the state-owned service, but without losing their autonomy. The experience of the Cochabamba water committees is an important example of alternative ways to manage the commons.

The question of "ownership" reveals the water committee's fundamental difference from the state company. When defining the notion of ownership of water, the committees rejected both the concept of "individual private ownership" as well as "state public ownership."

> What we are trying to defend in our neighborhoods is a type of ownership that is private in a sense (because it does not depend on the state but on the people directly), but at the same time is public (it does not belong to one individual, but to the entire community). That is why it is called collective or communal property. The main reason for the existence of such ownership is not economic, but to satisfy a social need, the administration of a public good such as water, which should never be considered a private good or an object to trade. Both Semapa and the water committees in our neighborhoods must understand it from the perspective of "communal public ownership" (ASIC-South 2003, 5).

This is very similar to the "private/social" concept formulated by Anibal Quijano to describe the predominant forms of ownership in Latin America's popular urban world. He argued that these anti-capitalist types of organization—collective, democratic, and based on solidarity—are "one of the most widespread forms of organization of everyday life and represent the experience of a large swathe of the population of Latin America" (Quijano 1988, 26). These forms of social experience rooted in the private/social are not, according to Quijano, cyclical or transitory but established practices in the urban peripheries in particular. These social organizations operating on the basis of reciprocity, equality, and solidarity "are not islands in the sea of the urban world dominated by capital. They are part of the sea that, in turn, modulates and controls the logic of capital." It is not "state power, but a power within society" that constitute these private/social islands; they are part of another society (Quijano 1988, 27–28).

Many consider Uruguay to be the most integrated country, in which the welfare state has achieved greater development and is therefore less troubled than other countries. The syndicalist movement and the left party Frente Amplio [Broad Front] have consolidated their grip on urban society since the nineties, with the result that Uruguay is not the best scenario for the formation of autonomous social practices.

However, at the peak of the economic and social crisis of 2001, thousands of unemployed residents of the Montevideo peripheries organized dozens of family and collective gardens. About 200,000 lived in informal settlements in the capital and its metropolitan area (of 1.5 million people), premised on collective labor with self-constructed family houses. Unemployment reached 20 percent at the peak of the crisis (July to December 2001), but 80 percent of the popular sectors had no stable employment and were shipwrecked among unemployment, self-employment, and various forms of informal work. The community gardens were a response to the food crisis hitting the poorest. Even though there has been economic growth since 2004, many of these plots continue to flourish.

During the crisis, more than two hundred collective family and communitarian gardens functioned in the urban zone. Families set up the first on privately owned land and cultivated them with the support of locals, while others set up the community gardens in public spaces. In both cases, garden activists established stable forms of organization, which became a unifying axis for neighborhood groups struggling for autonomy from political parties, trade unions, and the municipality. Although the first two years were difficult, groups began to grow, leading to a strengthening of ties that they themselves defined as "community." Women from the Amanecer Community Garden in the Sayago barrio reflected on the progress:

> At first we had a card upon which each person recorded hours worked. At harvest time, each received a certain quantity, according to the amount of time worked. And then during one meeting it was proposed, to our surprise, that we not note hours worked. This pleased us greatly, as it meant that the group was beginning to have a sense of communitarian consciousness. We operate on this basis to this day. Having worked in the garden, the member simply takes enough to feed their family (Oholeguy 2004, 49).

The group of *huerteros* [gardeners]—about forty of them, mostly women and youth—ultimately became self-sufficient and decided to stop accepting food from the municipality, indicating that they would rather the food go to soup kitchens or other groups that needed it.

Meanwhile in the Villa Garcia neighborhood on the periphery of Montevideo, some twenty collective family gardens began to network. After a shaky start, they formed a stable collective that met weekly, rotating the location among the gardens in the network. Without creating an organizational structure, the huerteros created a sort of "mobile network coordination" to support each other by exchanging seeds, knowledge, and cultivation techniques, and then looked into ways of marketing the produce. The weekly gatherings were divided into three stages: collective learning through work in the garden, sharing a common pot of the products harvested, and an evaluation and planning meeting. They were remarkably successful: Working groups were consolidated, the collective pot based on the production of the gardens was maintained, they depended less and less on food donated by the state, and a greenhouse and seed bank was created to supply all the gardens in the zone. The collective began publishing a monthly newsletter and coordinating with similar groups around Montevideo, which led to the First Gathering of Urban Agricultural Producers in October 2003, with the support of the Department of Agriculture and the municipality (Contreras 2004).

Huerteros in other zones also began to coordinate, organize workshops (in pruning, beekeeping, and poultry farming) and occasional fairs to market their harvest as well as canned goods and delicacies produced by families. In some zones, barter clubs participated in the markets. About seventy residents occupied a 19-hectare area owned by a private bank and began planting. The huerteros' ability—the term huertero became part of their collective identity—to reject urban solitude and anxiety about survival and act collectively shows popular sectors' capacity to overcome dependency on the state and the party system. Their gatherings stressed the need "to organize themselves into a network, as horizontally and openly as possible, without scheming leaders or becoming trapped in a bubble"(Contreras 2004).

Many community gardens were dissolved after the Frente Amplio occupied the government in March 2005 and implemented anti-poverty policies, but an Urban Agricultural Producers group still exists and brings together a large group of urban huerteros, including new groups testing out innovative production strategies. Despite the overall decline in the gardening movement, this experience demonstrates that, even in a "modern" and "complex" city like Montevideo, it is possible to produce autonomously and build non-market networks.

Finally, the peripheries of Argentinian cities have given birth to one of the most formidable and multifaceted social movements. The financial and social crisis that precipitated the uprising of December 19–20, 2001, brought many popular initiatives to the forefront, particularly economic alternatives. Expressions of the people's capacity to put this society in crisis back in movement came in the form of about two hundred recuperated factories, hundreds of local enterprises set up by neighborhood assemblies, and piquetero groups.

Each of these sectors has developed their own forms of action. The recuperated factories demonstrate that the workers are capable of the running factories and that there is no need for bosses, supervisors, or specialists. In some instances, the recuperated factories have formed strong relationships with one another, the local community, and with social and cultural organizations. Recuperated factories have opened their spaces to host cultural activities—workshops, community radio stations, and for discussion and exchanges, and so on—and in some cases they are building distribution networks that operate outside of the market.

The piquetero movement has secured major achievements, despite the uneven development and disorganization of much of it. Piquetero groups operating in neighborhoods forsaken by the state have built health clinics, popular kitchens, and food programs for local children. They have organized community gardens and bakeries to feed the communal pots, and others have set up carpentry and metallurgy workshops as well as training spaces organized around the principles of popular education.

The neighborhood assemblies have become centers for cultural and social activities, including the production of packaged foods, the cleaning and repair of computers, and so on. Across the big city of Buenos Aires, piquetero groups are organizing writing workshops, film screenings, cultural or political debates, popular markets where they sell their products, and their own distribution networks for their products. The three groups that we have identified—the recuperated factory movement, the piqueteros, and the neighborhood assemblies—are all taking the re-production of their lives into their own hands.

The popular movement offensive between 1997 and 2002 not only created thousands of alternative productive spaces but also generated a "new economy" around them, in the form of non-capitalist social relations between producers and consumers. Furthermore, in many of these enterprises, alienated or estranged labor is no longer the dominant form, and in others, the production of goods for the market—that is, the production of exchange value—is subordinate to the production of use value. Labor is de-alienated in different ways: either by rotating tasks or because producers control the entire work process. In these cases, we can speak of "free producers" rather than workers as appendages of machines who are alienated in a labor process that they do not control.

On the other hand, sometimes production occurs outside of the market and therefore non-commodities are produced, although this is more difficult to sustain over time. What difficulties and constraints do these enterprises face? How to make autonomous processes sustainable and should they take such processes even further?

I would like to enter this debate by taking a close look at one such alternative enterprise in Buenos Aires. There are many such projects, but I will focus on the self-run bakery in the Barracas barrio; it has been functioning for over three years, although the group of people running it have been working together collectively for almost a decade. These are youths who formed a cultural group in the late nineties and then, in the midst of the great turmoil that followed the uprising of December 2001, occupied the premises of a bank and were subsequently evicted. Today they have two illegally occupied spaces: a publishing house is run out of one, as well as a cinema for local children and adults, and in the other space they operate a popular library that serves two hundred members and a bakery employing twelve people, about half male and half female.

The story of the bakery is a remarkable one. For a couple of years, it operated with teams of two people who did the baking in an electric oven and sold the products in the neighborhood. They eventually secured the right to sell at the School of Fine Arts. The group decided to change from what they call "individual management"—deemed "unfair" because, for example, the group working Monday sold much less than the Friday group—to form a cooperative.

Now they have basically two "teams," one in the kitchen and one out selling. The money is divided equally among them and they earn almost double the salary that they would receive on welfare. Although some prefer certain types of work, tasks are still rotated. One of the main discussions they have is how to evaluate the different tasks. I should point out that the twelve bakers participated in struggles together for years and lived in the same squatted house, but most have never had formal "jobs." But how does one establish a correlation between work done and remuneration?

What is the equivalence? The answer is that there is no equivalence, because there is no abstract labor and, as we shall see, because the category of commodity does not exist. Let's look at some of the debates brought up by this experience.

Although they sell what they produce, *they do not produce commodities*. In fact, they do not go out to sell on the "market," as they have established a network of fixed buyers (80 percent of buyers are return customers). They have established a relationship of trust with their buyers, to such an extent that the Fine Arts school where they "sell" their goods also helps defend their squat and participates in local activities. That gives us a second clue: The "duality" of the commodity, as carrier of use value and exchange value has been—or rather, is being—deconstructed in favor of use value, or, *products that are non-commodities*. One cannot, in fact, speak of abstract labor but of useful or concrete labor. So there can be no equivalent between the labor of baking and the labor of selling, because an equal and abstract labor that is measurable by the socially necessary labor time does not exist. Although money is a means of exchange, I do not think it is a decisive factor.

There is no hierarchy between producers and distributors or between productive and unproductive labor, although those who sell the product have some advantage over those who produce it. Selling requires building social relations within the neighborhood, which, in fact, ensures the survival of the enterprise. Political economy is not applicable to these kinds of enterprises, and it is necessary to invent a new theoretical perspective.

What do we call this non-alienated labor, which produces non-commodities and in which the production is as "productive" as distribution? And what is produced? In this case, what is produced are non-capitalist social relations, or non-capitalism. And this very specific small experience, very micro if you will, is not unusual in Buenos Aires or other cities on the continent.

The appropriation of the means of production and the de-alienation of the production process are two steps taken by some recuperated factories and productive enterprises. They are certainly very valuable steps, but still insufficient. The next step is to produce, like the youth of the Barracas bakery, non-commodities. And with this concept we enter into the realm of exchange.

Marx notes that "the labor of the individual asserts itself as a part of the labor of society, only by means of the relations that the act of exchange establishes directly between the products, and indirectly, through them, between the producers. It is only by being exchanged that the products of labor acquire, as values, one uniform social status, distinct from their varied forms of existence as objects of utility"(Marx 1975, 89). In short, producers relate to each other in the market, but not directly, only as owners and sellers of commodities, they face each other through things.

This is why I have explored the case of the Barracas social bakery, though I could also add the example of the popular kitchens in Lima and a host of similar initiatives running across the length and breadth of the continent. Production is not for a market or through the market relationship of producers and buyers. However, it was not always so for the Barracas bakery, and it took three years to deconstruct the products—from commodities to non-commodities. At first, the bakery products were brought to the market "to see what happened." Some were sold and others were not. The relationship with buyers was a relationship mediated by the price of bread (i.e., if it was cheaper and better quality, more was sold). Buyers were not always the same but more likely to be those who happened to appear at a time and were able to buy. In short, it was a typical market relationship, impersonal and random. Over time, the producers/sellers and buyers began to get to know one another and established relations of trust. In other words, the relationship between things (bread and buyers with money) was becoming a relationship between people, or social relationships not mediated by things. Now the producers know the buyers, and now they produce the things the buyers need or want.

Many buyers have established direct links with the bakery, even visiting it in the social center that houses it. They are no longer bread sellers and buyers, but Peter and Jane who sell, and Eloisa and Felipe who buy. Thus they decode the "social hieroglyphic" that for Marx is "any product of labor" (Marx 1975, 91). Deciphering the hieroglyphic through social practice implies that something essential to capitalism has stopped functioning. The socially necessary labor time required for the production of bread is no longer the master key, and the sales price is not adjusted to that, simply because no similar "measure" exists, or it has ceased to operate as such. "Because, in the midst of all the accidental and ever fluctuating exchange relations between the products, the labor time socially necessary for their production forcibly asserts itself like an over-riding *law of Nature*" (Marx 1975, 92). The terms of trade are no longer random and fluctuating because the market is not impersonal. And the socially necessary labor time varies and depends on who is doing the work, if there are more boys or more girls, if they are very tired or if they are playing about while they work or listening to music or discussing things. And often they give the bread away, because that is how they are. Sellers and buyers no longer relate as "possessors of commodities" but in another context, in which solidarity between the "castaways" plays a central role.

This is not derived mechanically from the ownership of the means of production or even the de-alienation from the process of labor, but from something more profound: They are not focused on accumulating wealth and do not feel like possessors of commodities. The social function is above the possession of commodities, which is what allows them to produce use values for consumption by real people.

When Marx discusses these arid topics in *Capital*, he uses Daniel Defoe's famous Robinson Crusoe as an example. On the lonely island, Crusoe makes things and works to survive but, being a lone castaway, "the objects that form this wealth of his own creation are here so simple and clear," so that there is no fetishism in his life. Marx thought that in an association of free men, of free producers, "all the determinations of Robinson's labor are repeated here, only in a social manner, rather than individual" (Marx 1975, 94–96).

Those who try to establish non-capitalist relations are castaways in this system that marginalizes them. I would go further: Only the castaways, those who have a weak relationship with capital, and therefore with abstract labor, can undertake tasks like this. But unlike Robinson Crusoe, our compañeros are not passive victims of a shipwreck but are actually behind it—they are part of the wave that has been causing it since the sixties, in struggles like the Cordobazo in Argentina (1969), that began to call alienated labor into question, using sabotage, underground resistance, and sometimes open revolt. It was the generation of the sixties and the seventies that began to sink the ship of the capital-labor relation, and their children, the castaways of today, are building a new world around non-capitalist relations and upon the remains of this shipwreck.

I want to emphasize six aspects of the urban social movements I have reviewed, the second stage of these movements, which began during protests in Chile against Pinochet:

- The actors are not only rural migrants but also people born in the city with extensive experience in urban life. The barrios that they constructed in the first stage are now insufficient to house them and they tend to occupy new spaces, while it is becoming increasingly clear that there are no longer many "free" spaces left.
- The barrios/islands tend to become archipelagos or large

urban blotches (such as the peripheries of Lima). They are consolidated territories; the state enters only with great difficulty and must use armed force to do so, as happens in Santiago or Rio de Janeiro, since popular sectors have undermined the possibilities of state control.

- The production and reproduction of life *by* and *between* popular sectors grows and becomes the dominant form in those territories. Although non-capitalist relations are not yet hegemonic, they are growing. Territorial control facilitates the creation and maintenance of these relations, and the disconnection from capitalist cycles requires that popular sectors intensify them to survive.

- Popular sectors are in the midst of an offense, which began in 1989 with the Caracazo. Urban insurrections are the most visible form of this offensive, but there is also the invisible and subterranean sociability that is beginning to have an impact, from health and education to material production. Drug trafficking, which has expanded in the poor territories during this period, should be included in this long-term trend of popular counter-offensive.

- We are dealing with *two worlds*. Even the Venezuelan government must negotiate as an equal with the urban poor. They can provide stability or not to ongoing processes and are thus indispensable for the continuity of the capitalist model of accumulation. For this reason, those from below grouped into urban peripheries are "modulated and controlled" on a daily basis, as noted by Quijano. This other world cannot be represented in the formal world; it is not only different but also one outside the state-capitalist world.

- One issue that divides the popular world is *what kind of relations to maintain with the state* (the government and municipalities) and the party system. Two positions predominate. Those who support maintaining some kind of relation with the state because one must take advantage of every available space to strengthen the project of those from below, and those who are inclined to work autonomously without any relation whatsoever with the state, or with those from above, or capital.

Many collectives have divided as a result of these conflicting positions. Unlike the first period of the movement, this debate is no longer the prerogative of leaders or intellectuals outside of the movements but instead involves many activists within it. Another difference is that it is not an ideological debate but a strategic question. I think that working with state institutions weakens the movements, diverting strength from the main task, which is to strengthen what is "ours." I share the Zapatista position here. But there are many combative and consistent movements that fight for real social change that relate to the state and remain autonomous. The MST of Brazil is a case in point. These differences within the movements will not be resolved in the short term, and we will have to see what is the best way to process them with the least possible damage to organizations from below.

What Powers Are Found in the Peripheries?

I look at popular urban movements from a long-term perspective, one that can pick up on underground and invisible processes missed in other studies—to reconstruct the trajectory of the popular sectors during the last fifty to one hundred years, and to track their "historic project." This temporal distinction is important, too, because it can reveal the agenda that lies *below and behind* the visible actions, the major struggles and mass mobilizations, and can link several cycles of struggle that would otherwise have no apparent relationship. Comparing the situation of the urban poor in 1900 or 1950 with that of 2000 allows us to comprehend the path upon which they are traveling. Slow changes can be more readily understood over the long term.

The dominated do not act symmetrically in relation to those dominating them and, for that reason, do not formulate a rational program that they set out to implement. The popular sectors of our continent are creating their own project and history as they follow their trajectory but, just like Chilean settlers we have studied, they do not draw up plans as they construct their squatters' camps. There is no pre-planning, and those who do not understand this cannot understand the reality of our peoples. I advance, then, not a complete theory but rather a proposal for discussion and a set of conclusions about the experiences that I have studied in this overview.

1) A century ago, cities were the space of the dominant and middle classes, who maintained an uneasy relationship. Today they have been displaced or are surrounded by popular sectors. In other words, those from below are enclosing the physical and symbolic spaces from which the ruling classes historically established their power. Poverty is a question of power. From this point of view, the poor of our continent have settled in the cities without losing their connections to rural areas and are better able to corner the ruling classes. The ruling classes have had to emigrate to other areas, literally digging themselves in for fear of the poor. They are surrounded.

My hypothesis is that in the last half century, the urban peripheries of the large cities have formed their own world, traversing a long distance from the appropriation of land and space to the construction of territories; from the creation of new subjectivities to the constitution of new political subjects, quite different from the old industrial, unionized working class; from unemployment to the creation of new roles and thus opening up the way for oppositional economies. In my view, this long process has not been recognized in all its complexity, and we have yet to discover its full potential.

2) The foundation of popular sectors' activity is the expansion of a family/community logic focused on the role of the woman/mother. A new world of relations have been formed around this family/community logic, based on affection, mutual care, containment, and inclusiveness. These forms of living and doing have departed from the "private" realm in which they had sought refuge and, since the systemic crisis after the world revolution of 1968, have expanded into the public and collective sphere.

We can observe the expansion of the role of women/ mother in every current movement for social change. In some cases, such as among Argentina's piqueteros, women and their children make up 70 percent of the activists, although the implications go far beyond the quantitative. Women's presence breaks a relational episteme, says Alejandro Moreno (2006), and introduces another rationality, another culture. This ties in with understanding the idea of movement and life differently. It is a cosmovision in which relationships (and not things) play a central role, and is premised upon another way to knowing, of living, and of feeling. The main driving force of this other world is born in the affections: love, friendship, fellowship, and so on. They are creating a parallel system of economic relations on those foundations, one that is outside the market economy.

3) Another world exists in the spaces and times of this different society: feminine, based on use value, communitarian, centered on autonomy, spontaneous in the deepest sense of the term, natural, and self-determined. This world did not grow in opposition to the state/masculine world, one based in exchange values, polarization, institutions (political parties and associations) that are regulated by binary relations of order and obedience, cause and effect (planning). Its own internal dynamics prompted its birth and growth, and if it is unable to survive, by expanding and displacing the state/ masculine world, the survival of humanity will be in danger.

When I speak of feminine and masculine (or patriarchal) modes, I am referring to two opposing and complementary ways, two world views, or civilizations. With the advent of capitalism, a patriarchal, logocentric, Newtonian-Cartesian culture became hegemonic, grounded on the principle of the excluded third, a rationale of exclusion that implies an unspeakable violence against people and life. It is a culture of death, colonial and predatory, where the subject submits to the object. Among the Indian peoples of America, among the peoples of the East, and among the popular sectors, there is another cosmovision that we can call feminine or matriarchal:

it is holistic, relational, grounded in the complementarity of opposites and in reciprocity (Medina 2006). It is a culture of life and emancipation, where there is no subject-object relation, but rather a plurality of subjects. And this is not simply a matter of gender. Perhaps the best image for this would be the yin and yang of Taoism or the concept of chacha and warmi among the Aymaras. In this cosmovision, change does not consist of the annihilation of an enemy (revolution and dictatorship of the proletariat) but rather of the *pachakutik*, a cosmic shift, the world turned upside down.

4) And what of people's power? Of counter-powers from below? This remains an open question. The issue of power has been at the center of many ongoing discussions between social and political movements since the emergence of the Zapatistas. I believe that the very concept of power should be revised. I often speak of "non-state powers," but this still seems insufficient. The Good Government councils in the Zapatista autonomous municipalities exercise power on a rotating basis, so that all the inhabitants of a zone will eventually learn how to govern. But can we speak of power when the community exercises it?

The truth is that we live between the two worlds. One is out of control, having made domination and destruction its main source of nourishment. The other world offers the only chance that we have to remain human and preserve nature and the commons for the benefit of all. But the logic of life in this other world is not symmetrical to the hegemonic world. In that sense, it cannot grow by destroying and annihilating the world of oppression, but rather in its own way: by expanding, dilating, disseminating, transmitting, dissipating, radiating, and resonating. In other words, naturally. And this is how non-capitalism has grown in the urban peripheries for at least half a century.

It is not possible to impose this other world, as capital was imposed, but we can breathe life into it, nurture it, and help it expand and rise. The movement exists, and we cannot invent it or direct it. At best, we can be part of it, moving ourselves as well, improving the art of putting ourselves in movement. This is no small thing, because our capacity to move ourselves is our best hope for saving ourselves.

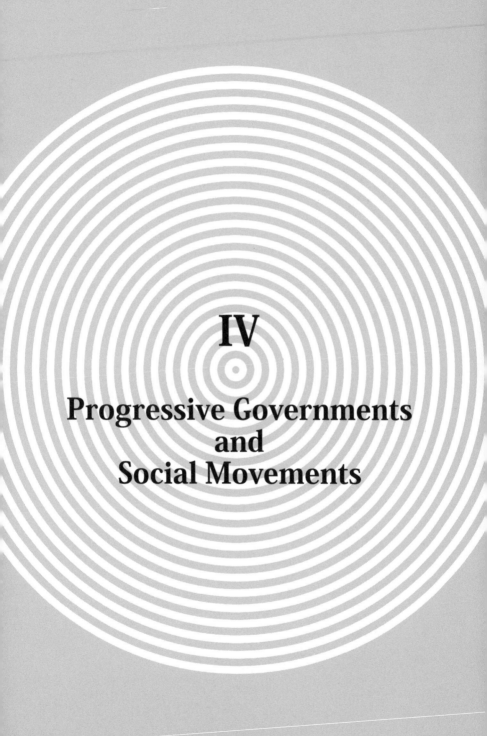

IV

Progressive Governments
and
Social Movements

The Art of Governing
the Movements

Since the early nineties, politics from below have had a powerful impact across Latin America, giving rise to a new political scenario. They have discredited the neoliberal model, opening cracks in hegemonic forms of domination. Broadly speaking, the rise of progressive and leftist governments is an indirect consequence of the struggles from below. Left governments have forged new forms of governance in response to the power of the social movements, just as elites have attempted to redirect the crisis within the model of domination. The situation is increasingly complex and understanding this "new governance" is an imperative for social and political struggles.

To begin, I argue that despite being the indirect consequence of the movements, the new forms of governance are not the answer, but rather something more complicated: They are the point of intersection between the movements (not as institutions but as the capacity to move itself) and the states, and from that "meeting point" new ways to managing states and populations are being formed. And rather than just one single point or points of intersection, I wish to convey the idea of something mobile and in permanent construction and reconstruction; the new forms of governance are not even a unilateral construction and do not occupy a fixed location. I will show that they are a collective construction and in movement.

But to speak of new governance implies that the old ways of governing are in crisis or have been overcome by the actions of an organized population. That is why we call them social movements, although the term is increasingly inadequate because it does not embrace the full extent of what is actually happening. We can talk then, and provisionally, of "society in movement," because I think this term—although it is vague, its vagueness is an advantage—does not refer to institutions but rather brings the idea of something moving to the forefront, and that "something" is in fact the "other" societies.

The starting point for addressing the new forms of governance could be a sentence from Eduardo Duhalde, Argentina's President after the insurrection of December 19–20, 2001: "One cannot govern from assemblies." That may be true, but it also reveals Duhalde's limitations; he was able to visualize the problem but tried to solve it using the traditional method of getting the people off the street through repression or deterrence. And what was missing—from the perspective of the dominant sector—was another way to address the "problem," which required not one but a set of measures, ranging from political economy to what I call "the art of governing the movement" (or, instead of "movement," societies in movement). This set of techniques or mode of governance does not replace the disciplinary modes of repression or deterrence that were used in the past, but is instead superimposed over the traditional ones, which recede into the background.

Nation-states govern movements in various ways. For the last few years, they have generally used two methods to intervene in movements: In the Andean region, particularly Ecuador and Bolivia, they enlist the poor in development projects; in other countries, notably Argentina and Uruguay (and perhaps Brazil), they implement government policies targeting poverty. However, the forms are not exclusive and both are usually found in almost all the countries; what they have in common is a need to go beyond disciplining bodies in closed spaces and to engage in something as complicated as governing the population.[1] The problem facing the art of government is that in recent decades, since the 1989 Caracazo, Latin American populations are insurgent and rise up regularly.

New forms of control to meet the challenge of societies in movement (unlike the previous focused on discipline, which represents a negative, normalizing, and regulatory impulse)

---

1   Much of my thinking on this topic is inspired by Foucault 2006.

seek "support in the reality of the phenomenon, and instead of trying to prevent it, making other elements of reality function in relation to it, in such a way that the phenomenon is canceled out" (Foucault 2006, 79). Rather than suppressing and prohibiting, they attempt to regulate the reality by making some elements act on the others, thereby annulling them. This type of control is more necessary when the oppressed have been overwhelming the disciplinary forms of control, when it is not just social sectors that are in movement but whole portions of societies that are now uncontrollable and impossible to discipline through repression. The question for government becomes, how to impose mandatory and negative laws on these "other" societies that are capable of disrupting and neutralizing disciplinary measures like coup d'états, states of emergency, and traditional forms of repression?

In this new reality, the panopticon has become archaic (though still functioning, it is not the primary means of control). What is required to govern large populations are more subtle forms of control that seek the "phasing out of phenomena through the work of the phenomena themselves" and that require a less transparent type of action, allowing the sovereign to make a "calculated, thoughtful, analytical" action (Foucault 2006, 95). The ruling classes must now act on a multitude of factors, but not in relation to the exteriority—as according to Machiavelli's Prince—but in terms of the immanence of the movements, in their attempt to domesticate, or rather redirect them so that they benefit the ruling class. When the sovereign attempt to prevent subjects from mobilizing, he puts his own position in jeopardy, so now the art of governance employs social mobilization as one of its techniques. The mobilization is not called, as before, in support of popular governments under pressure from oligarchies—as happened many times throughout the twentieth century—but to promote "just causes," such as human rights in Argentina or action against domestic violence in Uruguay.[2] This tactic of the left governments calling for street demonstrations in

---

2   The municipality of Montevideo, governed by the left, organized protests against domestic violence in late 2006.

support of various causes is one of the differences between the old and new forms of governance that have confused social activists. Who can better act in relation to the interiority of the oppressed than governments that have emerged from the bowels of the movements from below? Who is better placed to implement complicated tactics that represent the real art of governance than governments that emerge from the movements? Who better to implement these kinds of diversionary tactics than people forged as militants and with extensive experience in movements of the oppressed?

We can agree with Foucault that the "new" states led by Lula, Kirchner, and Tabaré Vázquez—to name the most obvious examples—are the sons of the art of governance or statecraft. They are not welfare states or hands-off, neoliberal states, but something previously unheard of that rests on a fragile base inherited from neoliberalism and organized around an attempt to keep state institutions standing and to legitimize them, despite the pressure from below. These arts of governance, and particularly of governing movements from below, merely serve to extend the life of decrepit nation states.

Armed with the conviction that the state is not a thing but a set of frozen social relations—that "the state is a practice" (Foucault 2006) that opposes the movement—I will try to address the two forms employed to "govern the movements" and cancel their anti-systemic effects. In the first case, the Andean model, I will rely on my experience as a militant involved in the movement for several years. The second case focuses on the southern cone where, unlike the Andean model in which development cooperation has been in place for over a decade, progressive governments are just now beginning to implement their social plans. For this reason, my analysis is provisional.

The Andean Experience: "Strengthening the Organizations"

Twenty years ago, the Aymara anthropologist Silvia Rivera Cusicanqui and a team from the Andean Oral History Workshop (THOA) denounced the role of development projects and NGOs in northern Potosí (Bolivia) for their responsibility in de-structuring the Indian communities. The research gave account of what they consider "a huge social and cultural misunderstanding that, in the name of development, led NGOs… to try to reform the 'archaic' *ayllus*[3] organizational structure, aiming to speed up the transition to an economic/mercantile rationale, and with that, or so they believed, desired but elusive economic well-being" (Rivera Cusicanqui 1992, 7).

According to their research, the NGOs never understood, or wanted to understand, that the circulation of money in the communities does not alter the functioning of their economy, which they call an "ethnic economy."[4] Furthermore, "money circulates within the ethnic economy as use value, whose itinerary and rules of trade are governed by principles of culture and kinship" (Harris 1987, 154). This is incomprehensible to advocates of development, who believe that money and the market go hand in hand. The development model depends on the expansion of the commercial component of the communitarian economy in order to solve what it regards as the intrinsic "constraints" of the Indian world. Worse still, since the programs do not reach all families, they cause divisions within the communities that, together with commercialization, accelerates the decomposition of the community structure.

The investigation identifies six problems resulting from development projects in northern Potosí: the erosion of communities and therefore their "autonomous spaces for reproducing the social organization and endogenous productivity"; the commodification of the communities/ayllus, leading to a dependency on external trade and a loss of autonomy; implementation of organizational models that lead to generational conflicts, divisions, and confusion, and a disconnection with community democracy; erosion of self-management skills to the point that "now the *ayllus* are less able to endure a drought or similar disasters"; cultural depersonalization and,

---

3   *Ayllu* is a word in the Aymara language referring to the network of families in a given area; it is a pre-Colombian, indigenous, local model of governance.
4   The term is from Olivia Harris (1987), who argues that goods and money circulate outside of the market.

finally, the ayllus become vulnerable to "political co-optation and clientelist manipulation, which expands the influence of the dominant Creole civilization into the *ayllus*" (Harris 1987, 191–92).

While these events occurred during the eighties, the problem intensified throughout the next decade. The number of NGOs operating in Bolivia rose from around 100 at the start of the eighties to about 530 at the beginning of the nineties. The process was similar in Ecuador: During the mid-nineties there were 519 NGOs, of which 73 percent formed between 1981 and 1994 (i.e., "on par with the launch of the various structural adjustment policies beginning from 1982") (Bretón 2001, 240). Over the years, the number of external financiers and planners increased, and they used NGOs to advance their policies. A similar process began in Ecuador in the mid-nineties, leading to the formation of the Indigenous Peoples and Afro-Ecuadorian Development Project (PRO-DEPINE) in 1998. Its purpose was to oversee cooperation in development with indigenous organizations.

> Questions arose about the appropriateness of an institution like PRODEPINE starting up only one year after the Indian uprising of 1994, which shook the pillars of the Ecuadorean state for a second time and when, simultaneously, far north in remote Mayan lands, an army of Chiapas Indians took up arms against the economic, political, social, and cultural exclusion to which the Mexican brand of neoliberalism condemned them...in that moment, development planners turned their attention to organizational strengthening as a strategy against exclusion and, incidentally, as an indirect way to co-opt and limit the scope of the emerging new social movements (Bretón 2001, 234–235).

The World Bank conceived of and financed PRODE-PINE. They consider it one of their most successful projects and an improvement upon previous efforts like the

Mexican PRONASOL, which state institutions directed (and undermined).[5] Unlike PRONASOL, PRODEPINE goes directly to the world of indigenous organizations and tries to strengthen them, seeking the "empowerment of the excluded" (Bretón 2001, 232). Let's look at some features of this project and the results.

"Never before have I experienced an initiative so decentralized, so participatory and so jealous of the Second-tier Organizations (OSG) advising and managing the evolution of its member organizations," says the Spanish anthropologist Victor Bretón (2001, 233).[6] PRODEPINE does not substitute for social organizations but places them in the center. Social organizations are the ones doing the "self-diagnostic," while PRODEPINE "simply puts the funds into an organization's account, provides it with a method, follow up, studies patterns, and the organization contracts for their own technicians or from outside," according to an assessment by its Executive Director (2001, 233). Then the second-tier organization executes the project. Thus, it is the organizations themselves that run the interventions made in their territory. They "learn" to set priorities, hire technicians, and execute the plan, "because PRODEPINE does not manage; it facilitates, accompanies, trains, advises and monitors; it resolves conflicts, but the OSG's are the ones running things" (2001, 233–34).

As can be seen, work methods have changed radically. PRODEPINE opened seven offices in Ecuador and the organizations contact it, contrary to what occurred before. It conducts a census of organizations to establish their "quality," identifying which are capable of taking charge of a project, and those that are not "are given more time to develop their organizational strength" (Bretón 2001, 234).

So we can see how the World Bank now promotes "community participation"—which had always been secondary

5   Starting in 1989, the World Bank has supported Mexico's National Solidarity Program (PRONASOL) efforts to facilitate education, health, transportation, and regional development.
6   In the sphere of development cooperation, second-tier organizations or NGOs provide support for base organizations and act as intermediaries to bigger entities like the World Bank.

before—as its most important concern. In doing so, they achieve direct access to the organized social bases, something that PRONASOL had failed to do in Mexico. Projects organized by PRONASOL had been plagued with "bureaucratization, centralization of information, and the superimposition of these organizational models to the detriment of natural leaders within organizations" (Díaz Polanco 1997, 120). According to Díaz Polanco,

> the programs' inability to bring substantial and lasting results is related to the weak economic organization of the communities and peoples, *especially at regional level*...the common lack of such strong organizations is a *handicap* for programs to find (supposing that they really are looking) *a social subject*—representative, legitimate and with moral force in the communities—*to make it work*" (Díaz Polanco 1997, 124; my emphasis).

This explains the birth of the policies of "organizational strengthening" that are applied to the second-tier organizations, which are the key to making state social programs "work," according to the World Bank.

In addition to seeking to resolve institutional weaknesses, "organizational strengthening" addresses problems that governments face when insurrections or "overflows from below" are a *fait accompli*. Two processes are in play. On the one hand, NGOs experienced substantial changes during the nineties—they went from playing an oppositional role to collaborating with the state, specializing in consultation, mediating in social processes, and managing or promoting people's local participation, but without questioning the macroeconomic policies of structural adjustment. The second is directly linked to the proliferation of second-tier organizations promoted by NGOs as instruments for channeling "cooperation" for development.

Victor Bretón studied the case of Guamote county, in southern Chimborazo, Ecuador, a province with a high concentration of indigenous people who played an important role in the first two Indian uprisings (1990 and 1994). The need for development agents (NGOs) to have local partners promoted the creation of numerous second-tier organizations (OSG). With only 28,000 inhabitants, the county had 158 first-tier organizations (OPG) and 12 OSGs in the late nineties. Although the municipality of Guamote has the greatest number of organizations in the Ecuadorian Andes and is among the top six in terms of concentration of NGO interventions, poverty is endemic (89 percent of households), it has the highest infant mortality rate in the country (122.6 per thousand), and it has one of the highest rates of chronic malnutrition among children under five. This shows the inefficiency of the NGO-led development model.

Perhaps the success of PRODEPINE can be found elsewhere. Bretón lays out six theses on the impact of the model on indigenous movements (2001, 246–48). The second-tier organizations were formed as a consequence of the action of external agents and are not "an emanation of a supposed Andean community spirit." Secondly, they establish a direct relationship "between the growing presence of development institutions and greater organizational density within the indigenous world," which, Bretón notes, causes splits in organizations' efforts to capture and channel external resources. The third is that the OSGs compete with each other to "ensure, maintain, and increase their 'clientele.'" Within each OSG, there are elite leaders who are increasingly distanced from their bases. The result is a relationship of hostility between organizations and activists: "Just as NGOs have to compete in a Darwinian manner to co-opt the OSG—in so much as development subjects legitimize their own institutional job— and to procure scarce resources from international cooperation agencies, so too must OSGs compete among themselves to become beneficiaries of NGO activities."

The fourth and fifth theses are of special interest. Due to NGO involvement, second-tier organizations are replacing a very militant leadership with a more project-focused technocratic one. OSG leaders, who in his opinion are becoming "newly minted local bosses," become administrators with the power to distribute monies from development agencies.

This favors relationships of patronage. Now the prestige of the leaders lays not so much in whether they are good fighters committed to the cause, but in their ability to garner resources from funding agencies. "Their own reproduction as leaders depends on success in this effort and strengthening their ability to manage a complex network of affiliates, with favors rendered in exchange for future support" (Bretón 2001, 248).

Finally, the leaders formed within the OSGs often collude with authorities, generating intense divisions within the movement. The result, in the Ecuadorean case, was the cooptation of leaders and the division of CONAIE. In August 2001, the government made the former leader of the CONAIE, Luis Maldonado, Minister of Social Welfare. CONAIE and Ecuarunari (a Quechua highland organization) opposed it, but Indian mayors and other elected authorities were in favor of the designation, which "could open up doors for the transfer of funds that municipalities desperately need" (Guerrero and Ospina 2003, 252). Over time, the political cost of these programs became clear and today few doubt their objectives, as "the government made explicit efforts to manage projects and programs in exchange for avoiding uprisings" (2003, 253).

The situation worsened considerably under the government of Lucio Gutiérrez, who came to power with the support of the indigenous movement. The government carried out an ambitious effort to neutralize the indigenous movement by means of division, repression, and co-optation. While CONAIE remained within the government, the government awarded grants directly to communities, without using their organizations as conduits, particularly in the Amazon and on the coast, in order to isolate Ecuarunari, the most militant and best-structured organization of the Sierra. But when the CONAIE broke with the Gutiérrez government, accusing him of betraying his popular mandate, the state's response was to appoint an established movement leader, Antonio Vargas, as social welfare minister. Gutiérrez took this step to co-opt the movement and, above all, to divide it. The appointment of Vargas was a severe blow to CONAIE, as he had been an activist leader and was held in high prestige.

A speech at a meeting of the Amazon confederation, CON-FENIAE, reveals Vargas's intentions: "I'm not in this position to divide the indigenous movement, I am here because the government wants to strengthen indigenous peoples... so I have checks totaling $300,000 ready...$118,000 per each nationality" (Chuji Gualinga 2004). The leaders of the organization consequently split and the whole structure was affected by co-optation.

CONAIE touched bedrock in June 2004 when the vast majority of the indigenous communities ignored its call for an uprising against the neoliberal government. The gap between the base and the leadership had never been greater. But the magnitude of the failure was a wake-up call, leading the organization to convene its Second Congress, in December 2004, and to find the right path once more. Most within the organization felt the need to change leadership and return the original founders, including Luis Macas. Macas was subsequently elected head of the CONAIE with a mandate to restore its capacity for widespread social mobilization (Zibechi 2005). However, the split within the organization almost destroyed it, as several leaders co-opted by the government threatened to withdraw and "refound CONAIE."

The CONAIE Congress defined some requisites for anyone who wanted to be a candidate for president of the organization. The conditions represent a clear assessment of the reasons for the crisis: The candidate must have the endorsement of the bases, must give up positions in NGOs and foundations, must not have participated in the government after the breakdown of the alliance, and must not have been accused of working against the organization.[7] With these criteria, CONAIE hoped to regain its autonomy and take control of its leadership. At the time of analysis, the new leadership appears to understand all that went on before. It has called into question the usefulness of participating in state institutions, noting that, during the Gutiérrez government, "an unfortunate process of institutional participation began that turned out to be a

---

7   "Perfil de los candidatos (as) al Consejo de Gobierno de la CONAIE", www.ecuarunari.org.

strategy for dividing the indigenous movement" (Cauja 2004). Indeed, the very existence of movements such as Pachakutik, created by CONAIE in 1996 to participate in the elections, was put into doubt.

The "opening" of state institutions to indigenous participation is part of the same strategy as enlisting cooperation in development—that is, both policies supplement each other by attempting to create a leadership body separate from the movement's base. After the experience of the late nineties and the early twenty-first century, many argue that there is "a deliberate strategy, or ploy, of opening up the movement to the government and then tricking it into co-option, canceling out its transformative potential, which, from its inception, had challenged the foundations of domination and exclusion"(Guerrero and Ospina 2003, 252). While CONAIE was able to gain ground after the disaster of the March 2006 uprising against the implementation of the Andean Free Trade Agreement (FTA), it still faces enormous difficulties. In order to recover as an organization, the leadership of CONAIE made an effort to return to the grassroots in 2005. More than 200 grassroots workshops were held to discuss the FTA; Macas attended at least 150 of them and CONAIE all but disappeared from the Ecuadorian political scene. That public absence allowed the reconstructing of the organization from below (Zibechi 2006d).

Involving the indigenous movement in the development cooperation model was a means for the government to "govern" the movements, creating a cadre of leaders and functionaries (teachers, government officials, and development project technicians) who tried to reshape the social movements. This cadre of leaders opened the door to new forms of co-optation and brought the movements into state institutions.

An Experience in the Southern Cone: Impact on the Territory, A Theoretical Analysis.

Let us go back to former Argentine President Eduardo Duhalde's line, "One cannot govern from assemblies." Once the people smashed the state of siege introduced by the government on the evening of December 19, 2001, occupying the streets en masse, it was useless to try to prevent assemblies. The assemblies are there to stay, and thereafter, the art of governing says they have to govern the assemblies or at least operate so that some factors override others. If they use force to suppress them, the assemblies will be strengthened. What to do? A government in this situation can take different strategies. It can try to manage the economy, which would be seen as "good economic policy," so people would not feel compelled to take to the streets or launch oppositional survival initiatives.

Another possibility is to refunctionalize some of the grassroots initiatives and guide them in another direction. This is what the government did. It replicated activities sponsored by autonomous neighborhood assemblies, like organizing kindergartens and popular kitchens, and some people stopped going to assemblies, concluding that the government or NGO can act more efficiently and has more resources than the movement. None of this is totally new. But now there are other initiatives that reflect the logic of "strengthening organizations," such as what occurred under the left-wing Uruguayan government.

I will look closely at a very concrete example in a neighborhood on the outskirts of Montevideo called Barros Blancos. It is a kind of "linear city" located along a road in the northeast of the city; there are about thirty settlements in the barrio, which is home to some 35,000 people. It is one of the poorest zones in the country, populated by an inundation of recent arrivals. Many of the families who came here had been forced out of central Montevideo because of unemployment and factory plant closings.

The new Frente Amplio government decided to implement the National Plan for Emergency Social Care, intended to tackle extreme poverty, a condition referred to as "indigence," that affects 320,000 people (86,000 households), or 10 percent of the population, which has a total 800,000 poor. The plan provides subsidies called "citizen's income" of about $50 per family to about 76,000 homes. There are also more focused plans: Work for Uruguay, which temporarily employs 7,000 people in community work, and Routes Out, which is a similar plan overseen by NGOs and university officials offered to 7,500 households. Marina Arismendi, General Secretary of the Communist Party (PCU) set up and ran the Ministry of Social Development (MIDES). It oversees various areas of work, each run by well-known leftist intellectuals, including a few former militants.

In addition to these plans, MIDES oversees innovative "territorial" work. This is implemented by the Guidance, Consultation and Territorial Coordination Services (SOCATA), formerly known as SOCAF (Guidance, Consultation, and Family Services). It was the Frente Ampio government that changed the name and focus from "family" to "territory." Why territorial? Seventy-five SOCATA groups have been created in poor areas across the country, where MIDES serves to about 617,000 people in a variety of forms—that is, there is a SOCATA group for every 9,000 people. There are three SOCATAs in Barros Blancos. Each one includes 10,000 people, but since they only serve very poor families, in reality, there is one for every 4,000–5,000 people. It is quite targeted work.

"Theoretical" Analysis

Social Development Minister Arismendi explained the reasons for the change of focus from familial to territorial: "SOCATA are weavers in the territory and articulators of the different services. Their task is *to weave and coordinate* throughout the country where there are problems and needs…to bring together and construct this social safety net within the territory." By "weaving," she means "promoting the organized participation of the people, creating Zonal Coordination Boards made up of residents, schools, clinics, etc., who build a program, after which Infamilia (a ministry program for children and adolescents) provides resources to support it" (Arismendi 2006).

In the same speech, the Minister said that the territory covered the confluence of the state (municipalities, ministries) and "organized society, of which you are part and which *is also part of the state institution."* She explains the name change from family to territory as an effort to "bind, articulate, and work together…in the territory, which is where life actually exists, and therefore, *if that is where life is, then that's where we all have to act*" (Arismendi 2006, my emphasis).

Meanwhile, the director of Infamilia, Julio Bango (sociologist, member of Socialist Party and the Frente Amplio and a former director of a youth NGO), says, "The SOCATA are *the voice of the territory*, they repair child and adolescent services in the territory and promote citizen participation." In one study, Bango asserts that the crisis of the welfare state imposes a need to establish a new relation between the state and civil society (Bango 2000). He argues that compensatory policies have failed because beneficiaries have not participated and, to work, they should not be based on state concerns but rather upon "existing expectations in young people's minds." He continues, "To think of the political from the perspective of the subjects rather than from the perspective of what services are available or can be given out." He promotes achieving this through "interactive and participatory diagnostic techniques such as motivational groups."

Bango consistently criticizes technocrats and defends youth culture as a starting point for policy. For him, the local is an ideal space "to renew the so-called association bond" and to promote the interests of young people. He goes further and introduces the concept of difference: "The rich concord between state youth agencies and youth organizations in implementing policies reflects the fact that both parties have built a consensus *presupposing a recognition of difference*, an affirmation of different identities, and the representation of different interests too" (Bango 2000, my emphasis). Bango insists that state agencies should not be limited to providing services, but "should promote youth participation in defining the services provided, so that they feel connected to and invested in the vital project." Project design must include "the values, motivations, cultural traditions, and different sensibilities that define the very content of the service, giving it specificity and allowing it to be more effective." This is how Bango interprets the construction of a social project that integrates young people through a policy of "dialogue" (inspired by Habermas) and democracy (through a recognition of diversity).

Bango's analysis is neither economist nor functionalist. He notes that "changes in the Uruguayan social structure and *growing social diversity have strained the capacities of the state institutions* that are responsible for social integration" (1999, my emphasis). He understands poverty as a complex, economic, social, and cultural problem. He wants to work on the "problem" of the stigmatization of behaviors that are different. Only with the contribution of civil society, he asserts, can exclusion be overcome. And this requires the "leadership of young people," who are the majority of the poor. How? Through the "generation of interactive spaces between the state services and their beneficiaries, and from the knowledge and recognition of young people's realities."

Ways of Working

The Inter-American Development Bank (IDB) funds SO-CATA to the tune of $40 million, while the national government provides $5 million. But the most interesting aspect is how it works.

In each assigned zone, SOCATA creates a Zonal Coordinating Board, involving residents and public and private institutions. An example: A typical board consists of representatives from local schools, churches, state-organized centers providing assistance to families and children, women's groups, neighborhood committees, incentive commissions, housing cooperatives, retiree associations, and cultural and sporting groups. In one neighborhood, of the twenty groups participating in SOCATA, about eleven are part of what we would legitimately describe as social movement groups. The rest are churches, schools, and groups of residents who attend on an individual basis.

Secondly, they operate democratically. An NGO manages each SOCATA. In Barros Blancos there are two: Vida y Educacion [Life and Education] and Juntos Somos Mas [We Are More Together], which have the distinction of having emerged "from below" after years of territorially based work, mostly by poor local women. The Ministry of Social Development provides each SOCATA group $3,000 every three months; the money is managed by an NGO known as the Regional Investment Fund (FIT). It's not much money, but we're talking about small neighborhoods of about 4,000 inhabitants. The local Coordinating Board, after long and hard debate, decides how to spend the money. Some SOCATAs have names: One chose a significant name—"We Are a Zone in Movement."

One thing to note is that SOCATA "are constructing a participatory diagnosis" that identifies the barrio's need. In Barros Blancos, they have done a great job, street by street, recording the opinions and needs of the neighborhood activists.

A third aspect concerns the background of the functionaries, most of whom hail from the NGO sector. They represent a relatively homogeneous group: They are usually young (around thirty years old), possess or are obtaining a university degree, and have extensive experience working in poor areas, whether as NGO staff or as social activists (or both). Because SOCATAs operate on the basis of plenary sessions and workshops, the functionaries use charts and other techniques designed to facilitate group participation. In general, they employ techniques of popular education.

Given these descriptions, I would like to make the following observations:

1) The boards are "coordinators," that operate in the neighborhoods or towns during struggles for specific demands (electricity, water, work, streets, sanitation, etc.). They are the so-called "live forces" that really move in the territory and are made up of leftists with years of experience working in the poorest barrios.

2) Their decision-making process is very similar to that found in social movements. Everything is discussed, and there is even talk of horizontality. While NGO functionaries generally take charge of the meetings, neighborhood leaders and activists also take the reins, as participants try to reach

consensus on an issue. Once the assembly decides how money will be used, it is left up to the MIDES functionaries to approve it, which they usually do. Photos of SOCATA territorial meetings (and also Ministries' meetings) show participants seated in a circle. One could be confused as to whether it is a meeting of a social movement or an NGO meeting.

These meetings generally employ popular education methods. This is a point worth dwelling upon. Toward the end of dictatorships in the late seventies and early eighties, popular education spread throughout the southern cone. There were no legal political parties, but nevertheless, the vertical manner of doing politics was in crisis. NGOs filled a void and did so in a "participatory" and democratic way, thereby innovating new modes of doing politics. Most NGOs worked in poverty and, at the end of dictatorships, sprouted like mushrooms. In the absence of unions and parties, layers of territorial activists emerged from the NGOs. The activists worked on poverty reduction and, with the withdrawal of the state from poor areas, did so very efficiently. Although the activists were formed outside of political parties and churches, they developed close relationships with them. Local NGOs eventually began intersecting with local municipal governments and, finally, with the progressive, national government. NGOs were like a factory for supplying functionaries to leftist governments, not only helping bring them to power but also helping sustain them there. Neighborhood NGOs, or at least a significant part of them, are part of the social movement, which leads to a certain amount of confusion about the dividing lines between social movements and institutions.

3) Officials at SOCATA, NGOs, and the Ministry of Social are, as I said, young, militant, well-educated, and familiar with popular education. They press the base social organization to address local issues, not national issues, and never call into question broader state policies. The Ministry of Social Development coordinates the work of SOCATA; that is, there is control from above, but not a traditional form of control. It is more "participatory," in the style of popular education.

In Barros Blancos, SOCATA and NGOs activists also work in the Permanent Assembly of Residents and Social Organizations, which is a militant territorial organization that unites all the barrios. NGO functionaries participate in the Assembly too, but it all seems to function well enough. The most conscious activists recognize that it is contradictory to have the state involved at such a local level, but see no way to avoid it because the NGO functionaries are so committed to the work they do, dedicating hours of unpaid overtime to it. In other words, they are both officials and activists, organizing meetings and ensuring the participation of the residents. Here also, we cannot but notice a significant level of ambiguity.

I hope it is now clear that this territorial intervention ties the state and the movements together, and this tie regulates and controls the movement from a distance; it controls the movement indirectly, using the methods and styles of activism derived from popular education.

Knowledge

All SOCATAs have a map of the territory and a detailed, quantitative study of the population provided by the state— age, percentage of the poor, level of education, births, etc. They analyze the data about children and youth—performance in school, disabilities, as well as so-called "vulnerabilities" in housing, family, education, and health. It is very detailed, even showing how certain variables have evolved over time. This is the discipline of statistics, a state "science" that allows for comprehensive knowledge of the population governed.

There are other qualitative approaches that do not rely on statistics and are constructed in a participatory manner through popular education techniques. Four social workers working in Barros Blancos did a study of youth culture, communication, and education (Gradin 2005). The social workers set out "to discover and learn about the spaces where youth gather" and their "codes of communication, practices, types of dress, ways of endo- and exo-group relating" with the aim of "building bridges of communication" between institutions and young people. They employ the full range of popular education techniques dedicated to "promoting young people's development, fostering their creativity" and "to promoting their reflection and critical discussion of topics of interest."

One result was that several dozen young people formed a communication group. It was made up of those youths more likely to participate in meetings, and not those "hanging out on the corners"; participants had probably attended high school and were a sort of elite among the poor. It was also these youth who were most likely to end up working for an NGO. The communication group learned to analyze newspaper articles, to produce a newspaper, and to make a video researching youth cultures in the barrio. This is important because in fact *they were being made into territorial leaders*, but in exogenous spaces created by NGOs and financed by the state.

At this point I would like to say something about my experiences with popular education. Beyond some interesting methods that encourage people to participate who would otherwise have difficulty doing so, popular education never intended to overcome the subject-object division and, in fact, actually consolidates it. Hence I draw two tentative conclusions; I feel that an assessment of popular education is necessary and overdue in Latin America. First, by maintaining and consolidating the subject/object division, I believe that popular education is useful for the state and party, and thus to the new governance. This is why new governments and other institutions have adopted it increasingly. Secondly, it leads to the formation of new groups of movement cadre, activists that specialize in leading the "masses."

SOCATA and the NGOs' use of popular education impacts only a small portion of youth, those "privileged" enough to have access to high school, and excludes "problematic" youths hanging out on street corners, who are stigmatized by the other young people participating in NGOs spaces.[8] The

8   According to Gradin, youth are divided between *planchas* [the most marginalized, in Uruguayan vernacular] and *chetos* [who are relatively better off]. The chetos see the planchas as the poor who don't go to school, hang out on street corners, and steal. The chetos say they want to "educate themselves and make something of themselves in life," go to high school, attend NGO meetings, and use the Internet.

NGOs provide special training to these youth, with the aim of reproducing a class of functionaries who will manage the new governance in poor areas. For example, when the NGOs carry out participatory assessment studies in the neighborhood, they compile a list of the neighborhood's needs and hand this information over to NGOs, who in turn pass it along to the government ministry. Those who oversee the work are placed in a position to take leadership roles in the community.

How to Govern the Movements

The Uruguayan Ministry of Social Development is attempting to build grassroots social movements, and not just any movement, but one that allows the state and its institutions to mold them from within, in a relationship of immanence. By means of SOCATA and the NGOs, the state has a role within the movements, which it uses to reconfigure and, ultimately, govern them. In the everyday practice of the Coordinating Boards, there is an illusion of horizontalism, but they have been created from above and lack real autonomy. They are, in fact, "developing the state within the conscious practice of men" (Foucault 2006, 290).

To summarize, I advance six theses about the state's territorial work and its influence on movements:

1) SOCATA creates a point of interaction between the state and society in movement. That space, which is not really a social or a state space, ties together the state and movement by means of a stable and permanent collective practice. We can call this practice *the new form of governance.*

2) This practice allocates resources, builds knowledge, and manages things that will affect the population. I want to emphasize that this is not a form of governmentality constructed by the state and assumed passively by the movements, but actually a joint construction in shared space/time. To oversee this strategy, it is not necessary to co-opt individuals, which could even be counterproductive. There must be a will to construct it together. This is why NGOs' role is so important—converging

in the spaces of militant struggle, bringing activists on board, and employing popular education techniques.

3) In reality, a dual recognition is at work. The state recognizes the role of territory and territorial movements, and movements recognize the new role of the state. And together, starting out from that dual recognition, they create something new: the new forms of governance. In this sense, there is no contradiction between the micro and the macro, and when we understand what is happening at the micro level, it helps us understand how they are fashioning the new form of governance.

4) SOCATA's practices ensure the coherent functioning of the state. Carrying out a diagnosis of the population at the barrio level, even if it is participatory, is an action of comprehending the barrio *from* a state point of view, focused on what functionaries deem "lacking" there. And, as some residents complain, the state then appropriates this data. SOCATA adopt the reason of the state, because preserving the state is the main objective. In other words, the goal of all this state action is to avoid revolution. SOCATA's practices make the state, and preserve it.

The SOCATA organizations test a new "way of governing." And who better to do it than civil society acting as a state? When the Coordinating Boards debate and decide how to spend the quarterly $3,000, they are overseeing a reading of what should be done to improve the neighborhood. They act on the basis of statistics (prepared by the state), qualitative studies (made by social workers), and participatory assessment (prepared by the movements themselves and residents); on the basis of this comprehensive knowledge of the barrio, they set priorities, calculate, and analyze. In other words, they develop a practice of government.

5) The poor are learning to govern their own spaces and territories. Is this not what they aspire to? Does this one positive factor override the negative ones? The movements are

addressing the fundamental problems of the new governance: health, education, and coexistence, etc. In short, they are occupying society, especially its most conflicted areas. This current state, product of a new form of governance, has an enormous legitimacy. It is now a capillary state; thanks to the art of governing, it has permeated poor territories and done so far more efficiently than the clientelist bosses of the neoliberal period. Those bosses acted in a vertical and authoritarian manner and therefore could always be overwhelmed from below.

6) Finally, SOCATA meets the four conditions of new governmentality: It governs the naturalness of society; it employs scientific knowledge to ensure good government; it takes charge of the population as a set of natural phenomena; and it manages but does not regulate. In other words, "the essential objective of this management will be not so much to prevent things as to ensure that the necessary and natural regulations work, or even to create regulations that enable natural regulations to work" (Foucault 2006, 403–404). It prioritizes "positive action"—like the initiatives sponsored by the Ministry of Social Development and leaves the negative role to the police, who will deal with the youth on the corners. The state as "a way of doing, as a way of thinking" is entering into zones that were previously reluctant to accept it.

The New Challenges for Autonomy and Politics from Below

The struggles of the social movements and societies in movement are a kind of tremor that affect the whole of society—the dominated (who change their place in the world) as much as the ruling class, its institutions, and states. Nothing remains in place, everything moves, as it adapts to the new situation. Those from below force elites to change their forms of domination and fashion more effective means of remaining the elite. The new progressive and leftist governments and their renewed arts of government are part of the state's adaptation to the new situation of widespread insubordination coming from below. Rebellion is no longer confined to a few spatially localized sectors because now the whole society—the "other" society—is rising up. The magnitude of the revolt makes it impossible for the ruling classes to completely erase it from the social and geographical map, since the very balance of power created, and the crisis of state institutions, make it difficult to employ a genocidal operation. I am not saying that the ruling class has renounced genocidal strategies, but that slaughter is not so straightforward in the current situation; indeed, instead of stifling revolt, it actually may encourage it.

For this reason, progressive governments are necessary for the preservation of the state. In this new situation, they are the most effective agent at disarming the anti-systemic nature of the social movements, operating deep within their territory and as the revolt brews. The cases analyzed above— both the Andean and southern cone experiences—are very different but share similar outcomes: In Ecuador, the government dismantled the bases of the indigenous and popular uprisings; in Uruguay, it prevented them from forming. The current process began during the nineties when the leaders of today's progressive governments began to integrate themselves into the state apparatus. The Workers Party in Brazil and the Frente Amplio in Uruguay began taking control of municipalities and regional states. In Argentina, the people accompanying Kirchner to power followed a similar trajectory (despite "ideological" differences). In Mexico, there was a political shift when the PRD won the elections in the Federal District in 1997 and thus, in principle, began governing. In Ecuador, the creation of Pachakutik in 1996 denoted a similar path. From that time, an important part of the left began to govern the institutions, and key leaders came to occupy space leased from the state apparatus.

But this is only a first step. The second occurs when the left embraces the politics of the right: when it takes over portions of the state apparatus and begins to turn rightward, leaving the social movements without a reference point, given that their leaders occupied those state spaces with the promise of resolving popular demands. This ideological and political disarmament produces an organizational crisis, and those leftists responsible for carrying out rightwing policies within the institutions are the leaders of these movements. This triple disarticulation of the movements (ideological, political, and organizational) represents a beheading of popular struggle and lays the foundation for co-opting what remains of it. In essence, left parties accomplish tasks that the right could not achieve through repression: a historic defeat of popular forces, without massive bloodshed but every bit as effectively as authoritarian states of yesteryear.

The social movements that created the conditions for the rise to government of Nestor Kirchner, Lucio Gutiérrez, Tabaré Vázquez, and Lula are now isolated, divided, and on the defensive. Some movements leaders try to defend government policies while still supporting the social movement. The divisions within the movement and the difficulty of mobilizing for common objectives increases governments' freedom to implement neoliberal policies. Although they are more subtle and less predatory than during the days of savage privatization and devastating structural adjustments, neoliberalism is just as intense as before. Let us look at how people who were once friendly to the governments of Lula and Kirchner address this phenomenon.

In Brazil, the general secretary of the National Conference of Bishops, Odilio Scherer—historically, an ally of Lula—says that the current government has transformed Brazil into "a financial paradise." The Archbishop of São Paulo, Claudio Hummes, a friend of Lula, is also disappointed with his management. The Bishop of Salvador, Geraldo Majella Agnelo, was terse: "Never has there been a government so submissive to bankers" (Lavaca 2006). In the case of the frustrated demand for agrarian reform, the bishops believe that Lula wagered on the "modernization" of the agrarian sector via agribusiness to strengthen exports and to meet the demands of the financial sector. As a result, far from introducing agrarian reform, these policies have led to a higher concentration of rural property in fewer hands, while throughout Brazil income concentration continues to grow.

In the case of Argentina we cede the floor to an economist who was elected deputy for a list akin to Kirchner.

Claudio Lozano, an economist at the Central de Trabajadores Argentinos (CTA), is not a radical but argues that
"we are now worse off than in the 1990s," during the years of
Menem. He insists that the policies of the previous regime
have not changed under Kirchner—not the high concentration of wealth, the regressive pattern of income distribution,
the role of the state, or even the country's international integration. On the contrary, there is "a greater exploitation of
the workforce and further impoverishment of society." Despite the significant economic growth registered in the last
three years, "in 2004 and 2005 inequality was exacerbated."
Lozano points out that Kirchner's economic model focuses
externally "toward placement of cheap natural products on
the world market" and is also "a model from the top, in the
sense of meeting the demands of the most affluent sectors
of the population. This model organically maintains a more
regressive distribution" (Lavaca 2006).

In both cases the continuation of neoliberalism is accompanied by policies targeted to address extreme poverty.[9] But
these policies do not address fundamental universal rights
and instead attend to certain sectors that the state has deemed
a priority based on their own criteria. This is because, as noted
by Lozano, "universality puts into question a very good part
of the political system," which functions on the basis of clientelism. The popularity enjoyed by Lula and Kirchner is due to
the crucial factor of clientelism, allowing them to keep winning elections. In parallel, both manage to weaken and isolate
the social movements by means of explicit politics aimed at
creating "reasonable" movements—that is, those with whom
they can negotiate and bargain—while considering other
movements as "radical," destabilizing forces that should be
suppressed. In Argentina this is very clear in relation to the
piquetero movement; in Brazil the government is privileging and building bridges with rural movements who are less

---

9   The concept of "targeted policies" should be revised, given that in Brazil
social plans serve 40 million people, over 20 percent of the population, and in
Argentina they exceed 10 percent. Although it is too early to evaluate, it is likely
that progressive governments are giving birth to a new way of tackling poverty,
different to Keynesian and neoliberal models.

combative than the landless movement (MST), with whom they tend to establish more fluid ties.

It should be understood that this is not a question of the intrinsic evil of the left project or of any particular animosity of their leaders toward social movements. The divorce between the electoral left and social movements has no solution: There are too many material interests and too much complicity with the state apparatus to think there could be a shift. The electoral left is not the enemy of movements, but its access to state power can do it irreparable harm if the movements do not have sufficient autonomy.

Recent experiences in countries such as Argentina, Uruguay, Bolivia, and Brazil suggest some reflections on the problems therewith and possible replies. I do not intend to advance a "political line" that social movements should apply, but simply to outline future possibilities for the movements. I want to indicate some of the unavoidable challenges facing the movement in order to help us continue moving within this new reality.

1) *To understand the new governance in all its complexity, as a result of our struggles, but also as an attempt to destroy them.* The new strategy of the powerful is most apparent during the most critical times for movements, such as during the treachery of Lucio Gutiérrez's government in Ecuador, when this attempt to destroy movements was revealed in all its nakedness and cruelty. However, the problem is not so much the "traitorous" character of this government as the fact that it represents a deep attack on the autonomous spaces won by the movements.

One of the clearest—and totally sincere—arguments made by defenders of progressive governments is that at least they are better than right-wing governments and offer movements an opportunity to consolidate and build upon gains.

This argument is valid, but it is a short-term perspective and a view from above. Under progressive governments, current movements are weaker, more fragmented, and more isolated than ever. The piqueteros in Argentina, militants of the MST in Brazil, and many other activists in other countries recognize this fact. Oscar Olivera, leader of the Cochabamba Water Coordination, evaluates the first year of the Evo Morales government as follows:

> Now that the Movement Toward Socialism occupies state space, it has begun trying to co-opt and control the movements, in order to demobilize them by means of their own specific demands and tame them according to the government's interests. The state is expropriating capacities that we recovered at great cost: the capacity to rebel, to mobilize, to organize, and advance proposals. They give institutional positions to movement spokespeople, embassies to social leaders, and dismiss and stigmatize those of us who do not want to enter the state institutions but rather want to break with them, alleging that we are funded by the Rightwing (Olivera 2006).

New "progressive" governments bring a great deal of confusion and ambiguity, as we have seen in Uruguay and Ecuador, especially when long-term militants support them. The first, unavoidable step to deal with this is to unravel and understand how the new art of governing functions. This study aims to be a small contribution to the task, seeking to address phenomena that are just starting to reveal their long-term goals.

2) *Protect our spaces and territories.* The new governance aims directly at the heart of the "other" societies in movement. It invades their spaces without armed troops but with functionaries supported by international financial institutions. This silent invasion is just as dangerous as a military intervention and seeks to achieve the same goals in a less conspicuous manner. Even worse, it inevitably takes activists and militants on-board. The elites who rule the world seem to have understood the importance of spaces and territories for those from below, which is why the number of development projects in

our territories continually increases. What is new is that the projects employ the same tools we use to rebel and participate in the "strengthening" of grassroots organizations.

3) *To not submit to the agenda of power, it is better to create or maintain our own agenda.* It is increasingly apparent that there are two agendas: the agenda of those from above, which either the left or the right can implement, and the agenda of those from below. Many find it difficult to distinguish one from the other, especially when the agenda of those from below is a presence in mass mobilizations. Moreover, it can be difficult to differentiate between movements and mobilizations, given the ambiguities that we have seen, and as official discourse includes some of the demands of those from below and calls mobilizations and employs modes of action and codes specific to those from below.

How can we differentiate between mobilizations from above and those from below when they appear so similar? Clearly the number of people mobilized is not the best indicator. In attempting to disarticulate the "historiography of the elite," Indian historian Ranajit Guha argues that "elite mobilization in the political field tends to be done vertically, while that of the subaltern is achieved horizontally" (Guha 2002, 37). The former is "more cautious and controlled," while the latter is more "spontaneous"; mobilizations organized by the elite tend to be "more legal and constitutional," while those of the subaltern tend to be "relatively more violent" (Guha 2002, 37). The paradigm of the former is electoral mobilization, that of the latter, popular insurgency. However, it is only in a long-term perspective that we can grasp the totality of confusions and ambiguities, which are not accidental but rather "calculated," and implemented by the elites as part of the art of governing movements.

Points two and three can be considered ways of protecting the autonomy of movements from below from elite attempts to destroy popular autonomy. Elites use elections as a platform to expand the ambiguities and strike against the cultural and political autonomy of the popular sectors.

4) *It is essential to hold our ground.* Although the situation is ambiguous and confusing, that does not mean that we should be passive. Speaking out against those from above has repercussions, including hostility from the left institutions. Until recently, major movement events like the World Social Forum and other counter-summits were spaces with a diversity of political perspectives that allowed for resistance. Now, parallel "counter-summits" are held with support from progressive governments every time there is a major elite event. This happened in Mar del Plata in November 2005, in Córdoba in July 2006, and in Cochabamba in December of the same year, where a People's Summit occurred at the same time as the summit of South American presidents.

The National Coordinator in Defense of Water, Basic Services, the Environment, and Life (2006) took an exemplary position in refusing to participate in this event organized "with the support of the Bolivian government and under the watchful eyes of some NGOs." It issued a statement pointing out that "politics from below and autonomy are not constructed from above." Critical of intellectuals and professionals who maintain a "paternalistic position toward what social movements must do and how we should organize and struggle," they declared that "we do not accept the guardianship" of NGOs. Regarding the summit, the statement declared that "we believe that it did not originate in a horizontal or inclusive manner" and that "the scheduled events do not represent all the organizations and their places of work and living." They took a firm position, despite the prospect of being isolated within the wider movement. This is the price one pays to avoid mortgaging movements from below to the state.

5) *To enhance plebeian politics.* Elites can use calls for unity among the popular sectors to their advantage. Even though the idea that unity can serve the popular sectors still persists, history teaches us that those from below never needed unitary structures—which are always centralized—to rebel. Unity is achieved though other means: in the act of insurrection, in rebellion, or in sharing horizontalities.

The idea is gaining ground that unity can be an imposition or a way to slow down social movements. "Defending unity as a value above all others only opens the way to the forces that oppose social transformation. Indeed, at certain junctures, the slogan should be 'divide and struggle better,'" says Brazilian sociologist, Francisco de Oliveira, who co-founded the Workers Party over a quarter of a century ago and who was eventually forced out (De Oliveria, 2006). To sum up, the objective of popular politics should never revolve around creating unity.

Moreover, in cultures from below, unity does not have the currency it does among those oriented toward state power. State-focused political currents attempt to develop state forms in movements from below, from which they gain visibility and that they eventually attempt to co-opt. One of the most important tasks for the social movements today is to bolster the various forms of doing politics from below, to enhance their spaces and their times, their ways of doing. Unity is one of the biggest barriers to this. What is often dismissed as "fragmentation" is actually a way of avoiding co-optation, which, as we have seen, is one of the goals set by elites. Efforts at "strengthening organizations" sponsored by the World Bank and implemented by the local elites with the help of opportunistic movement leaders are attempts to create "strong" organizations that avoid division and can unite fragments. They understand that unity, set in large political structures, can pave the way for co-option under the guise of gaining visibility for the movement. Social movements have learned this lesson the hard way in recent years.

Plebeian politics are not always so visible. They are impermanent in the eyes of those from above, because the mainstream media tends not to focus on them. Intellectuals only deal with them when they make an impact on the "grand" stage. The rest of the time, those from below simply exist— they resist in their own spaces, far from the cacophony of above. However, it would be folly to overlook the new reality constructed from below in Latin America and the thousands of spaces emerging out of the successive uprisings in the region.

Governments and Movements: Autonomy or New Forms of Domination?

The end of 2008 marked the ten-year anniversary of Hugo Chávez's first electoral victory (December 6, 1998) and initiated a new period marked by the emergence of progressive and left governments in South America. His clinching of the presidency was the result of a long process of struggles from below, beginning in February 1989 with the Caracazo, the first great popular insurrection against neoliberalism, which drove the party system that had sustained elite domination for decades into crisis.

In the years that followed, seven other presidents embodying the ongoing political-institutional changes came to power, accounting for a total of eight out of ten governments in the region: Luiz Inácio Lula da Silva in Brazil, Néstor and Cristina Kirchner in Argentina, Michelle Bachelet in Chile, Tabaré Vázquez in Uruguay, Evo Morales in Bolivia, Rafael Correa in Ecuador, and Fernando Lugo in Paraguay. These administrations were made possible—to a greater or lesser degree—by social movement resistance to the neoliberal model.

In some cases, admittedly, this change at the top arose from years of steady electoral growth (notably, in Brazil and Uruguay), while in other countries it was the fruit of social movements capable of overthrowing neoliberal parties and governments (Bolivia, Ecuador, Venezuela, and Argentina, to an extent). More than a decade after the start of this process, it is time for a brief evaluation of what has happened:

1. Beyond the differences between these experiences, they share something fundamental: the return of the state as the main agent of change.

2. Movements that were the central protagonists of resistance to neoliberalism in the nineties and early 2000s have been marginalized.

3. The dominant contradiction in this period is between the governments and right-wing sectors, a change that has sucked movements into a statist whirlwind from which most have been unable to escape.

4. There are some tendencies—still dispersed—that seek to rebuild the movements on new foundations, based on new issues and new forms of political action.

The twilight of the "progressive" decade as a source of social, political, and economic change makes it necessary for social movements to take stock of the gains and losses that this decade has brought to popular forces.

The Risks of Subordination

Initially, governments were subordinate to movements, and movements were demobilized, divided, and fragmented. Only small nuclei remained in open confrontation with the governments, whereas most slid toward government collaboration in exchange for economic subsidies (known as *planes sociales*) and other material benefits. Many other movement collectives simply dissolved.

By contrast, movements in Chile, Peru, and Colombia are experiencing an era of vibrant activity. In all three, indigenous groups are taking the lead. In Chile, the Mapuche are recovering from the ravages of the Pinochet-era anti-terrorism law, which was reactivated by "socialist" President Ricardo Lagos (2000–2006). The Mapuche, along with high-school students and workers from various sectors, particularly mining and forestry, have generated a major reactivation of social struggles.

Indigenous communities affected by mining in Peru are vigorously resisting through the grassroots Quechua organization, CONACAMI, paying a high price in lives and arrests for their efforts. The group is leading the fight against genocidal mining projects that leave behind contaminated waterways and polluted air just to line the pockets of the multinationals.

CONACAMI fiercely opposes the U.S.–Peru Free Trade Agreement and President Alan García's neoliberal policies.

In Colombia, the long struggle of the indigenous Nasa represented by the ACIN and CRIC has been doubly fruitful. The broad social mobilization known as the "Minga" (literally, collective work), which brought together dozens of indigenous groups in October 2008 in Cauca, managed to break through a military siege and challenge the militarization of society that had immobilized indigenous communities. Cane cutters—most of them Afro-Colombians—service workers, neighborhood organizations, and human rights activists all joined the indigenous-led Minga.

The example set by these movements, which are beset by and born out of adversity, should be a source of inspiration for the rest of the continent's movements. Mapuche advocate Patricia Troncoso's long hunger strike, which lasted from November 2007 to January 2008, and Colombia's indigenous Minga share the potent mission of breaking through the isolation and "soft" genocide that seeks to wipe indigenous groups off the map and undermine their existence as a people.

The panorama for the movements in other countries is extremely complex. Perhaps the most emblematic case is that of Argentina. The state has co-opted the vast majority of the piquetero movement with economic subsidies to families (the planes sociales) and by the awarding of government posts to leaders. The human rights movement—particularly, the Association of the Mothers of the Plaza de Mayo, which had played a prominent role in resisting neoliberalism during the nineties—has joined officialdom, becoming an unequivocal defender of government policies. Meanwhile, many neighborhood assemblies have simply disappeared.

Nonetheless, not everything has been a step backward. Over the last five years, innumerable collectives have sprung up, many of them focusing on environmental issues, such as open-pit mining, forestry, and soy mono-cropping. Out of this, some one hundred local assemblies have emerged and are organized into the Union of Citizen Assemblies (UAC), which has become one of the most active opponents of the multinational mining companies.

Also in Argentina, campesinos and small farmers formed the National Campesino Front, made up of some two hundred rural organizations, to militate for family and community agriculture against the impetuous advance of soy agribusiness. The organization represents long-standing movements (such as MOCASE from Santiago del Estero) as well as new organizations of small producers, including a handful of collectives from urban peripheries.

In Brazil, the movements have been incapable of advancing beyond their long-standing defensive footing—a position aggravated by the Lula government. In Uruguay, despite organized labor's growing strength, which is primarily attributable to state protection of labor leaders' activities, the movements are far from being an anti-systemic actor, and organizational levels among the urban poor remain local and fragmented. The planes sociales are largely responsible for this weakening of the movements.

In Bolivia, the situation is quite different. The movements have not been defeated and maintain a significant capacity to mobilize and pressure the government and right-wing sectors. The September 2008 crisis, for example, was resolved in favor of popular sectors, thanks to the movement's intense mobilization, which included the cordoning off of Santa Cruz and resistance to Plan 3000—the poor and indigenous peripheral suburb of the oligarchic mestizo city.

Raquel Gutiérrez has noted that Bolivian movements have "recovered a margin of political autonomy in relation to the government," particularly when they see the government as incapable of stopping the oligarchy. "And they have no inclination to be subordinated," she continues, "when it comes to the fulfillment of their demands" (Gutiérrez 2008).

The pressure exerted by the movements, however, comes up against statist logic, which is firmly enmeshed in bloated state bureaucracies (military, judicial, legislative, ministerial, and municipal). Those bureaucracies are resistant to change. Bureaucracies are not only conservative by nature, but these are also managed by newly empowered officials—both elected (deputies, senators, council members, mayors, etc.) and the unelected (ministers and hundreds of advisers)—whose main ambition is to maintain their positions.

The New Forms of Domination

It is not possible for movements to overcome dependency on and subordination to the state without understanding that the new "left" and "progressive" governments are exercising new forms of domination. The planes sociales aimed at "integrating" the poor play a central role in these novel modes of social control. I recently had the following conversation with a top-level official in Uruguay's Ministry of Social Development:

The official said, "For us, social policies are emancipatory policies, not a way of disciplining the poor."

"Is this your personal opinion or is it the ministry's as well?" I asked.

The official replied, "It's not just mine, it's also that of the national government and of the Ministry of Social Development. The national government did not come here to placate the poor; it came to generate opportunities for integration and emancipation."

Such affirmations are doubtlessly honest in their intent but implicitly undermine social movements by adopting their discourses and even their practices. This raises three central questions:

1. *The end of the old right*: The new governments were born from the crisis of the first stage of neoliberalism—the period of privatization and deregulation—and consolidated their rule by destroying right-wing elites' traditional bases of domination. These elites had built extensive clientelistic networks with local political bosses, who used their role as mediators with state institutions and the electoral system to subjugate the poorest sectors.

The movements arose to fight these elites. The piquetero case is symptomatic: The piqueteros' struggle for direct control of the planes sociales sought to rupture caudillos ability to control patron-client networks. In confronting the right directly, this wave of mobilizations strengthened the piquetero movement and modified Argentina's political map.

With mixed results, the new governments have tried to displace these clientelistic networks, putting government-directed state bureaucracies in their place. This is arguably the main "progressive" action of the new governments. In the process of dismantling the old elite networks, the governments have employed the same language and codes used by the movements.

2. *New forms of control:* The crisis of discipline as a way of molding bodies in closed spaces was one of the most prominent characteristics of the "Revolution of '68." The overwhelming of patriarchal hierarchies and defiance of authority in the workplace, school, hospital, and the barracks forced capital and the state to create new forms of open-air social control. They had to find new ways to deal with the population and to maintain security.

The state-backed planes sociales, directed by a coterie of NGO officials, introduce these new forms of domination into spaces that are impervious to discipline. In these sites, the state becomes capillary, working from within, stretching its reach into ramshackle neighborhoods that were once bastions of revolt. It works with the very sectors that had been organized as movements, but its aim is to disorganize them.

The state's presence no longer manifests itself in the grotesque form of the police baton—though, for sure, it is never absent—but rather in the subtler form of generating "opportunities for integration and emancipation." To do this, the state relies on the knowledge accumulated by NGOs over decades of local "cooperation," during which they adopted the "participatory" practices of popular education.

Young NGO officials are a new army of functionaries who no longer wait for children at schools or tend to patients at hospitals, but who instead go directly to the territories of poverty and rebellion. And they have something that makes this job much easier: They have insider knowledge of these popular sectors, because many of these officials at one time participated in resistance against the neoliberal model; they had been militants or were at least deeply tied to social activism.

Echoing Brazilian sociologist Francisco de Oliveira, it could be said that the planes sociales are instruments of biopolitical control in which the state classifies people according to their material needs and "restores a type of clientelism" (let's call it state-scientific) in which politics become irrelevant (de Oliveira 2006).

Although the planes sociales help alleviate poverty, they do not change the distribution of income and don't touch the growing concentration of wealth, thereby leaving the fundamental aspects of the model intact. And by affecting the movements' organizational capacity and undermining their growth, the planes sociales serve the neoliberal drive to turn all of life into a commodity. Given this, it is alarming that left intellectuals are nearly unanimous in viewing the planes sociales as a progressive achievement.

3. *An offensive against autonomy*: States now adopt the language of the movements, even claiming to support the "critical autonomy" of those receiving the planes sociales. States have devised coordinating mechanisms that prompt the movements to participate in the design of the planes sociales and implement local policies (never general policies, though, or those that might challenge the model).

The movements are persuaded to undertake a "participatory diagnosis" of the neighborhood or town; in fact, they are even put in charge of carrying out local charity work. This is all consistent with the World Bank's policy of "capacity building."

All of this is aimed at "state building" within the everyday practices of popular sectors, and it is done precisely in areas where people had learned "movement building." The planes sociales are directed straight at the heart of territories that were incubators of rebellion. These programs seek to neutralize or modify networks and forms of solidarity, reciprocity, and mutual assistance that were created by those from below in order to survive neoliberalism. Once the social ties and knowledge that assured their autonomy have disappeared, these sectors will be easier to control.

None of this should be attributed to a supposed malevolence on the part of the progressive governments. Whenever the poor have overturned existing forms of domination, new and more perfected ones have necessarily taken their place. Only by neutralizing these planes sociales and overcoming their offensive against the autonomy of the poor will the movements be able to get back on their feet and resume their march toward emancipation.

Epilogue:
Interview by Michael Hardt
and Alvaro Reyes[1]

Democratic Organizational Experiments

In several of your books, you describe and analyze the horizontal, autonomous, and democratic modes of organizing that characterize the latest wave of movements. What are the primary organizational characteristics that differentiate these movements from the major political movements of the previous era? What do you consider the chief benefits of these organizational experiments? What have been the greatest concrete successes of this new mode of action? Do you see any significant shortcomings or dangers presented by such democratic organizational models?

The most important difference is that these are not state-centric organizations, or hierarchical, with a strict division between the leadership and bases, between those who give orders and those who execute them, between knowing and doing. We can say that the old union movement follows a Fordist and Taylorist organizational model and is, in that sense, symmetrical to capital; being hierarchical, it is also symmetrical to the state in general terms. Large gatherings have a special arrangement: They focus on a table, where the leaders who organize and run meetings are seated, while the "mass" is physically at a lower level, listening passively, and able to speak only when the table authorizes it. This type of organization is no longer the most active or creative in Latin America.

The new organizations are smaller, they don't have leadership teams that are so separated from the base, and sometimes

1   This interview first appeared in the *South Atlantic Quarterly* 2012 Volume 111, Number 1: 165–191

they don't have permanent leadership teams at all. But the most notable difference is evident on the micro scale. Here meetings, gatherings, or assemblies are smaller; people usually sit in a circle; the "leaders" simply spread the word and are often appointed to that role during that gathering only. The word flows, sometimes like a "turbulent waterfall," to quote Carlos Lenkersdorf's description of a Tojolabal assembly. These are face-to-face relations, direct and without intermediaries. Of course most of the time what predominates are forms of intermediate organization between, say, the association and the community.

When these new organizations become too large, it is quite common that things will function more or less as described at the base level, but as one ascends the hierarchy, it will start to look more and more like the traditional model. Something like this happens in both the MST and the CONAIE, indicating that it is not easy to find alternative forms of organization on a scale larger than a local or community-based group.

I think the big advantage of this model is that—by not being state-centric organizations—they tend toward reducing bureaucracy, which is a traditional, elementary, and very old form of domination. Not only is the state a bureaucracy, but the civil and military bureaucracies are also among its constitutive features. Most of the poor in Latin America live their daily lives on the margins of the state, and in order to struggle, they are discovering that they don't need to be organized in a state-like manner. In my view, this is a positive structural change with respect to the manual laborer of yesteryear, whose daily life in the factory was spatially and temporally regulated by capital and the state to such an extent that, to defend their interests, they had to organize themselves in a way that reflected the organization of the state. That was one of the great successes of the welfare state.

But now the new movements are experimenting with something different, with marginalized sectors of the population, and are organizing themselves in ways that do not differ much from forms practiced in everyday life (for example, from how the women organize themselves in the markets or neighborhoods). The trend, at least when progressive governments appear, is to institutionalize the ways and means of making everyday life in the broader political-social organization. You can see meetings with styles similar to "meetings" of young people or women in their neighborhoods, which are non-Taylorist, unordered, and non-hierarchical forms of being together.

In *Dispersing Power*, I tried to show how this type of organization rooted in everyday life enabled the inhabitants of El Alto and the Bolivian Altiplano to block the repressive machinery of state (i.e., the army and police). Organizational dispersion was more potent than the centralized state or union, because the unions did not play the least role in the Bolivian revolt. Something similar occurred in Argentina on December 19–20, 2001, in Caracas during the coup d'état against Chávez, and in other situations in which the population drew from resources taken from everyday life and was able to remove those from above.

I wouldn't call this type of organization democratic. I think it is something more complex. Felix Patzi says that the Andean community is not a democratic but rather a form of "consensual authoritarianism." To be honest, I do not advocate democratic forms as if they were superior. The family cannot function democratically, because not all members have the same responsibilities and duties or the same abilities to contribute to the collective. I think that what we call democracy is a mode of domination created by the West, but that is an altogether different question.

Organizing on the basis of modes of everyday life is slow, and using it to make decisions can be a time consuming process. It probably cannot be exercised much beyond local groups, where there is a lot of personal trust and many small, everyday interests in common. So I do not think it is a perfect paradigm for opposing large bureaucracies but it is, nevertheless, a way that thousands of grassroots groups have found to resist autonomously. We can't ask it for more than it can provide. For instance, we have the crisis of the Social Forums, which have weakened because, among other things, they were taken over by those who were most capable of "leading" assemblies and raising money for travel, and so on—in other words, professionals from universities and NGOs. This reveals one of the limits of this new "way of doing," a name I prefer to "organization," which always has an air of Taylorism to it.

Origins

It is impossible, of course, to establish the specific date of origin of a complex phenomenon such as a political movement, but we find such periodizations interesting and useful in part because they often reveal our assumptions about the nature and dynamics of the movement. Some people, for example, date the birth of the current wave of Latin American movements to the Zapatista uprising on January 1, 1994, thus placing emphasis on both its challenge to neoliberal policies, such as NAFTA, and its experimentation with autonomous and horizontal modes of organizing. Others date the origin to 1989 in ways that emphasize similar qualities. Conceiving as origin, on the one hand, the Venezuelan Caracazo (the riots and looting in response to the IMF-imposed privatization policies) can serve to underline the opposition to neoliberalism. If, on the other hand, if one locates the point of origin as the FMLN's final offensive in El Salvador—and interprets that as the extreme point and final drama of foquismo—this could point toward the subsequent development of autonomous and horizontal strategies of social struggle. We find it interesting instead that in several of your works, you imply that this current wave of movements has been in gestation since 1968. What do you think we gain when we cast our view of the movements back as far as 1968? Does that help us see differently, for instance, either the analysis of power prevalent in the movements or their organizational forms? And, more generally, what do you think is primarily at stake in such periodizations?

I point to 1968 in order to identify the root of this process. Two important processes begin in that period. On the one hand, women and youth begin to play a new role and there is a crisis or change in patriarchy, which is very visible in small, base organizations. My understanding of patriarchy at this point, which is not unique of course, is as a way to lock down and prevent the circulation of social energy. When patriarchy begins to be eroded, creative energy starts to flow. Patriarchy principally affects women and poor young people, the vast majority of whom are Indian, black, or mestizo. I emphasize that date, because it seems obvious that the process that Wallerstein called the "Revolution of 1968" began to break down an embankment, and those who did it—here in the South, there is a different story to the North, one that has yet to be written—were perhaps not women in general but young men and young women. They were not helped by factory employment or access to education but above all by the shared experience of Christian base communities (liberation theology), Guevarista militancy in armed or unarmed groups, the breakdown of the traditional communal order, and so on. This led an entire generation to enjoy a different cultural experience than their parents. However, this is not something "given" by the system—the contraceptive pill, better factory conditions, and so on—but something created from below by diverse young actors. In Brazil alone, there were 80,000 ecclesiastic communities, and something like 8 to 10 million people who, in the sixties, had collectively experimented with something different. That's what interests me when I say 1968.

The second point is to periodize the appearance of new organizations. To understand the Bolivian revolt of 2000–2005, one must go back to what happened in the nineties, the huge marches for the sovereignty and livelihoods of coca growers, Amazonian groups, and others. And we can't help but to look back at 1973, when the Tiahuanaco Manifesto was issued and the Katarista current was born. To read the Tiahuanaco Manifesto and compare it with the Pulacayo Thesis written by the miners' union in 1947 is to compare a traditional Trotskyist statement—very revolutionary but Eurocentric—with a text written by literate Aymara after the 1952 Revolution that places the problem of oppression beside that of exploitation.

To understand the Zapatistas, one also has to go back to 1974, when the Indigenous Congress met in San Cristóbal de las Casas, the first meeting among all the ethnic groups in Chiapas, who had never been gathered together before. This Congress is at the root of the Zapatista movement, just as the founding of the Ecuarunari in 1972 is at the root of the CONAIE, which led the uprisings in Ecuador after 1990 and brought Correa to government. We find similar patterns across the entire continent—the first land occupation in Brazil took place in 1979 in the south; the first demonstration of the Madres de Plaza de Mayo, which did not yet have that name, was in 1977; and so on.

So when I speak of 1968, I do so in a double sense: as a means of referring to cultural changes within the popular world that are translated into a new form of doing politics, which I frame as a crisis of patriarchy (not as an end of domination but as the impossibility of containing creative energies) and, on the other hand, what we could call a renovation, which I periodize in the dates mentioned. This renewal is related to the limits of the state-centric ways of doing and the emergence of a new generation of collectives. In my view, Bolivia is the most eloquent case of this, transparently demonstrating the limits of the old and the rise of the new, where the old is nothing less than the COB, a parallel power of immense potency, that falls apart in just a few years, as analyzed brilliantly.

The important thing here is to understand that the old is collapsing, so to speak, not only externally with the eroding of the Washington Consensus but also internally, a reality in which the spread of the communal logic has played a major role. In Bolivia, the great failure of the 1952 Revolution was its defeat within the communities in the rural areas, where it failed to impose the union as an alternative modernizing force to community forms seen as archaic. Here, patriarchy had a name in the union, which was a kind of power over the community. While the community did not reject the union, it ate away at it, weakening it step by step, day by day, with its style of doing, which, if I may say, is more feminine than masculine, more subtle than frontal. That cultural/political victory of the community is key to understanding everything that came afterward, which is to say—Katarismo, the reclaiming of Tupac Katari and Bartolina Sisa (never one or the other but always both), a process of decolonization from below that is amazing and that is still far from over.

The Map of Differences

We are struck by the remarkable continuities of political thought in this wave of Latin American struggles and the communication among movements from Chiapas to Patagonia. Indeed, your work throughout the continent has revealed and analyzed these commonalities, but you have also emphasized the differences and the singularities of national and local situations. In terms of both progressive governments and social movements, what do you think are the most important lines of division or continuity? In terms of progressive governments, for example, some observers pose Chávez on one side as representative of the aggressive approach to wielding state authority against neoliberalism with Lula and the Kirchners on the other side as representatives of a more moderate approach. If you were to draw a map of Latin America in terms of either progressive governments and/or social movements, what would be the most important lines of division and connection?

It's difficult to establish boundaries with any hope of being definitive because of ongoing instability and movement within the field of progressivism, a field decisively influenced by the politics of the United States. There is something in common in all the processes: the continuity of the extractive model, whether it be open-pit mining, the extraction of hydrocarbons, or monocultures. In all cases, it is about commodity production, which is the form that neoliberalism takes in the region today. Nevertheless, what happens in Venezuela or Bolivia is not the same, where the exportation of oil and gas prevails and has prevailed even though we have had ten years of the Chávez government.

In Brazil, there has been a re-primarization of exports, the same as in the rest of the region, but we must remember that we are dealing with an emerging power that has the second largest oil company and the second largest mining company in the world and that exports aircraft through Embraer, the third largest aircraft producer globally behind Boeing and Airbus. If in Brazil there is a tendency toward de-industrialization relative to the brutal increase in commodity exports, you can imagine what is happening in the rest of the region, which does not have the resources of BNDES, the largest development bank in the world, and which loaned more money than the World Bank and the IDB combined in 2009 and 2010.

In addition to the export of commodities, what all Latin American countries have in common is the expansion of social policies that seek to neutralize the social movements and cushion or prevent conflict. Even in Colombia, the armed conflict is no longer the focus of state action, which was characterized by repression and disappearances. It now concentrates on social movements. This is particularly important because, alongside the improvement of the economic situation, it is at the base of the current reflux of social action—albeit more important than that. The states, progressive or not, through means of the Bolsa Familia, the social plans of the Argentinean government, and the Colombian Ministry of Social Action, are managing to create a social base for the state, something that was previously achieved through welfare programs. And the important thing is that these policies are not a mere continuation of the World Bank's anti-poverty efforts but are responsive to input and critique from social movements, to the point where the think tanks of these policies are agencies such as FLACSO and social development ministries, as I argue in my latest book.

The map of progressive and leftist governments must reflect the difference between countries in which social action entered into major conflicts with the political system, such as Venezuela, Bolivia, and Ecuador, and those like Brazil and Uruguay, where stability has prevailed, with Argentina being somewhere between the two. This helps us define the current role of these movements. They are weak in Brazil, where they have already fulfilled their historical purpose and are now in a prolonged decline. They are strong in Bolivia, where they continue to prevent the state from imposing its stabilization policies, as demonstrated in the wake of the recent *gasolinazo* protests on December 26, forcing Evo Morales to suspend its implementation. And the situation in Ecuador is complicated; there the regime's pressure against Indians is very intense, combing isolation, repression, social policies, and the delivery of water to mining multinationals.

In Argentina, I see interesting trends in the restructuring of the movements, even though they are on the defensive in the face of a very active and intrusive state. But social creativity has been maintained, as shown by the hundred assemblies against the mining business organized by the UAC (Union of Citizen Assemblies), the educational initiatives of the recuperated factories, and what survives of the piquetero groups. The forty high schools under popular control and the creation of a university in IMPA, as well as the occupation of the nations oldest company, show that there are still new conquests and that the government's attempts to co-opt and neutralize social movements also have their limits.

In summary, I believe that there are countries such as Brazil, in which there is a clear crisis in the social movements, which cannot be separated from the economic and political strength of the new emerging force, to the intermediate situations that we find in other countries, where there is a kind of chess game between movements and governments—a sort of war of positions, a delineation of ground and spaces. Movements' quest to maintain their autonomy is counterbalanced by a concerted effort on the part of governments to co-opt them. What I am trying to say is that outside of Brazil, there are open and uncertain scenarios, where the various forces are moving cautiously and one cannot conclusively say whether one or the other is winning. Maybe the positive exception for the social movements is in Peru, where there is a strong response to one of the most right-wing governments in the region.

Latin American Anomaly

Although anti-neoliberal sentiment has been widespread throughout the world, anti-neoliberal political projects have been particularly intense and coherent in Latin America. When we consider the direct and indirect influences of the Zapatistas on movements on just about every continent, for example, or the resonance and circulation of the Argentinean que se vayan todos, or even the popularity and influence of a figure like Hugo Chávez far beyond the borders of the Latin America, even taking into account its massive internal differences, the continent seems to stand out as an anomaly to the ongoing global status quo. Does this conclusion seem valid to you, or is this phenomenon mere appearance? What social conditions and political initiatives might account for this anomaly?

I dare say that Latin America was an anomaly during the 1990s and the first half of the first decade of the 2000s, until progressive politics began to move and influence the various sectors from below. However, now it is not so clear and I think we are experiencing a transition. I spent a decade studying the Brazilian case, which I think is going to have an enormous influence throughout the region now that it is becoming a power capable of displacing the influence of the United States, which has played an "ordering" role for more than a century. This hegemonic change cannot help but to influence social movements, as always. That is why studying Brazil is so important.

On the other hand, as a region, Latin America has had a higher level of economic growth for the last seven or eight years, which has allowed for a return of political and social stability and a greater state presence (what we call governance). This suggests that the two factors that contributed to the strengthening of the social movements—the confluence of economic crisis and the de-legitimization of neoliberal governments—have come to an end.

We can understand the emergence of progressive governments as a necessary step in re-establishing stability. As such, I think the cycle of struggles has ended in most of the principal countries, although there is still a crisis of governance in two of them—Venezuela and Bolivia. This is due in large part to the clumsiness of empire, but also to a popular power that has not allowed itself to be domesticated and that seeks to maintain its autonomy through inorganic means. Its unconventionality has actually helped it succeed. By inorganic, I mean outside of the established bodies or institutions. In my view, the failure of reform in these countries is an indicator of the success of the quest for autonomy.

However, another trend is also evident. To the extent that the economic model continues to focus on extractivism, there is no way to prevent the ongoing marginalization of large sectors of the population. The massive occupation of the Parque Indoamericano that just happened in Buenos Aires shows that the soybean industry does not create jobs and in fact concentrates more and more people in urban neighborhoods. Social conflict is inevitable in this scenario. The cycle of struggle may be over, but the state's social policies are still unable to contain the turmoil. Therefore, even assuming that we are living through the end of the anomaly, there is no impasse among popular sectors, pressure is becoming more intense, and conditions are once again being created that will facilitate the return of outbursts of rebellion or mass social movements. These ensuing two years will offer clues to the future, because governments are facing financial difficulties that force them to intensify the model that brings in fresh money even though the political strategy is a dead end in the medium term.

Reverse Flow of Influence

When José Carlos Mariátegui returned from Europe to Peru in 1923 he brought with him a wealth of knowledge about European Marxist theory as well as communist and socialist movements, which he adapted in creative ways to the Andean reality. Today, however, influence and inspiration flow primarily in the opposite direction. How do you see the role and significance of contemporary Latin American political thought for those in other parts of the world, particularly Europe and North America? What part does indigenous thought play in this? In contrast, what is (and/or what should be) the continuing relevance of European and North American thought for Latin American political movements?

I think European and North American thought remains hegemonic within the core militants, and not only among university students. I believe that Latin America can be an inspiration, an example, and even have some political influence, but the categories with which they think and reflect upon reality remains, with a few exceptions, Eurocentric. The best example is that people understand conflict in terms of the concept of social movements, which is an idea coined by intellectuals from the North to explain movements in the North. I think that the various currents of what has been called the sociology of social movements are interesting and important, especially when they work on concrete reality. Studies such as McAdam's *Freedom Summer*, and the work of Tilly, Tarrow, and Melucci, among others offer contributions that we cannot ignore even though they are of little use to reflections about our reality in Latin America.

The theories about social movements start from the assumption that there is *one* society and that a part of it—a social class or disadvantaged or oppressed sector—demonstrates before the state in an effort to make itself heard and satisfy its demands. This leads to analyses of the organizational forms of collective action, of the structure of opportunities, of the cultural resources that are put in motion, and so on—in other words, different ways of explaining how *one* unified society with *one* state, *one* system of justice, and *one* political system of decision making resolves or expresses differences, inequalities, and oppression.

However, we do not have *one* society in Latin America. In addition to classes, ethnic groups, age ranges, genders, and sexes, there is another reality that is often not even understood by our own intellectuals. There are two systems, although even the word "system" seems inadequate, because they are not symmetrical. We have an official society, hegemonic, of colonial heritage, with its institutions, modes of doing, forms of justice, and all that. But there is also another society, which may be based in remote rural areas and organized in communities or even found in the peripheries of large cities. It has different ways of organizing itself, including its own system of justice, forms of production, and an organizational model for making decisions that is parallel to or on the margin of the establishment. Non-capitalist social relations are the mortar of this other society. The purpose of the relations is not to accumulate capital and power but to reproduce the life of those who have no place in the hegemonic society.

This other society does not exist as a state alongside another state. It is a fragmented, non-institutionalized society and, most importantly, is only visible when it enters into movement, when it operates in ways that contract the established society, precisely because it is not organized around state institutions. And this does not have much to do with social movements: What we call social movements are a product of that difference, not its cause. In other words, the social mobilization emerges not to demand rights or goods from the state, which would be the traditional way of doing things, but so that the state recognizes it, visualizes it, and respects it. It is true that many leaders talk of rights and employ statist language, but that is not important at all. It also doesn't matter whom that other society chooses to represent its interests within the state bureaucracy, because that state continues to be experienced as alien. This is even true in Bolivia, where the state has allegedly been re-constituted. Understanding this takes a good bit of time and philosophical reflection, but it can't be grasped within the politics of the possible, which is always the realm of the politics of the state. This is why the work of Clastres, an anthropologist-philosopher of people without a state, is so helpful.

There are very few studies that can explain this reality. I am aware of the most recent work of James Scott (*The Art of Not Being Governed*), but in it he reduces his studies to rural areas and argues that that world no longer exists. In Latin America, I know only of Alejandro Moreno's work on peripheral areas of Caracas, the Peruvian group PRATEC on rural communities, some of Silvia Rivera's studies of the urban Aymara, some by Luis Tapia (who is also from Bolivia), Rodrigo Montoya on the Quechua in Lima, and a few more. In some senses, all the theoretical work of Subcomandante Marcos points in that direction, insofar as it shows that another world exists down below and to the left and that, to see it, books are no help but rather active participation in the educational, health, productive, and decision-making processes of the communities.

I think the worst thing we can do is try to understand this reality based on concepts such as social movements, because this involves applying categories alien to what we are trying to comprehend. I find it striking that thinkers dedicated to decolonization still insist on this view of reality. Incidentally, this is not just a problem for intellectuals and activists from the North—it often occurs in the South as well. It would appear that the remarkable cycle of struggles that we have lived through between the 1990s and 2000 have not transformed the intellectual certainties and acquired politics of these thinkers, as if revolutionary theory was impervious to reality. Ultimately there is an epistemological problem, rooted in determining how, when, and where it is possible to learn. I think the moment of revolt is that which illuminates the other society, which returns to going unnoticed when the rebellion dissipates. Taking that moment as an epistemological axis supposes an understanding *in* movement, *in* the spaces of revolt, *in* its time, and this completely dismantles sociology and institutional politics.

I think that Indian practice challenges important elements of Western revolutionary concepts. I do not see non-Indian intellectuals who are willing to give Indian collective action and reflection the status of revolutionary theory, despite having shown their capacity for combativeness and transformation. Apparently only state-centric practices are theorizable. I ask what a theory of revolution would look like if the *tabula rasa* was set aside and the Pachakutik taken seriously, for example. What would rebellious thought—better to say rebellious than revolutionary—look like if it held that the masculine and feminine are complementary rather than antagonistic opposites? Ultimately, how could we go beyond the dialectic, avoiding the concept of syntheses, which is non-existent in the Indian cosmovision, and work with other categories? Marx has said that the new world exists within the old and could think in non-exclusory terms, which is to say non-dialectically, but this now seems very strange in the small critical circles that are more familiar with Deleuze and Nietzsche than with Felipe Quispe and Luis Macas.

Indigenous Movements

In many parts of Latin America, indigenous movements have played a particularly inspirational role in this latest wave of mobilization, and one could certainly argue that the organizational innovations of these movements have been central to the effectiveness of this wave. (The Zapatista Good Government Councils and El Alto's Neighborhood Councils are just two examples that come to mind in this regard.) That is, whether in Southern Mexico, Bolivia, Chile, or Colombia, it certainly seems that since the seventies indigenous movements have moved from the position of a marginalized sector, even within the left, to the central protagonists of social change throughout the region. What might account for the notable success of these movements? What in your opinion have been the greatest fruits of this shift? In what ways do you think that the indigenous left and, perhaps more importantly, the non-indigenous left have changed in recent decades in order to make this outcome possible?

It's hard to say. Honestly, to explain a change of this magnitude, which is so deep and complete, and that resulted in the triumph of the community against the association, to put it in a few, overly schematic words, one cannot appeal to the political scenario. I think that there has been a turning point in history in the last half century, certainly in Latin America, that is related not only to the social sectors but also to something we can more correctly describe as civilizational.

The question is, why, after five centuries of repression, genocide, marginalization, cultural assimilation, and domestication, do indigenous peoples emerge with so much capacity to act? Clearly there are many possible answers and one single argument would not be satisfactory. I think there are long-term changes, such as the installation of community logic, to which we should add the short-term like the neoliberal reforms that forced the other world to move in order not to disappear. Perhaps a dialogue between the short and the long-term can help us understand these changes.

Perhaps most significant is that what I call community logic, or the Indian cosmovision, relates empathetically with the worlds that arise from non-Indians, specifically in peripheral urban neighborhoods. For example, if we look at the slums of Buenos Aires, where two million people—or 15 to 20 percent of the city—live, we find that indigenous ways of doing things are now common sense within popular barrio organizations. When the population of these barrios build churches, they do so through *minga* (community work), whether they are Paraguayans, Bolivians, or Argentines from the North, because this is the most practical way to address such challenges. The festivals are community based and the names of churches and festivals are indigenous, although a substantial part of the population is not Indian. I mean to say that ethnicity is not that important, and that what should be taken into account are the ways of doing things and the collective practices, which are undoubtedly communitarian. We find a sort of mixture between practices associated with the Christian world (such as base communities) and others linked to the Indian and also rural world, which are experiencing a strong interpenetration. This sector is now the most active, even in countries like Argentina and Chile. What we can learn pertains to that other way of doing, of face-to-face ties, that leads us not to create instrumental organizations but rather bodies in which people are not the means but the ends.

Social Movements and Progressive Governments

The core dynamic of left politics in Latin America in the last decade is often posed in the relationship between social movements and progressive governments. Many emphasize (rightly, in our view) that the leftist governments all came to power riding on the backs of social movements. We are more interested, though,

in your views about the relationship after power is won. We rec-
ognize at least three widely expressed conceptions about the form
this relationship should take. First is the hegemonic position that
sees the progressive government as the primary directive force and
the social movements as secondary, aiding the pursuit of its poli-
cies. Second is the collaborative position, which argues that the
state and the social movements should come together as much
as possible to pursue united projects. Some of the authors in this
collection, however, such as Roland Denis and the Grupo Acon-
tecimiento, argue for a third option, an otra política *in which the*
social movements would maintain their autonomy from state di-
rection and projects. How do you understand the current dynam-
ic between progressive governments and social movements? What
stance do you think social movements should take with respect to
progressive governments?

I sympathize with the position of Denis and the Acontecimiento Group, in the sense that social change and a truly different politics cannot come from governments but rather must
come from the diverse sectors from below. However, there is a
significant problem that we are just beginning to perceive: The
movements are already other when progressive governments
come to power. One cannot keep thinking about those movements because they have already changed and therefore their
relation to the governments is not the same as it was when
they fought alongside leftists on the barricades.

By definition, a movement exists against or in conflict
with a government: To put it more accurately, it is that conflict
that gives form and life to the movement. During this period,
the groups that are the least impacted by the state and the market, or by its social policies and consumerism, are the most active. Often they create other organizations, like the young hip
hoppers from Quito, or the Amazonian Indians who oppose
extractivism like the Yupka from Venezuela, and so on in all
the different countries. It usually happens that the sectors that
were at the head of things during a cycle of struggle are the
most privileged by the new government and thus become its
most sympathetic supporters.

The thing to understand is that a substantial part of the movements of the nineties—not all but a decisive part—have become key to the new form of government. And, therefore, new movements are emerging out of that relationship, because the new way of governing has been built halfway between progressive forces and social movements. I do not criticize this relationship, and I'm not against what the Madres de Plaza de Mayo are doing today, but it is clear that stronger creativity is emerging in other spaces.

State Power
What do you consider the primary dangers and benefits that come with achieving state power? Has winning state power been in some ways and in some cases a poisoned gift, or has it been simply one further step in the project of the movements?

I usually say that to understand what happens we have to look at three scenarios: inter-state relations (or the question of governments); the relationship between social movements and states (or the question of emancipation); and the relationship between development and good living (or post-development). If we look at the state question, the existence of progressive governments is very positive because what is at stake is the relationship with the United States and big multinationals from the North. These questions accentuate the crisis of imperialist domination. However, if we look at the issue of emancipation or development, these governments represent a step backward.

The problem is that some social and political forces are destined to become managers of the state. Brazil's Partido dos Trabalhadores [Workers' Party] and the Frente Amplio, which emerged out of the labor movement, started winning municipalities, and then joined the government, focuses necessarily on the state. Even Brazil's landless movement fails to think beyond change through the state, although their actual practice is much richer than their articulate political views. This is the case for the MAS of Bolivia as well, which comes out of the coca growers' unions, and not the ayllus of the Altiplano.

There are two logics or approaches: that of the union which has a tradition inherited from the COB and the 1952 revolution, and that of the reconstruction of the Aymara nation, which is based in katarismo. But this perspective spans over the long term and does not give answers to the problems of today, and this is the reason why it was defeated by the MAS.

To solve the problems of today, one must be in government. The problem is when continuities with the colonial state, with the old political way, begin to emerge. The left has still not understood the limits of the nation state, including that the state cannot be re-founded. That is the historical significance of the December 26 *gasolinazo* protests in Bolivia, of a state that wants to be strong but is impeded because those from below will not tolerate being treated or addressed as before. This leads to a situation of permanent crisis, because on a national level the governments are not going to rule in favor of the social movements, because post-state institutions have still not being born.

Developmentalism

Some observers criticize the progressive governments in Latin America of repeating the old economic strategies of modernization, especially in terms of export strategies regarding the extraction industries such as petroleum and the monocultural agricultural production of crops such as soy. Do you see developmentalism or neo-developmentalism as a significant danger? Do you see in practice or can you imagine beneficial economic alternatives to development or, perhaps better, alternative forms of development that break with the old strategies of modernization and focus instead on the development of not only economic but also social and community goods? Could we redefine the concept of development to make it adequate to our contemporary political projects? Does the concept of buen vivir *[good living] indicate such an alternative?*

The main problem of growth based on the export of commodities—that is, extractivism—is that it generates exclusion. There are no workers in its production; in fact, there are very few in either the production of soybeans or in mining, and consumers are not needed because everything is exported. So we have a huge growth in production, while maintaining inequality and increased levels of informal and black market employment. Without compensatory social policies, this kind of growth will inevitably produce social conflicts. Furthermore, this type of production favors large foreign multinationals or, in some cases, Brazilian companies.

Small rural farmers are losing the struggle for the land and agribusiness is winning. Governments are subject to the economic cycle of fluctuating prices for raw materials, which is leading us up a blind alley, except, once again, in Brazil, because when the cycle of high prices terminates, there will be no alternative and once again prosperity will remain in few hands. I understand the government officials when they say they need money to pay their bills, which leads them to accept this economic model. But I do not agree at all when they claim that extractivism is good, thereby bypassing the debate on how to find and build alternatives.

In fact, the main problem is that we have don't have any alternatives. The *buen vivir* is something declarative, something with which I agree completely, but it has no relation to reality. The only country in Latin America to have another model is Cuba and, as we know, it is not a model for others because, among other things, it would produce a generalized impoverishment of the middle classes. At this moment of systemic, civilizational crisis, the great challenge for anti-systemic movements is to find non-capitalist ways of producing and living. I truly believe that we are still far from that. Throughout history there have been periods of systematic crisis in which no alternatives emerged, as in the long transition from antiquity to feudalism, for instance. We are in the early stages of the decomposition of the current system, and I think it will have to go much deeper and for much longer before different forces are born. As far as I can see, we still have a long way to go. Some settlements of the landless movement in Brazil serve as an inspiration, as well as the Caracoles in Chiapas, but the system is still very powerful and capable of reigning in members of these movements with the illusion of a better life offered by capitalism.

In summary, I believe that a profound revolution or cultural mutation is needed if we are to find an alternative to developmentalism, one that will change the way we sense wealth and poverty, life and death, time and space, the human and non-human, and so on. There is a need to establish non-hierarchical, complementary relationships that are not mutually exclusive, for humans to return to the simple life and in hopes of living in harmony with others and oneself. The buen vivir goes in that direction, but those who practice it, like some Andean and Amazon communities, are impoverished minorities that do not excite anyone, even the intellectuals who formulated the constitutions of Bolivia and Ecuador, within which these concepts are so important.

Indigenous Alternatives

The indigenous aspects of this latest wave of movements has also been particularly interesting in that it has been quite productive of new modes of thinking. Some might even claim that the indigenous movements have been the most "radical" in that through their conceptual production they pose the question of a "civilizational"—rather than a strictly "economic" or "political"—impasse and thus claim to offer alternatives beyond the imagined given political spectrum. For example, how might the concept of Pachakutik open spaces for action that are simply not available given the liberal notion of "progress" or the more Marxist inflected idea of "revolution?" How has this conceptual development altered the nature of political struggle in Latin America? Do you see that they have had a practical effect within the actions of the movements themselves? Have they been taken into account or implemented by any of the current governments?

The Indian movement brings several issues to the table. The first is its conception of time, the present-past relationship. The second is the idea of social change or revolution, the Pachakutik, in respect to the tabula rasa as I said. The third relates to rationalism and the relationship between means and ends, which involves ideas of strategy and tactics and also the

question of program and plan. These are some of the corner-
stones of modern revolutionary action that the Indian cosmovision questions in practice, although in most cases it is not
explicitly formulated.

On the first issue, an Indian leader from Ecuador says,
"We walk in the footsteps of our ancestors." This means that
the past—not a modernist future—inspires action. The past
is not dead, as Marcos says in *Votan Zapata*, a central Zapatista text. This questions the very roots of enlightenment
revolutionary theory, both Marxist and anarchist, which are
forward-looking theories. One could say that French revolutionaries looked back in order to make the Phrygian cap a
symbol, but always looked toward the future theoretically—
"to construct a different future" out of the revolutionary rupture. The three concepts to which I refer are summarized in
that statement.

If the revolution looks to the past, it is because it is looking to balance what has become unbalanced, not to create a
new world. It becomes more like placing something back on
its feet, to put it back in order—not in the sense of state order
but rather in cosmic order—to align ourselves with the higher
order that is the world or nature or the cosmos, depending on
what one chooses to call it. And here the second issue appears,
the Pachakutik. Since what is important is not the creation of
something new but rather restoring equilibrium, the Pachakutik is the return, the return of what has been marginalized,
separated, or hidden. This can refer to the Indian world itself,
or the lost equilibrium, or a concept of non-linear but cyclical
time, because the revolution/Pachakutik is the beginning of
a new/old cycle, the end of something and the beginning of
something else, not like the tabula rasa but more akin to the
restoration of what has been lost/forgotten. I have said that
this resonates with ideas expressed in Marx's *The Civil War in
France*, particularly when he reviews the Paris Commune and
says that the workers have no ready-made utopias to introduce
but rather must "set free" the other world that already exists
within the collapsing bourgeois society. Here the revolution
does not create anything new, but gives birth, as Marx says,

to something that already exists in embryonic form, because one cannot give birth to something that does not exist. The revolution is not something created but that which is brought forward and, in this sense, relates to the Pachakutik.

The third issue relates to what Marcos says when he argues that the means are the ends, using our language to question modern rationalism. I think this says at least two things: that society is not planned as if it were the mud with which God formed Adam and Eve, but something much more complex and unpredictable. It also confronts us with a double challenge: to question the colonial subject/object relationship and the idea that someone may shape the future as if it were an object. If the means are the ends, it is because there are no ends beyond an ethic of doing good or of good governance, which is the same thing. This has nothing to do with the traditional idea of revolution or a new world, but rather with the other world that we must sustain, grow, give birth to, and so on.

Clearly, this touches on some Nietzschean themes, such as eternal return, the roll of the dice, and others, and I think this is a very fertile field for reflection that can help us think about how we can relate the best of the West with the best of the East, as pointed out by Anuar Abdel Malek. This dialogue between these two shores of civilization has its best chances in Latin America because that's where the two civilizations have co-existed for the longest period of time, in an asymmetrical relation, but co-existing nonetheless. The Zapatista movement is part of that from a theoretical and also practical point of view. It incorporates feminism, critical theory, autonomy, and other Western ideas. And are we willing to incorporate some of the Indian cosmovision? Here the challenge is ours, because otherwise we're trying to pass off the Zapatistas as the "Caudine Forks" of modern revolutionary theory and read it with Marxist, anarchist, post-modern, or whatever eyes. If we don't unseat our current position, we will see the indigenous struggle as merely an interesting contribution, almost cosmetic, and undoubtedly folklorist. But now is the best chance we have to thoroughly review everything that Western revolutionaries have done badly. Moreover, if we do not do it, the chances of overcoming capitalism will be greatly reduced.

Role of the Intellectual

Just as the recent wave of mobilization challenges the foquismo *that characterized much of the Latin American left even up until the eighties and the "mass insurrectionary" character of many of these new movements challenges the centrality of "guerilla warfare," so too a widespread critique of vanguardism has also led to a reassessment of the role of intellectual production within the movement. How have you seen the critique of vanguardism and new role of the intellectual play out in the various movements that you have analyzed? Has this new relation proved productive? How do you imagine a beneficial role between intellectual work and radical politics? Or perhaps, more precisely, how have you imagined the ways in which your own work can be inserted and has been into the larger panorama of struggle in which these movements participate?*

The social movements from below are in a period of transition in which the old ideas and ways of doing continue to exist but are weaker and have not yet been displaced by new ones. So party/vanguardism and autonomy/horizontalism are co-existing, to put it very simply. The important thing is that no one fully supports the notion of vanguardism, although quite a few still practice it. A few others criticize horizontalism, but in reality their practice is indebted to that style. As with all political cultures, transitions are slow, maddeningly slow, like glaciers.

I would not call myself an intellectual but rather an activist/militant and thinker/educator. It also sounds pretentious. But it starts from there. I started in 1969 as a militant in a Tupamaros' mass organization in high school and have been active ever since. Now, on the one hand, I write for newspapers and write books to earn a living while, on the other hand, I give workshops and training courses with new movements in various countries. Working with movements and militants allows me to ensure that the many ideas that come from us—meaning everyone who works in a similar direction—are the heritage of the many people in the movements. Of course, they use these words and ideas as they wish or as they can. There are many compañeros who speak of autonomy and horizontality and yet act as a vanguard; sometimes reality is hard and things are not as we imagine when we write or think.

I do not believe in the intellectual role as defined by Lenin or Gramsci: the intellectual who takes theory from outside and inserts it into the movement or the organic intellectual who is with the movement. I believe that movements form their own intellectuals, good or bad, but they do it, and that is very valuable. What I can do is contribute to their disappearance, as Marcos says about his role in the Zapatista Army. Two years ago, I took a course with peasants and groups from marginalized urban areas in Paraguay that aimed to create research groups that would enable militants attending the course to replicate it in their communities and neighborhoods. It worked and they can now oversee their own training, thereby facilitating the gradual dissolution of the external intellectual. Now we're doing the same in Uruguay with neighborhood groups. The starting point may seem similar, but the path we follow helps us leave the place from which we started.

A question of ethics, not of method, emerges here, because popular education has been institutionalized and now works in the service of progressive governments and is doing great harm. The issue is who is at the center. If the intellectual/political party is at the center, then its work will tend to consolidate that site; if the people in movement are at the center, then the intellectual tends to be only one among many others in the movement.

After all, what is movement? If it is organization or institution, then it functions in the traditional role. We are now arriving at other formulations of movement that prioritize the aspect of moving-of-itself, of moving away from identity and the inherited material and symbolic sites. This means that a real movement is one in which its members change place, something feminists and Indians teach us. Movement is not, like a workers' union, what confirms and screws the workers in place in relation to capital. This is why, as intellectuals, we must also put ourselves in movement and move ourselves from this place of being above the people.

Prospects for the Future?

The question of origin, which we addressed earlier, leads us also to ask about the end point. Are the essays we present in this volume, many of which were written five to ten years ago, primarily of historical interest, or are they politically relevant today? It seems to us that in regard to the historical trajectory of these movements, most commentators take one of two very different views. Some claim that the wave of movements was defined by a specific conjuncture, primarily characterized by struggles against neoliberal governments, and that we have thus now passed into a different period requiring different political practices. Others maintain that these movements are expressions of an epochal, rather than a conjunctural shift, and that the forms of power they contest remain in place and their mode of doing politics continues to be necessary. Do you consider the era of this wave of political movements to be over? Or, what might we expect from these or other movements in the near future? What do you see as the most promising initiatives by these various movements? And what do you think are their biggest obstacles to overcome in the near future?

The cycle of struggle has ended, as we have seen, but these movements have began a new era of social or class struggle that is still in its early stages. This new era is that of the self-construction of another world, without the need to go through the seizure of the state. This marks the main difference from previous periods. The axis of the struggles is changing radically, going from being focused on the state to concentrating on the areas where these new worlds are being constructed.

The most obvious case is that of the Zapatista Caracoles, where they have created a complex of bodies representing the new world: health clinics that combine the cure of pills, which is how they refer to allopathic medicine, and herbal medicines

' and other forms of treatment coming from the Indian world, such as bone healing; education with their primary and high schools where it is the community that decides what is taught and how; justice imparted by the Good Government Councils; production overseen by family and cooperatives, with trade and exchange in transparent markets where everyone relates equally because there is no monopoly; and community *fiestas* and entertainment, sports, and the Internet. I think the novelty of this other world is that it has been able to build supra-community forms of power, like the councils that are regional powers comprised of several municipalities, which bring together hundreds of communities in each one. And most importantly, they are non-state powers, with rotating positions, where everyone learns to govern. This is a historic achievement that has never before existed in the struggles of those below except during the sixty-nine days of the Paris Commune and the brief period of the Soviets before the Stalinist state reconstruction.

In the rest of Latin America, we have experiences that are not as complete and not so encompassing that they can be called new worlds; there are bits and pieces, or something similar to the threads of a tapestry that is being woven, and unraveling. In the landless movement settlements of Brazil, production is overseen in a different way, collectively, in some cases without the use of pesticides, and they are experimenting with new forms of interchange and education. In thousands of Andean communities, they produce use-values for non-capitalist markets; in some regions of the Bolivian Altiplano, the indigenous are experimenting with different forms of military power such as the Qalachaka headquarters that are based in hundreds of militarized communities. In the peripheries of Buenos Aires, Caracas, Bogotá, São Paulo, Salvador, and Asunción they produce, they teach, they provide health care, all collectively. There are hundreds of recuperated factories that teach how to produce in a non-Taylorist way, with minimal division of mental and manual labor. I think all this points toward the constitution of other societies, which are still in varying degrees of development.

There are multiple obstacles. The state and capital are doubtlessly among them—the first because of its social policies and the second because of its power of seduction. Both tend to dissolve alternative experiences. But the other world must erect material and symbolic defenses to keep going and grow. The material aspect consists of its physical ability to defend itself against the inevitable armed attack—to construct a non-centralized, non-hierarchical defensive apparatus that does not become a parasite on the emerging new world. As for symbolic defenses, it requires understanding a different culture, based upon practices that are unlike the hegemonic, with enough potency that the egomaniacal dreams of consumption and power with which capital appeals are dissolved by an ethics of life. In this regard we have advanced very little, while capital continues to seep into our minds and our hearts, infecting our bodies with an attraction so compelling that it is destroying not just humanity but also the planet itself. One overcomes this situation not by destroying capitalism, because capital is within us, but by developing a love for life, something that cannot be created artificially. Maybe that kind of love will only be reborn when humanity's fear of self-annihilation becomes so strong that it compels us to put a sense of responsibility before the whims of our desires.

REFERENCE LIST

ACERO, Gloria and María DALLE RIVE
1989 *Medicina indígena*, Abya Yala, Quito.
ACOSTA, Alfredo
2004 "Resistencia indígena ante una nueva invasión," in *La resistencia civil. Estrategias de acción y protección en los contextos de guerra y globalización*, PIUCP, Bogotá.
AGAMBEN, Giorgio
1998 *Homo sacer. El poder soberano y la nuda vida I*, Pre-Textos, Valencia.
2003 *Estado de excepción*, Adriana Hidalgo, Buenos Aires.
AMERICA'S WATCH
1991 *La "guerra" contra las drogas en Colombia*, Universidad de los Andes, Bogotá.
AMNESTY INTERNATIONAL
2004 *Colombia: un laboratorio de guerra. Represión y violencia en Arauca.*
ANTILLANO, Andrés
2005 "La lucha por el reconocimiento y la inclusión en los barrios populares: la experiencia de los comités de tierras urbanas," *Revista Venezolana de Economía y Ciencias Sociales*, Vol. 11, no. 3, Caracas.
2006 Interview, www.espacioalternativo.org /node/1698
ARISMENDI, Marina
2006 "Trabajar políticas sociales sobre un mismo plan," August 16, www.presidencia.gub.uy.
ASICA-SUR
2003 *Yaku al Sur*, bulletin, August, no. 2.
BALCAZZA, Mario and Jose Luis URBINA (Zanón workers)
2005 Author interview, Montevideo, December 1.
BANCO INTERAMERICANO DE DESARROLLO
2006 Seminar "La faceta ignorada de la violencia juvenil: estudios comparativos sobre maras y pandillas," October 6, http://www.joveneslac.org/portal/000/violencia/BID-seminario-violencia-juv-octubre06.pdf.
BANGO, Julio
1999 "Ponencia: Jóvenes, formación y empleo," www.cinterfor.org.uy.
2000 "Políticas sociales y políticas de juventud," *Revista*

Iberoamericana de la Juventud, www.iica.org.uy

BELLINGHAUSEN, Hermann
2004 "La fiesta zapatista de la educación abre paso a una *enseñanza verdadera*," *La Jornada*, México, August 7.
2006a "Llama Marcos a juntar las luchas dispersas, para transformar el país," México, *La Jornada*, January 25.
2006b"Los procesos de autonomía nos mantienen en pie," México, *La Jornada*, February 9.
2006c "Los zapatistas nos enseñaron a revalorar nuestro sentido del futuro," México, *La Jornada*, February 11.

BENGOA, José
2000 *Historia del pueblo mapuche*, LOM, Santiago.

BENSAID, Daniel
2005 "Teoremas de la resistencia a los tiempos que corren," *Globalización*, www.antroposmoderno.com.

BLANCO, C.G.
2005 "Mara Salvatrucha 13," *Instituto Nueva Mayoría*, August 5.

BLONDET, Cecilia and Carmen TRIVELLI
2004 *Cucharas en alto*, IEP, Lima.

BOGADO, Aura
2006 "Entrevista con el subcomandante Marcos," www.rebelion.org.

BORAZ, Steven and Thomas BRUNEAU
2006 "La Mara Salvatrucha y la Seguridad en América Central," *Military Review*, November–December.

BOURDIEU, Pierre
1999 *La miseria del mundo*, FCE, Buenos Aires.

BRECHA
2000 "La desaparición del Estado," Montevideo, May 5.
2003 "Encuentro de huertas urbanas. De sembrar y cosechar," Montevideo, November 7.

BRETÓN SOLO, Víctor
2001a *Cooperación al desarrollo y demandas étnicas en los Andes ecuatorianos* Flacso, Quito.
2001b "Capital social, etnicidad y desarrollo: algunas consideraciones críticas desdelos Andes ecuatorianos," *Yachaikuna*, no. 2, ICCI, Quito.

BREVÉ, Federico
2007 "Las Maras: Desafío Regional," *Military Review*, March–April.

BROWN, Ross A.
2007 "La evaluación de un comandante: Bagdad del Sur," *Military Review*, May–June.

BURBACH, Roger
2007 "Ecuador's Nascent Leftist Government Victorious in Confrontation with Right," *Countercurrents*, March 26.

CAFARDO Analía and Paula DOMÍNGUEZ
2003 *Autogestión obrera en el siglo XXI*, Centro Cultural de la

Cooperación, *Cuaderno de Trabajo*, no. 27, Buenos Aires.

CALDART, Roseli Salete
2000 *Pedagogia do Movimento Sem Terra*, Vozes, Petrópolis.

CALDÓN, José Domingo
2004 "Pueblos indígenas y resistencia a la guerra," in *La resistencia civil. Estrategias de acción y protección en los contextos de guerra y globalización*, PIUCP, Bogotá.

CAUJA, Adriana
2004 "Movimiento indígena, trayecto difícil," *Jatarishun* (Levantémonos), CONAIE, July.

CASTELLS, Manuel
1986 *La ciudad y las masas*, Alianza, Madrid.

CECEÑA, Ana Esther
2006 "2006: entre la promesa y la tragedia," *OSAL*, no. 20, May–August. Clacso, Buenos Aires.

CHIARELLI, Peter W.
2005 "Lograr la paz: el requisito de las operaciones de espectro total," *Military Review*, November–December.

CHUJI GUALINGA, Mónica
2004 "Asamblea Extraordinaria de la Confeniae," www.alainet.org

CLASTRES, Pierre
2004 *Arqueología de la violencia: la guerra en las sociedades primitivas*, Fondo de Cultura Económica, Buenos Aires.

COLECTIVO SITUACIONES
2002 *19 y 20. Apuntes para el nuevo protagonismo social*, De mano en mano, Buenos Aires.
2005 *Bienvenidos a la selva. Diálogos a partir de la Sexta Declaración del EZLN*, Tinta Limón, Buenos Aires.

CONTRERAS, Mariana
2003 "De sembrar y cosechar," *Brecha*, November 7, Montevideo.

CORPORACIÓN TALIBER
1998 "Potosí-La Isla. Historia de una lucha," Bogotá.

COSTA, Luix
2006 "Conmemoración de las Reducciones guaraníticas," February 19, www.sinpermiso.info.

CRIC (CONSEJO REGIONAL INDÍGENA DEL CAUCA)
1988 *Cartilla de Legislación Indígena*, CRIC, Cali.

DÁVALOS, Pablo
2001 "El ritual de la 'toma'en el movimiento indígena," in Leonela CUCURELLA and Kintto LUCAS (eds.), *Nada solo para los indios*, Abya Yala, Quito.
2001 "Movimiento indígena ecuatoriano. La constitución de un actor político," *Cuestiones de América*, no. 7, November, www.cuestiones.ws.
2002 "Movimiento indígena ecuatoriano: construcción política y epistémica," in Daniel MATO (ed.) *Estudios y otras prácticas*

interculturales latinoamericanas en cultura y poder, Clacso, Caracas.
2007a "Movimientos ciudadanos, Asamblea Constituyente y neoliberalismo" January 16, www.alainet.org.
2007b Author interview, April 12, Montevideo.

DAVIS, Mike
2001 *Control urbano: la ecología del miedo*, Virus, Barcelona.
2006a "De la ciudad de Blade Runner a la de Black Hawk," interview, July 30, www.sinpermiso.info.
2006b "La pobreza urbana y la lucha contra el capitalismo," interview, July 25, www.sinpermiso.info.
2006c "La ciudad imperial y la ciudad miserable," interview, May 21, www.sinpermiso.info.
2007 "Los suburbios de las ciudades del tercer mundo son el nuevo escenario geopolítico decisivo," *Rebelión*, March 2, www.rebelion.org.

DE OLIVEIRA, Francisco
2006 "A política interna se tornou irrelevante," *Folha de São Paulo*, July 27, San Pablo.

"DECLARATION OF QUITO"
1990 in *El levantamiento indígena y la cuestión nacional*, Comisión por la Defensa de los Derechos Humanos, Abya Yala, Quito.

DEGREGORI, Carlos Iván and Romeo GROMPONE
1991 *Demonios y redentores en el nuevo Perú*, IEP, Lima.

DELEUZE, Gilles y Félix GUATTARI
1994 *Mil mesetas*, Pre-Textos, Valencia.

DÍAZ, Miguel
2007 "La otra guerra que Washington no está ganando," *Instituto Nueva Mayoría*, March 16.

DÍAZ POLANCO, Héctor
1997 *La rebelión zapatista y la autonomía*, Siglo XXI, México.

DÍAZ POLANCO, Héctor and Consuelo SÁNCHEZ
2002 *México diverso*, Siglo XXI, México.

ECO-EDUCACIÓN Y COMUNICACIONES
2001 "Democracia y poder local," May, Santiago.

ENERO AUTÓNOMO
2003 "El movimiento en conjunto es quien cura," Taller de salud, www. lavaca.org.

ENGELS, Federico
1976 *El problema de la vivienda*, Akal, Madrid.

ESPINOSA, Yuderkys
1999 "¿Hasta donde nos sirven las identidades?," June, www.creatividadfeminista.org.

ESTEVA, Gustavo
2005 "Desarrollo del mandar obedeciendo: Chiapas y Oaxaca," in COLECTIVO SITUACIONES *Bienvenidos a la selva. Diálogos a partir de la sexta Declaración del EZLN*, Tinta Limón, Buenos Aires.

FAJN, Gabriel (ed.)
2003 *Fábricas y empresas recuperadas. Protesta social, autogestión y rupturas en la subjetividad*, Centro Cultural de Cooperación, Buenos Aires.

EZLN
Documentos y comunicados, Volumes 1, 2 and 3, (1994, 1995, 1997), Era, México.
2004 *La Marcha del Color de la Tierra*, Rizoma, México.
2005 *Sexta Declaración de la Selva Lacandona*, México, June, www.ezln.org.

FERNANDES, Bernardo Mançano
2000 *A formaçao do MST no Brasil*, Vozes, Petrópolis.
1996 *MST, formaçao e territorializaçao*, Hucitec, San Pablo.

FERNÁNDEZ DURÁN, Ramón
1996 *La explosión del desorden*, Fundamentos, Madrid.

FERRARA, Francisco
2004 "¿La clínica en el galpón?," mimeo, Buenos Aires.

FOUCAULT, Michel
2006 *Seguridad, territorio, población*, Fondo de Cultura Económica, Buenos Aires.

FREYERMUTH ENCISO, Gabriela
1993 *Médicos tradicionales y médicos alópatas*, Instituto Chiapaneco de Cultura, Tuxtla Gutiérrrez (Chiapas).

GARCÉS, Mario
2002a *Tomando su sitio. El movimiento de pobladores de Santiago, 1957–1970*, LOM, Santiago.

GARCÉS, Mario *et al.*
2002b *El mundo de las poblaciones*, LOM, Santiago.

GARCÍA DE LEÓN, Antonio
2002 *Fronteras interiores. Chiapas: una modernidad particular*, Océano, México.

GARCÍA LINERA, Álvaro
1999 *Reproletarización. Nueva clase obrera y desarrollo del capital industrial en Bolivia (1952–1998)*, Muela del Diablo, La Paz.
2001 "Multitud y comunidad: La insurgencia social en Bolivia," *Chiapas*, no. 11, Era, México.
2004 *Sociología de los movimientos sociales en Bolivia*, Diakonía/Oxfam, La Paz.

GILBERT, Alan
1997 *La ciudad latinoamericana*, Siglo XXI, México.

GILLY, Adolfo
2003 "Historia desde adentro: la tenaz persistencia de los tiempos," in HYLTON FORREST et al., *Ya es otro tiempo el presente*, Muela del Diablo, La Paz.
2005a "El restablecimiento neoliberal del orden," *La Jornada*,

México, June 22.

2005b "Navegar es necesario," *La Jornada*, México, 7 July.

GÓMEZ, Luis A.

2004 *El Alto de pie. Una insurrección aymara en Bolivia*, Comuna-Indymedia, La Paz.

GÓMEZ LEYTON, Juan Carlos

2006 "La rebelión de las y los estudiantes secundarios en Chile. Protesta social y política en una sociedad neoliberal triunfante," *OSAL*, no. 20, May–August.Clacso, Buenos Aires.

GONZÁLEZ, Fernán

2004 "Una mirada de largo plazo sobre la violencia en Colombia," *Bajo el volcán*, no. 7, Puebla.

GONZÁLEZ CASANOVA, Pablo

2006 "Una nueva forma de pensar y hacer," *La Jornada*, México, September 26.

GRADIN, Valeria et al.

2005 "Da un espacio a los jóvenes," Montevideo, www.liccom.edu.uy.

GRANDIDYER, Alan (President of ASICA-SUR)

2005 Author interview, June.

GRUPO IDENTIDAD DE MEMORIA POPULAR

2007 *Memorias de la Victoria*, Quimantú, Santiago.

GUERRERO, Fernando y Pablo OSPINA

2003 *El poder de la comunidad. Ajuste estructural y movimiento indígena en los Andes ecuatorianos*, CLACSO, Buenos Aires.

GUHA, Ranajit

2002 *Las voces de la historia*, Crítica, Barcelona.

GUTIÉRREZ, Raquel

2004 "Bolivia: El temblor viene de abajo, carajo," *Ojarasca, La Jornada*, November 8.

HARRIS, Olivia

1987 "Economía étnica," Hisbol, La Paz.

HARVEY, David

2003 *Espacios de esperanza*, Akal, Madrid.

HERNÁNDEZ NAVARRO, Luis

2004a "Autonomia sin pedir permiso," *La Jornada*, México, September 7.

2004b "Desarrollo desde abajo," *La Jornada*, México, September 28.

2006a "El romper de la ola," *La Jornada*, México, Febraury 14.

2006b "Oaxaca: sublevación y crisis de un sistema regional de dominio," *OSAL*, no. 20, May–August. Clacso, Buenos Aires.

HERNÁNDEZ NAVARRO, Luis and Ramón VERA HERRERA (Eds.)

1998 Acuerdos de San Andrés, Era, México.

HIDALGO, Francisco

2001 "El movimiento indígena en el Ecuador," in CUCURELLA, Leonela y Lucas KINTTO (eds.), *Nada sólo para los indios*, Abya Yala, Quito.

HOLLOWAY, John
1997 "La revuelta de la dignidad," *Chiapas,* no. 3, Era, México.
HUENCHUNAO, José
1998 Interviewed by Sergio MAUREIRA, http://www.mapuche.info/
mapuint/Marinan980700.htm.
2007 "Carta abierta desde la cárcel de Angol," March 21, www.lavaca.
org.
HYLTON, Forrest and Sinclair THOMSON
2003 *Ya es otro tiempo el presente,* Muela del Diablo, La Paz.
INDYMEDIA ARGENTINA
2004 "Encuentro por la Resistencia desde la Diversidad," October 3,
http://argentina.indymedia.org.
KINTTO, Lucas
2007 "Endémica crisis institucional," March 8, www.ipsenespanol.
net.
LANDER, Edgardo
2000 "Ciencias sociales: saberes coloniales y eurocéntricos," in
LANDER, Edgardo (ed.), *La colonialidad del saber: eurocentrismo y
ciencias sociales,* Clacso, Buenos Aires.
LAVACA
2004 *Sin Patrón. Fábricas y empresas recuperadas por sus trabajadores,* Buenos Aires.
2006 "Estamos peor que en los 90," interview with Claudio Lozano,
www.lavaca.org.
LEE TELES, Anabel
2004 "Los gérmenes de nuevos modos de vida comunitaria," *Campo
Grupal,* no. 58, July, Buenos Aires.
LEFEBVRE, Henri
1972 *La vida cotidiana en el mundo moderno,* Alianza, Madrid.
1976 *Espacio y política,* Península, Barcelona.
LEFF, Enrique
1998 *Saber ambiental: sustentabilidad, racionalidad, complejidad,
poder,* Siglo XXI, México.
LEMOINE, Maurice
2007 "Ecuador, una victoria por consolidarse," *Le Monde Diploma-
tique,* January, Buenos Aires.
LIMPIAS ORTIZ, Víctor Hugo
2002 "Ciudad de El Alto: una aproximación a la arquitectura y el
urbanismo de la nueva metrópoli altiplánica," *Revista Arquitextos,*
www.vitruvius.com.
LIND, William S.
2005 "Comprendiendo la guerra de cuarta generación," *Military Review,* January–February.
LISCANO, Carlos
2000 "La desaparición del Estado," *Brecha,* May 5, Montevideo.

LLAITUL, Hectór
2007 Interviewed by Alvaro Hilario, April 24.
LOJKINE, Jean
1999 *La clase obrera hoy*, Siglo XXI, México.
LOMNITZ, Larissa A de.
1975 *Cómo sobreviven los marginados*, Siglo XXI, México.
LÓPEZ ECHUAGÜE, Hernán
2002 *La política está en otra parte*, Norma, Buenos Aires.
LOINGSIGH, Gearóid
2002 *La estrategia integral del paramilitarismo en el Magdalena Medio de Colombia*, www.prensarural.org.
MACAS, Luis
2002 "¿Cómo se forjó la Universidad Intercultural?," *Boletín Rimay*,
no. 19, October, ICCI, Quito.
MACAS, Luis y Alfredo LOZANO
2000 "Reflexiones en torno al proceso colonizador y las característi-
cas de la educación universitaria en el Ecuador," *Boletín Rimay*, October 19, ICCI, Quito.
MAGNANI, Esteban
2003 *El cambio silencioso*, Prometeo, Buenos Aires.
MALDONADO ALVARADO, Benjamín
2003 "Reflexiones sobre comunalidad y medicina indígena tradicio-
nal," www.antorcha.net
MAMANI RAMÍREZ, Pablo
2005 *Microgobiernos barriales*, Cades, El Alto.
MARX, Karl
1975 *El Capital*, Libro Primero, Vol. 1, Siglo XXI, Buenos Aires.
1980 *La guerra civil en Francia*, Progreso, Moscú.
MATE, Reyes
2006 *Medianoche en la historia. Comentarios a las tesis de Walter
Benjamin "Sobre el concepto de historia,"* Trotta, Madrid.
MATOS MAR, José
1989 "¿Informales o contestatarios?," in Carlos ARROYO, *Encuen-
tros, Historia y movimientos sociales en Perú*, Memoriangosta, Lima.
2004 *Desborde popular y crisis del Estado. Veinte años después*, Fondo
Editorial del Congreso del Perú, Lima.
MEDINA, Javier
2006 *Suma Qamaña*, Garza Azul, La Paz.
MERKLEN, Denis
1995 *Identidad y acción colectiva. Las ocupaciones ilegales de tierras
urbanas en la Argentina de fin de siglo*. Tesis de Maestría in Investigación en Ciencias Sociales. Universidad de Buenos Aires.
MIGNOLO, Walter
2001 "Descolonización epistémica y ética. La contribución de Xavier
Albó y Silvia Rivera Cusicanqui a la reestructuración de las ciencias

sociales desde los Andes," *Revista Venezolana de Economía y Ciencias Sociales*, Vol. 7, no. 3, Caracas.

2003 *Historias locales/diseños globales: Colonialidad, conocimientos subalternos y pensamiento fronterizo*, Akal, Madrid.

MILITARY REVIEW

2005 www.military.com, November–December.

MORENO, Alejandro

2000 "Superar la exclusión, conquistar la equidad: reformas, políticas y capacidades en el ámbito social," in LANDER, Edgardo (ed.), *La colonialidad del saber*, Clacso, Buenos Aires.

2006 *El aro y la trama. Episteme, modernidad y pueblo*, Ediciones USCH, Santiago.

MORISSAWA, Mitsue

2001 *A história da luta pela terra e o MST*, Expressao Popular, San Pablo.

MUÑOZ RAMÍREZ, Gloria

2004 "El Centro de Capacitación 'Compañero Manuel': ejemplo de autonomía, resistencia y encuentro," revista *Rebeldía*, no. 21–22, México, July–August.

2005 *El fuego y la palabra*, Tinta Limón, Buenos Aires.

MURACCIOLE, Jorge

2003 "Economía asamblearia en acción," *Proyectos 19/20*, no. 4, May–June.

MST

2001 "O que levar em conta para a organizaçao do assentamento," Cuaderno de Cooperación Agrícola, no. 10, Concrab, San Pablo.

MTD SOLANO AND COLECTIVO SITUACIONES

2002 *La hipótesis 891. Más allá de los piquetes*, De Mano en Mano, Buenos Aires.

MST (Movimento dos Trabalhadores Sem Terra)

1999 "Como fazemos a escola de educaçao fundamental," *Caderno de Educaçao*, no. 9, November.

NACHMAN, Eduardo Luis

2004 "Educación en tierras zapatistas," September, 2004, www.fzln.org.mx.

NATIONAL COORDINATOR IN DEFENSE OF WATER, BASIC SERVICES, THE ENVIRONMENT, AND LIFE

2006 "Declaración de la Coordinadora Nacional de Defensa del Agua, los Servicios Básicos, el Medio Ambiente y la Vida," Cochabamba, October.

NAVARRO, Fernanda

2005 "Reseña de una visita a Chiapas," *La Jornada* de Michoacán, México, March 14.

NEGRI, Antonio and Giuseppe COCCO

2006 "La insurrección de las periferias," April, www.

universidadnomade.net.

NOCHTEFF, Hugo y Nicolás GÜELL

2003 *Distribución del ingreso, empleo y salarios*, Instituto de Estudios y Formación de la CTA, Buenos Aires.

NUESTRA LUCHA

Periódico de los obreros ceramistas, www.obrerosdezanon.org

NUN, José

1969 "Sobrepoblación relativa, ejército industrial de reserva y masa marginal," *Revista Latinoamericana de Sociología*, July.

OBSERVATORIO   LATINOAMERICANO   DE   CONFLICTOS AMBIENTALES

1999 "Aproximación crítica al modelo forestal chileno," OLCA: Santiago.

OHOLEGUY, Cristina

2004 "El arte de sembrar," *Alternativas desde la diversidad. Saberes y prácticas de educación popular*, no. 13, Montevideo, Multiversidad.

OLIVERA, Oscar

2006 Author interview, Montvideo, October 30.

ORNELAS, Raúl

2004 "La autonomía como eje de la resistencia zapatista," México, unpublished.

PÁEZ, Pablo

2004 "'Ferias libres: espacios residuales de soberanía popular' de Gabriel Salazar," www.bifurcaciones.cl.

PÁGINA 12

2004 "Un jardín piquetero en La Matanza," Buenos Aires, May 5.

PATZI, Félix

"Rebelión indígena contra la colonialidad y la trasnacionalización de la economía: triunfos y vicisitudes del movimiento indígena desde 2000 a 2003, in HYLTON, Forrest et al., *Ya es otro tiempo el presente*, Muela del Diablo, La Paz.

PÉCAUT, Daniel

1987 *Orden y violencia: Colombia 1930–1954*, Siglo XXI, Bogotá.

PERRO MUERTO

2006 "La ciudadanía sin ciudadanos," Santiago.

PLATAFORMA COLOMBIANA DE DERECHOS HUMANOS, DEMOCRACIA Y DESARROLLO

2004 *Reelección: el embrujo continúa. Segundo año de gobierno de Álvaro Uribe Vélez*, Plataforma Colombiana de Derechos Humanos, Bogotá.

PORTES, Alejandro et al. (eds.)

2005 *Ciudades latinoamericanas*, Prometeo, Buenos Aires.

PORTO GONÇALVES, Carlos Walter

2001 *Geo-grafías. Movimientos sociales, nuevas territorialidades y sustentabilidad*, Siglo XXI, México.

2006 "A reinvençao dos territorios: a experiencia latino-americana e caribenha," in Ana Esther CECEÑA, *Los desafíos de las emancipaciones en un contexto militarizado*, Clacso, Buenos Aires.

PORTOCARRERO, Gonzalo and Isidro SORAYA
1991 *Sacaojos. Crisis social y fantasmas coloniales*, Tarea, Lima.

POVEDA, Pablo
2003 "Trabajo, informalidad y acumulación: Formas de producción y transferencia de excedentes de la industia manufacturera boliviana," *Cuaderno*, no. 30, Cedla, La Paz.

QUIJANO, Aníbal
1977 *Imperialismo y "marginalidad" en América Latina*, Mosca Azul, Lima.
1988 *Modernidad, identidad y utopía en América Latina*, Sociedad y Política, Lima.
2000 "Colonialidad del poder, eurocentrismo y América Latina," in LANDER, Edgardo (ed.), *La colonialidad del saber, eurocentrismo y ciencias sociales*, Clacso, Buenos Aires.
2006 "Estado-nación y 'movimientos indígenas' en la región andina: cuestiones abiertas," *OSAL*, no. 19, January–April, Clacso, Buenos Aires.

RAMÍREZ, Jesús
2005 "Más allá del sistema político," in COLECTIVO SITUACIONES, *Bienvenidos a la selva. Diálogos a partir de la sexta Declaración del EZLN*, Tinta Limón, Buenos Aires.

RAMÓN VALAREZO, Galo
1993 *El retorno de los runas*, Comunidec, Quito.

RANCIÉRE, Jacques
2002 *El maestro ignorante*, Laertes, Barcelona.

REGALSKY, Pablo
2003 *Etnicidad y clase. El Estado boliviano y las estrategias andinas de manejo de su espacio*, Plural, La Paz.

REVILLA, Marisa
1991 "Chile: actores populares en la protesta nacional 1983–1984," *América Latina Hoy*, vol. 1, July, Salamanca.

RIVERA CUSICANQUI, Silvia
1983 "Luchas campesinas contemporáneas en Bolivia: el movimiento katarista: 1970–1980," in René ZAVALETA MERCADO (ed.), *Bolivia hoy*, Siglo XXI, México.
1990 "El potencial epistemológico y teórico de la historia oral: de la lógica instrumental a la descolonización de la historia," *Temas Sociales*, no. 11, La Paz.
1992 *Ayllus y proyectos de desarrollo en el norte de Potosí*, Aruwiyiri, La Paz.
1996 *Bircholas*, Editorial Mama Huaco, La Paz.
2004 "Metáforas y retóricas en el levantamiento de octubre," *Bolivien*

Studies Journal, Vol. 4, no. 1.

RODRÍGUEZ, Alfredo y Ana SUGRANYES
2005 *Los con techo. Un desafío para la política de vivienda social,* Ediciones SUR, Santiago.

ROJAS, Bruno y Germán GUAYGUA
2003 "El empleo en tiempos de crisis," Avances de Investigación, no. 24, Cedla, La Paz.

ROMERO, José Luis
1976 *Latinoamérica, las ciudades y las ideas,* Siglo XXI, Buenos Aires.

SAAVEDRA, Luis Ángel
2003 Interviewed by Alexia Guilera Madariaga, Agencia Prensa Rural, November 26, http://www.prensarural.org/alexia20031126.htm.

SALAZAR, Gabriel y Julio PINTO
1999 *Historia contemporánea de Chile II. Actores, identidad y movimiento,* LOM, Santiago
2002a *Historia contemporánea de Chile IV. Hombría y feminidad,* LOM, Santiago.
2002b *Historia contemporánea de Chile V. Niñez y juventud,* LOM, Santiago.

SALETE CALDART, Roseli
2002 *Pedagogia do Movimento Sem Terra,* Vozes, Petrópolis.

SALGADO RUIZ, Henry
2004 "Plan Colombia: ¿Guerra contra las drogas o contra las poblaciones amazónicas?," *Bajo el volcán,* no. 7, Universidad Autónoma de Puebla, Puebla.

SALUD REBELDE
2004 www.solidaridadesrebeldes.kolgados.com.ar.

SARMIENTO, Libardo
1996 *Un modelo piloto de modernización autoritaria en Colombia,* CREDHOS, Barrancabermeja.

SANABRIA, Mauricio
2007 Author interview, Bogotá, November 1.

SCHERER, Julio
2001 "La entrevista insólita," *Proceso,* México, March 11.

SCOTT, James
2000 *Los dominados y el arte de la resistencia,* México, ERA.

SEOANE, José and Clara ALGRANATI
2006 "Los movimientos sociales en la geopolítica continental," *OSAL,* no. 19, January–April. CLACSO, Buenos Aires.

SEOANE, José and Emilio TADDEI
2004 "Movimientos sociales, democracia y gobernabilidad neoliberal," *OSAL,* no. 15, September–October. Clacso, Buenos Aires.

SKEWES, Juan Carlos
2005 "De invasor a deudor: el éxodo desde los campamentos a las viviendas sociales en Chile," in RODRÍGUES and SUGRANYES, *Los*

con techo. Un desafío para la política de vivienda social, Ediciones SUR, Santiago.

SOPRANSI, María Belén
2004 *Nuevos movimientos sociales y salud*, Buenos Aires, mimeo.

SOPRANSI, María Belén y Verónica VELOSO
2004 "Contra la subjetividad privatizada: la creación de lo colectivo, *Herramienta*, no. 27, Buenos Aires.

SUBCOMANDANTE INSURGENTE MARCOS
2003a "El mundo: siete pensamientos en mayo de 2003," *Rebeldía*, no. 7, May, México.
2003b "La treceava estela," México, August, www.ezln.org.
2004 "Leer un video, México, August, www.ezln.org.
2005a "Palabras finales en la reunión con organizaciones y movimientos sociales," August 21, www.fzln.org.mx.
2005b "Plenaria del 16 de setiembre de 2005," *Rebeldía*, no. 35, September, México.

SVAMPA, Maristella
2004 "Cinco tesis sobre la nueva matriz popular," *Revista de Estudios SobreCambio Social*, no. 15, Spring, http://lavboratorio. fsoc.uba.ar/textos/15_6.htm.

TAMAYO, Eduardo
2007 "Consulta popular se perfila como salida a la crisis," March 23, www.alainet.org.

TAPIA, Luis
2002 "Movimientos sociales, movimiento societal y los no lugares de la política," in *Democratizaciones plebeyas*, Muela del Diablo, La Paz.

THOMPSON, E. P.
1989 *La formación de la clase obrera en Inglaterra*, Volume 1, Crítica, Barcelona.

TOKESHI, Juan
2006 "Cambios socio-culturales, vivienda y urbanización in Lima," April, www.interculturalidad.org.

UNIDAD INDÍGENA
2004 periódico de la ONIC, no. 119, Septembér, Bogotá.

URIBE, María Teresa
2004 "El republicanismo patriótico" in *Reelección: el embrujo continúa. Segundo año de gobierno de Álvaro Uribe Vélez*, Plataforma Colombiana de Derechos Humanos, Bogotá.

VERMEREN P., CORNU L. y VERMEREN, Benvenuto A.
2003 "La actualidad de El maestro ignorante. Entrevista a Jacques Ranciére," *Cuaderno de Pedagogía*, no. 11, Libros del Zorzal, Buenos Aires, November.

WACQUANT, Loïc
2007a *Parias urbanos*, Manantial, Buenos Aires.
2007b *Los condenados de la ciudad. Gueto, periferias y Estado*, Siglo

XXI, Buenos Aires.

WALLERSTEIN, Immanuel

1996 *Después del liberalismo*, Siglo XXI, México.

1998 "Braudel y el capitalismo o todo al revés," in *Impensar las ciencias sociales*, Siglo XXI, México.

1999 *El legado de la sociología, la promesa de la ciencia social*, Nueva Sociedad, Caracas.

2001 (1999) *Conocer el mundo. Saber el mundo: El fin de la aprendido*, Siglo XXI, México.

2004 "Paz, estabilidad y legitimación: 1990–2025/2050," in *Capitalismo histórico y movimientos antisistémicos*, Akal, Madrid.

WALSH, Catherine

2004a "Las geopolíticas del conocimiento y colonialidad del poder. Entrevista a Walter Mignolo," in *Indisciplinar las ciencias sociales. Geopolíticas del conocimiento y colonialidad del poder. Perspectivas desde lo andino*, USAB/Abya Yala, Quito.

2004b "Geopolíticas del conocimiento y descolonización," *Ary Rimay*, no. 60, March, ICCI, Quito.

WEBER, Max

2002 *Economía y sociedad*, FCE, Madrid.

WILLIAMS, Raymond

2000 *Palabras clave*, Nueva Visión, Buenos Aires.

ZANÓN BAJO CONTROL OBRERO

2005 Folleto de la cooperativa Fasinpat, October.

ZIBECHI, Raúl

1999 *La mirada horizontal. Movimientos sociales y emancipación*, Nordan, Montevideo.

2003ᵃ *Genealogía de la revuelta, Argentina: una sociedad en movimiento*, Letra Libre, Buenos Aires.

2003b "Los movimientos sociales latinoamericanos: tendencias y desafíos," *OSAL*, no. 9, January, Clacso, Buenos Aires.

2005 "Los limites del neoliberalismo," *La Jornada*, January 3.

2006a *El arte de gobernar los movimientos*, unpublished.

2006b *Dispersar el poder*, Tinta Limón, Buenos Aires.

2006c *De multitud a clase. Formación y crisis de una comunidad obrera, Juan Lacaze (1905–2005)*, Multiversidad Franciscana, Montevideo.

2006d "Dilemas electorales de la CONAIE," *La Jornada*, April 14.

2010 *Dispersing Power: Social Movements as Anti-State Forces*, AK Press, Oakland.

ZULUAGA NIETO, Jaime

2003 "Colombia: entre la democracia y el autoritarismo," *OSAL*, no. 9, January, Buenos Aires.

INDEX

Symbols

9/11/2001 193
1968, Revolution of 194, 304, 311, 312

A

Abdel Malek, Anuar 329
affect 25, 56
affects 216
Agamben, Giorgio 193, 194, 201
agenda 86
Agnelo, Geraldo Majella 155, 291
agriculture
  crisis in 123
  industrial 123
  multinationals and 123, 124–125
  organic certification 124
agroecology 123–124
Alarcón, Fabián 180
alienation 17
Allende, Salvador 218
alliances 15
alternative medicine 34, 132
Americas Watch 163, 164
Amnesty International 163
Andean Free Trade Agreement (FTA) 278
Andean Oral History Workshop (THOA) 270–271
"another world is possible" 101
anti-capitalism. See non-capitalist social relations
Antillano, Andrés 245–246

Aquino, Joel 148
architecture 69, 121, 122–123, 137, 171–172, 214, 221–222, 224–225
Argentina 13, 62, 70, 84. See also assemblies; piqueteros
Agrarian Missions Movement 99
aguante 96
Barracas bakery 253–254, 255
Buenos Aires 85, 98
  mass expulsions of urban poor, 1977 65
Carapachay 96
Central de Trabajadores Argentinos (CTA) 73, 155
Cooperativa Asamblearia 99
Cordobazo (1969) 257
Cutral Co roadblocks (1996) 84
December 19–20, 2001 43, 79, 81, 98, 251, 268, 279, 309
El Aguante bakery 95–96
El Tigre 99
General Mosconi 84
IMPA 96
Madres de Plaza de Mayo 18, 230, 301, 312, 324
MOCASE 302
National Campesino Front 302
New Hope 96–97
Panificadora Cinco 96
Parque Indoamericano 317
Popular Assembly of Pompeya 95
Ronda de Pensamiento Autónomo 27

Sindicato de Obreros y Empleados Ceramistas de Neuquén
   102–103
solidarity economy in 97–100
Titrayjú 99
Union of Citizen Assemblies
   (UAC) 301, 315–316
Universities of Comahue (Neuguén) 104
University of Buenos Aires 104
Zanon 101–108
   Nuestra Lucha 105
Arguedas, José María 8
Arismendi, Marina 280
Arteaga, Rosalía 180
"asking we walk," 56–57
assemblies 96, 98, 252, 278–279
authoritarianism
consensual 309
autonomy 15, 43, 68, 73, 128–129,
   130, 139, 143, 152, 157, 177,
   211, 217, 221, 222, 234–235,
   293
   and difference 129
   as process 129
   material and political 127
   preservation of in contact with
      state apparatus 247–248
   production and social reproduc-
      tion 38
   state assault on 305–306
awti pacha 80
Ayala, Turbay 161
ayllu 271
Aylwin, Patricio 118

B
Bachelet, Michelle 117, 234, 299
Balcazza, Mario 102
Ballén, Sixto Durán 180
Bango, Julio 281–282
Bánzer, Hugo 84
Baptista, Asdrúbal 85
bare life 194

Barrantes, Alfonso 236–237
barter 97, 99
Bengoa, José 114
Benjamin, Walter 193
Bensaid, Daniel 43
Bernate, Evaristo 173–175
Betto, Frei 155
biopolitics 192–193, 197, 305
Bolivarian Alternative for the
   Americas 182
Bolivia 20, 76–78
   1952 revolution 29, 311, 312,
      325–326
   2000–2005 revolt 311
   Association for the Management
      and Production of Water and
      Sanitation (ASICA) 246–247
   Association of Community Wa-
      ter Systems in the South 247
   Aymara headquarters 85, 333
   Aymara uprising in September
      2000 18
   Bolivian Peasant Confederation
      (CSUTCB) 86
   COB 312
   Cochabamba
      water committees in 246–248,
         294
   El Alto 67, 69–72, 85, 246, 309
      neigborhood councils 73, 321
   gasolinazo protests 325
   gas war 83
   indigenous movements 39–40
   insurrection in 75, 79–80
   "masacre del valle" (Cochabam-
      ba, 1974) 84
   mass expulsions of miners, 1985
      65
   Movement Toward Socialism
      (MAS) 294, 324, 325
   National Coordinator in
      Defense of Water, Basic Ser-
      vices, the Environment, and
      Life 296
   NGOS and development 271

Plan 3000 302
Pulacayo Thesis written by the
    miners' union in 1947 311
Raqaypampa 30
Semapa 246, 247–248
September–October 2003 insur-
    rection 62, 69, 72
social movements 207–208
Tiahuanaco Manifesto 311
Unique Confederation of Rural
    Laborers of Bolivia (CSTUB)
    208
uprisings in 2003 and in 2005
    43
urban peripheries in 246–248
Villa Sebastián Pagador 246–
    247
Water War 14, 84, 247
bottom up 134–135, 136
Bourdieu, Pierre 203
Braudel, Fernand 8, 26, 98
Brazil 13, 20, 22, 121–125. See
    also landless movement,
    MST
agrovila 121–123
as economic power 316
as global economic power
    313–314
Asociação Nacional dos Trab-
    alhadores em Empresas de
    Autogestão (ANTEAG) 93
BNDES 314
Bolsa Familia 314
Cooperminas 93
Embraer 314
National Conference of Bishops
    155, 291
rubber tappers 14, 66, 78, 209
solidarity economy in 97
Workers' Party 290, 297
Workers' Party 324
"Zero Hunger" 197
Zero Hunger Plan 155
Bretón, Victor 273, 274–275
Bucaram, Abdalá 180

buen vivir 326, 327
bureaucracy 135, 302–303, 308
Bush, George H.W. 182
Bush, George W. 161

C
Calfunao, Waikilaj Cadim 109
Camdessus, Michel 184
capillarity 206, 208
    and the state 289, 304
capital flight 65, 70, 78, 87
capitalism 20, 39, 68, 135, 256,
    334, 334–335. See also
Caracazo 42, 45, 228, 244, 258,
    268, 299, 310
Castells, Manuel 203–204, 218
cattle industry 114
Caupolicán 115
centralization 41–42, 46, 47
Chávez, Hugo 181, 182–183, 243,
    244, 299, 313, 316
Chiarelli, Peter W. 191–192
children 17, 39, 173–174, 215,
    239–240
Chile 218–219. See also Mapuche
    Angelini group 112, 117
    Bosques Arauco 117
    Cañete 115
    Central Bank 112
    Chilavert 95
    Civility Assembly 231
    Commando of United Residents
        231
    Concertation 116–117, 118
    Corporación de la Madera 112
    dictatorship, end of 231
    dictatorship, protests against
        228–229
    Esteban Gumucio de Yungay
        Cultural Center 235
    FLACSO 314
    La Legua 235
    La Victoria 212–213, 214,
        215–216, 217, 218, 234–235
    Pedro Mariqueo Cultural

Center 234
Matte group 112
Pablo Quintriqueo 115
Primero de Mayo radio station 234
Safe Neighborhoods Program 235
Santiago 218
Settler Women's Movement 231
student protests 117, 234, 300
transportation struggles 117
Zanjón de la Aguada 211–212
Christianity 13. *See also* liberation theology
class 64, 209–210, 214
Clastres, Pierre 28, 319
Colectivo Situaciones 47, 57
Colombia 159–169
    authoritarian government of 161
    Barrancabermeja 165–166
    Bogotá 159–160, 171, 176–177
    Bogotá Sin Hambre 177
    Bogotazo (1948) 160
    Caracoli 177–178
    Cerros del Sur school 171, 173–178, 177–178
    Ciudad Bolivar 172, 175, 176
    COB 324–325
    Constitution of 1991 161
    CRIC 169
    demilitarized zones 166, 168
    drug traffickers 164
    ELN (National Liberation Army) 163, 172
    FARC (Revolutionary Armed Forces of Colombia) 163, 164, 169, 172, 182
    geography of 162–163
    geopolitical importance 160
    guerillas 162–163, 166–167
    homosexuals, repression of 165–166
    Indian Guards 168, 169
    indigenous movements 167–
    168, 169, 301
    Inredh 166
    JERUCOM 174
    Jerusalén 172, 174
    La Violencia 163
    M-19 guerrilla camps 172
    Magdalena Medio 164–165
    militarization of 159–162, 161–162, 164–166
    Minga 168–169, 301
    Ministry of Social Action 314
    National Indigenous Organization of Colombia (ONIC) 167
    oligarchy 160, 162, 163, 164
    paramilitaries 159, 163–164, 164–166, 178
    Peasant University of the Resistance 168
    Plan Colombia 161, 164–165, 166
    Potosi 176
    Potosí 171–178, 178
    Regional Indigenous Council of the Cauca (CRIC) 32, 167
    San José de Apartadó 168
    Second Meeting of Communities of Civil Resistance 168
    Statute of Security 161
    United Self-Defense of Colombia (AUC) 164
    war, effects of 160
colonialism 54
commitment 56
commodities 254, 256
commons 248
communication 46, 151
communitarian ties. *See* social ties
community 215–216, 250
    decomposition of 271
community gardens 249–251
community organization 173–177
competition 275
CONAIE (Confederation of Indigenous Nationalities of

Ecuador) 19, 27, 32, 86, 180,
181, 182, 276–278, 278, 308,
312
Second Congress 277
concentration 69
concentration camp 194, 204
control 160. *See also* new governance
cooperatives 99, 138, 253
co-optation 231–232, 233,
235–236, 272, 278, 279, 291,
294, 301, 315–316
of leadership by NGOs 275–276
coordination 19, 43–44
Corporation of Social Studies and
Education 221
Correa, Rafael 179–180, 181,
182–183, 184, 185, 186, 299,
312
counter-hegemonic economy. *See*
counter-summits 296
coyotes 138
creation 52
crisis 317, 325
crisis in Uruguay in the winter of
2002 62
Crusoe, Robinson 257
Cuba 326
Cuenca, Lucio 111
culture 16, 22

D
Dávalos, Pablo 185
Davis, Mike 190, 195, 198–199
debt 92
Declaration of Quito 211
decolonization 312–313, 320
deforrestation 112
deindustrialization 78, 92
Deleuze, Gilles 321
demands 83
demobilization 300
democracy 234–235, 235,
282–283, 309
and indigenous struggles 118

as defeat 231
as pacification 192
participatory 107–108
Denis, Roland 323
deterritorialization 65
of production 14
development 268, 324
as means of governance 270–
275
dialogue 282
Díaz Polanco, Héctor 274
dictatorships
legacy of 91–92
difference 70, 71, 76, 77, 88, 143,
211, 281
and autonomy 129
defense and affirmation of
83–85
discipline 75, 268–269
crisis of 304
dispersion 41–42, 69, 73, 88, 151,
297
displaced protagonists 82
displacement 9, 171, 172
division of labor 40–41
dollarization 186
domestic space 82
domestic violence 178
drug trafficking 164, 202–203,
258
Duhalde, Eduardo 268, 278

E
economic growth 202, 316
economic solidarity 238–239. *See
also* solidarity economy
economy
informal 225
Ecuador 13, 18, 20, 85, 179–186.
See also CONAIE
Alianza País 182–183
Christian Democratic Union
184
CONFENIAE 277
constituent assembly 179–180,

183, 184
Democratic Popular Movement
    182
dollarization 180, 186
Ecuarunari 276, 312
Free Trade Agreement with the
    United States 182
Guamote 274–275
indigenous movements 15–16,
    16, 179, 180, 181–182,
    274–278
Indigenous Peoples and Afro-
    Ecuadorian Development
    Project (PRODEPINE)
    272–273, 275
Institutional Renewal Party of
    National Action (PRIAN)
    184
Intercultural University of
    Indigenous Peoples and
    Nationalities 16, 27
middle classes 186
NGOS and development in 272
oligarchy 184–185
Pachakutik (party) 182, 278,
    290
Patriotic Society Party (PSP)
    184
political instability 179
political reform 185–186
Social Christian Party (PSC)
    181
Social Christian Party (PSC))
    184
Supreme Electoral Tribunal
    (TSE) 183–184
education 16–17, 21–30, 22, 23,
    25, 28, 40, 132, 136–138,
    171–172, 175, 177, 213,
    286–287, 315–316. See
    also popular education
and emancipation 26
contestation of 28
educational matrices 24
in movement 24, 26–27

reintegration 28
electoral politics 116, 150, 151,
    153, 157, 233, 234, 299
refusal of 233
elites 7, 162, 179, 197, 221, 244,
    267, 289, 295, 297, 303
El Salvador
    FMLN 310
emancipation 26, 37, 51
limits of 51–52
process 135
Engels, Frederick 198–199
epistemology 52, 320
equality 55
discourse of 64
ethnic economy 271
Eurocentrism 204, 318
everyday life 129
as mode of organization
    308–310
exclusion 16, 53–54, 55, 87,
    325–326
expansion 45
expression 79, 80
extractive industries 313,
    325–326
EZLN. See Zapatistas, EZLN

F
factories, recuperated 91–108,
    252
and egalitarianism 94–95
and unions 102–103
community support 104,
    104–105
in Argentina 94–108
in Brazil 93
indigenous solidarity 103, 104
linkages to community 95–97
self-organization of production
    105–108
support for culture 96–97
workplace safety 102, 104
factory occupations 94–95

fair trade 98
family 17, 38–39, 74
   as economic unit 71–72
Ferras, Daniel 103
First Continental Gathering of
   Indigenous Peoples (1990)
   211
First Latin American Gathering of
   Worker-Recuperated Facto-
   ries 105
food security 38, 122, 138, 176,
   236–237, 239, 249, 250
foquismo 310
Fordism 202, 307
Foucault, Michel 210, 268–270
fourth generation war 191–192
fragmentation. *See* dispersion
Franco 235
Franco, Carlos 226
Free Trade Area of the Americas
   (FTAA) 165
FTAA 167
Fujimori, Alberto 227, 237

G
Gaitán, Jorge Eliécer 160
Garcés, Mario 212, 218
García, Alan 237, 240, 301
García Linera, Alvaro 72,
   207–208
Garzón, Luis 176
Gelman, Juan 101
genocide 290, 301
gentrificaton 192
geography 162–163
globalization 87, 92, 146, 223
Gradin, Valeria 286
Gramsci, Antonio 331
Grupo Acontecimiento 323
Grupo Identidad de Memoria
   Popular 212
Guaraní Reductions 125–126
guerilla warfare 330
Guevarism 13, 311
Guha, Ranajit 44, 82, 87, 295

Gustavo Noboa 180
Gutiérrez, Lucio 154, 180–181,
   184, 186, 276, 277, 291, 293
Gutiérrez, Raquel 302

H
Habermas, Jürgen 282
Harvey, David 201
health care 31–35, 34–35, 41, 132,
   213, 332
hierarchy 18, 47, 83, 307
homogeneity 65–66, 74
homosexuality 165–166
horizontalism 19, 88, 283,
   307–309, 330
   illusion of 287
Huenchunao, José 109, 115,
   116–117
Hummes, Claudio 155, 291
hydroelectric industry 109–110,
   119

I
identity 16
immanence 269
indigenous movements 8, 13, 14,
   15, 16, 39, 64, 67, 167–168,
   167–169, 179, 180, 181–182,
   185, 210–211, 274–278, 301,
   311–312, 321–322, 327–329.
   See also Zapatistas; Mapuche;
   CONAIE
   "back seat driver" politics 81
   cosmovision 31–32, 54, 80, 261,
      320–321, 322, 327–328, 329
   economy 224, 271
   education in 22, 29
   health care in 31–32, 32–33,
      35–36, 133
   identity 76
   land struggles 200–201
   vs. concierto Indians 15
   women and 17
inequality 155, 292, 305

instability 7
insurrection 75
leaderless 73
intellectuals 16, 330–331
intensification 45
intensity 9
Inter-American Development
Bank (IDB) 235, 282, 314
International Labor Organization 118
International Monetary Fund (IMF) 181, 184
Iraq
US war on 191–192, 192

K

katarismo 84, 311–312, 313–314, 325
Keyserling, Hermann Graf 52
Kirchner, Néstor and Cristina 154–156, 156, 204, 270, 290, 291, 299, 313
knowledge 22, 55, 134
control and 285, 288
Ko Wo, Ruperto 148

L

labor
nonalienated 254–255
labor unions 7, 63, 68, 70, 82–83, 102–103, 196, 214, 307
Lagos, Ricardo 300
land 118–119, 121, 125–126, 139, 160, 173, 199, 211–212
reform 111, 291
seizure 211–212, 213–214, 217, 220–221, 223, 234, 312
and women 214
landless movement 8, 14, 15, 18, 22–23, 26, 62, 67, 175, 199, 324, 333
Movimiento dos Trabalhadores Rurais Sem Terra (MST) 16,

22, 28–29, 48–49, 121–125, 122, 156, 259, 293, 308
Filhos de Sepé (Sons of Sepé) settlement 121–125
language 7–8
Latin American Coordinating Agency of Campesino Organizations 122
Latin American Observatory of Environmental Conflicts (OLCA) 111
Lautaro 113
law 193–194
"lead by obeying" 144
leaderless revolt 45, 73, 80, 244
Lefebvre, Henri 200–201, 209
Left 143, 154–155, 293
co-optation by state apparatus 154–155, 156, 157, 181
theoretical framework of 63
left governments 13, 267, 299–300, 316–317, 322–324
and new governance 303–304
as state apparatus 290–291
Leninism 16
Lenin, Vladimir Ilyich 331
Lenkersdorf, Carlos 308
Leyton, Gomez 116–117
liberalism 194–195
liberation theology 13, 237, 311
Lind, William S. 191
linearity
and history 198–199
and time of capitalist production 88
listening 150
Llaitul, Héctor 109–110, 115
Llanquileo, Jose 115
logocentrism 29
Lomnitz, Larissa 205
López Obrador, Andres Manuel 151, 153, 156
Lozano, Claudio 155–156, 292
Lugo, Fernando 299
Lula da Silva, Luiz Inácio 62,

154–155, 156, 204, 270, 291, 292, 299, 302, 313

M

Macas, Luis 182, 277, 278, 321
Mahuad, Jamil 180
Makerly, Calzados 93
make the road by walking 189
Maldonado, Luis 276
Manifesto of Tiahuanaco (1973) 76
manqhapacha 44, 75
manufacturing 71
Mapuche 103, 104, 109–119, 300, 301
  Arauco Malleco Coordinating Group (CAM) 109–110
  CAM 115
  conquest by Chile 114
  history 113–115
  independence 114, 116
  nonhierarchical social relations, and 114
  Parliament at Quilín 113
  precolonial 113
Mara Salvatrucha 190
Marcos, Subcommandante 53, 56, 58, 62, 64, 127, 128, 133, 137, 146–147, 147–148, 150–151, 156, 157, 319–320, 328, 329, 331
marginalization 62–63, 75, 76–78, 92, 203–204, 205
Mariátegui, José Carlos 317
markets
  community-controlled 98–99
  popular/informal 236
Marxism 198–199
Marx, Karl 48, 52, 77, 89, 198, 255, 256, 257, 321–322, 328
Matos Mar, José 205–206, 224, 225
McAdam, Doug 318
Melucci, Alberto 318
Mendes, Chico 209

Menem, Carlos 94, 155
Mexico. *See* Zapatistas
  Assembly of Chontales and Zapotec Authorities of the Sierra Norte 148
  Democratic Revolutionary Party (PRD) 151, 152–153, 154, 290
  Indigenous Congress (1974) 312–313
  Mexico City 205
  National Solidarity Program (PRONASOL) 273–274
  PAN 152
  PRI 152
  PRONASOL 274
micropolitics 236
middle class
  as politically stabilizing force 196–197
  declasse intellectuals 16
Mignolo, Walter 55
militant research 57, 331
militarism 159–162, 161–162, 164–166, 169
  and social movements 166–169
militarization 197, 301
minga 31–32, 322
minka 224
Monsanto 123
Montoya, Rodrigo 319
Morales, Evo 247, 294, 299
Moreno, Alejandro 85, 261, 319
movement 24, 25, 26–27, 41, 57, 231, 323, 331
multiculturalism 30
multiplicity 80, 142–143, 150
Muñoz Ramírez, Gloria 127, 128, 131, 133

N

nationalization 182–183
nature 17
Navarro, Luis Hernández 131

negativity 204
Negri, Antonio 204
neocolonialization 66
neoliberalism 7, 13, 21, 54, 67, 85,
    92, 155–156, 156, 161, 175,
    228, 243–244, 246, 267, 270,
    291, 292, 303, 312, 313
  Latin America as epicenter of
    resistance to 315–316
network 46–47, 250–251
new governance 267–269,
    268–269, 287, 288, 289, 293,
    294, 303–306, 314–315, 324
new protagonists 57, 61–64, 229
new social movements 63
new world 20, 37, 47–48, 52–53,
    77, 87, 88, 89, 133–134, 258,
    261–262, 328–329, 332, 334
Nietzsche, Friedrich 321, 329
Noboa, Álvaro 180, 182, 184, 185
non-capitalist social relations
    40–41, 41, 46, 72, 223, 227,
    250–251, 252–253, 254–256,
    255, 256–257, 258, 319, 326,
    333
non-citizens 66
non-governmental organizations
    (NGOs) 157, 176, 271, 272,
    274–275, 277, 287, 296, 304
  poverty and 275
  relationship to state 284
  relationship to the state 274
non-state forms 80, 81, 82, 83

O
Occidental Petroleum 182
occupations. See factory occupa-
    tions; land seizures
oil 182–183
de Oliveira, Francisco 297, 305
Olivera, Oscar 294
oppositional economy 225
oral history 55
orality 29

"organizational strengthening"
    273–274
Organization of American States
    163
organizations
  second-tier 273–274
  "strengthening" 279, 297
Ornelas, Raúl 144
otra politica 323
overflow 7, 205–206
ownership 17, 248–249

P
Pacari, Nina 181
Pachakutik 226, 262, 320, 327,
    328, 329
Palacio, Alfredo 181, 182
panopticon 69, 78, 221, 222, 269
Paraguay 13
paramilitaries 159, 164–165, 178
Paris Commune 48
participation 283, 304–305
  as control strategy 281
parties 46
party 214
patriarchy 39, 311–312, 312
Patzi, Felix 309
Pécaut, Daniel 163, 166
pedagogy. See education
Pedro Vargas 172
Peru 13, 205–206
  American Popular Revolution-
    ary Alliance (APRA) 236
  CONACAMI 300–301
  First Meeting of Self-Managed
    Kitchens 238
  Free Trade Agreement with US
    301
  from below 206–207, 226
  indigenous struggles 300
  Lima 205–206, 223, 224
    collective kitchens 236–239
    Federation of Women Orga-
      nized in Committees of

Self-Sustaining Kitchens
(FEMOCCPAAL) 239
Glass of Milk Committees
236–237, 241
popular assistance programs
236–242
San Cosme 224
National Commission of Kitchens 238
popular kitchens 241
sacaojos 240
sacaojos rumor 239–240
Sendero Luminoso (Shining
Path) 238, 240, 242
Pinochet, Augusto 218–219, 227,
228, 300
legacy of 110–111, 118
Pinto, Julio 229
piqueteros 14, 15, 18, 33–35, 67,
76–77, 84, 156, 252, 292, 301,
303–304
Movimientos de Trabajadores
Desocupados (MTD) 34–35
MTD Allén 34
MTD La Matanza 27
MTD Neuguen 103
MTD Solano 27, 34–35, 47, 57
planes sociales 301, 303–304, 305,
306
Polar, Cornejo 8
politics 19, 44
from below 152, 267
popular education 283–284, 285,
288, 331
consolidation of subject-object
division 286
Porto Gonçalves 66, 78
Porto Gonçalves, Carlos Walter
209
postmodernism 69
poverty 55, 134, 156, 268, 292,
308
criminalization of 222
power 262
"change the world without taking power" 48–49
PRATEC 319
privatization 13, 111, 181
production 40–41, 71, 138–139
productivity 108
project 86, 259
property 213–214
Proudhon, Pierre-Joseph 198–199
psychology
social movements and 34–35
public housing
as control strategy 219–222

Q
"que se vayan todos" 81
Quijano, Anibal 248–249, 258
Quispe, Felipe 321

R
Ramírez, Jesus 153
Rancière, Jacques 21, 26
rationalism 329
rationality 77
recuperated factories. See factories, recuperated
reform 185
Regalsky, Pablo 29, 86
remittances 186
representation 9, 19, 78, 80, 149,
214–215, 226–227
crisis of 68, 77–78, 79
repression 16, 109–110, 229
inadequacy of 269
reproduction
control of the means of 68
research 55
resource extraction. See extractive
industries
revolution 48
rhizomatic flows 8
right 300
crisis of 303–304
Rivera, Silvia 43–44, 55, 75,
79–80, 270–271, 319

roadblocks 84–86. *See also* piqueteros
Rodrigo Cisternas 117
Roman, Angela 216
Romero, José Luis 223
de la Rúa, Fernando 98
Ruiz, Samuel 56

S
Saavedra, Carlos 106
Saavedra, Luis Angel 166–167
Salazar, Gabriel 114, 118, 215, 229, 231, 232, 234
Salete, Roseli 23–24
Scherer, Odilio 155, 291
Scott, James 67, 190, 319
self-awareness 77
self-government 211
self-management 237–238
self-organization 16, 212–213, 214
self-reproduction 85
self-sufficiency 250
separation 135
sexual abuse 35
Sisa, Bartolina 313
Skewes, Juan Carlos 221–222
Social Forums 296, 309–310
socialism 16, 42, 183
"social movement" 70
social movements 7, 21, 23, 166–169, 267–268, 289
as "mestizaje" or mix 13
change and 47–48
concept of 207, 210, 230, 318, 320
co-optation of leadership 278
division and isolaton of 290–291, 292–293
electoral politics and 180–182, 184
internal logic 83, 86–87, 88
isolation and division. *See also* co-optation
Left and 293
limits of 44–45
marginalization of 300
relationship to the state 279, 295
relative strengths of 314–315
structure of 46
Social networks of reciprocal exchange 205
social planes 314
as pacification 192, 204–205
social relations 24, 229–230
social services 21
social theory
necessarily incomplete 47
social ties 37, 41, 46–48, 80, 88
"society in movement" 8, 208, 268, 289
and the state 287
sociology 210
solidarity economy 97–99, 97–101. *See also* non-capitalist social relations
space 14–15, 18, 19, 36, 38, 40, 65, 68, 85, 149–150, 150, 200–201, 209, 210, 227
spatial discipline. *See* panopticon
spontaneity 38, 76, 87
state 7, 19–20, 21, 48, 82, 87, 267, 270, 334–335
anti-statist theory 319–320
apparatus 152, 153–154
as protest sponsor 269–270
"black holes" outside of control of 190
capillary 289, 304
crisis of 194–196, 196
education and 26, 29, 30
globalization and 146
instrumental relationship with 217
limits of 312
logic of 63, 74, 261, 302–303, 307

overflow of 206
perspective of 42, 45, 54, 66,
    133–134
power 324
progressive 290
relations to 258
return of 299
social base of 314
society in movement and 287
statist organization 14, 68
threats to 191
state of exception 193
Stédile, Joao Pedro 48–49
structure 46
subalterity 54, 66, 82, 295
subject 23–24, 66, 134
    emergence of new 53
    national 211
    territories and 209
subjectivity 203–204, 213–214
subject-object relation 54, 329
synthesis 57–58

T
Tabaré, Vazquez 154, 270, 291
Tapia, Luis 208, 319
Tarrow, Sydney 318
Taylorism 18, 25, 37, 307, 310,
    333
territorialization 14–15, 85, 97
territory 18–19, 28, 38, 62–63,
    64, 66, 68, 78, 129, 167, 199,
    201–202, 209, 210, 214–215,
    227–228, 229, 288
    consolidation of 258
    co-optation of 280–289
    new goverance attack on
        294–295
    protests and 228–229
    state and 211
    state attacks on 293
    struggle for new 66–67
    versus land 70
terrorism 109–110, 119

theory 7, 51, 53
    antistatist 319–320
    inadequacy of Western 329
    Latin American export of
        317–321
Thompson, E.P. 66, 70, 209–210
Tilly, Charles 318
timber industry 109–112, 119
time 328
Tiraju, Sepé 125–126
totalitarianism 193, 194, 201
transformation. *See* movement
Treaty of Madrid (1750) 125
Troncoso, Patricia 301
Tupac Katari 313

U
understanding 52
unemployment 92
unification 46
unions. *See* labor unions
United Nations 163
unity 296–297
universality 77, 292
urban counterinsurgency 70,
    190–191, 219–220, 235–236
urban crises 78
urban geography 68–69
urban insurrections 258
urbanization 227, 246
urban peripheries 8, 192
    and state of exception 194
    as oppositional geography 260
    control of 197
    control through economic subsi-
        dies 190
    cooperative production i
        245–246
    economic organization of 249
    generation of oppositional ter-
        ritories 206
    historic project of 259–263
    indigenous cosmovision preva-
        lent in 322

in the US 202–203
in the world system 195,
    198–199
misunderstood by academics
    198
popular settlements 211–221,
    222–223
recent revolts in 189
role of women 260
shantytowns 213
turn to insurrection 228
urban poor 63, 190, 201–202
and economic growth 202
displacement and containment
    of 219–220
growth of 197
misunderstood by academics
    202–203
networks of mutual aid 205, 220
urban religion 225
urban social movements 62, 67,
    171–178, 204, 208
Urbina, Jose Luis 102
Uribe, Álvaro 160–161, 164
Uribe, María Teresa 161–162
Uruguay 77, 249–251, 280
    Barros Blancos 279, 282–283,
        285
    Communist Party (PCU) 280
    First Gathering of Urban Agri-
        cultural Producers 251
    Frente Amplio 249, 279, 281,
        290, 324
    Guidance, Consultation and
        Territorial Coordination Ser-
        vices (SOCATA) 280–289
    Infamilia 281
    Ministry of Social Development
        (MIDES) 284, 287
    Montevideo 85
        comunity gardens 249–251
        expulsions of the poor 65
        July 31–August 1, 2002 70
    National Plan for Emergency
        Social Care 279

Routes Out 280
state-sponsored protests against
    domestic violence 269–270
Work for Uruguay 280
use value 217

V
de Valdivia, Pedro 113, 115
Van der Linde, Maria 237
vanguardism 330
Vargas, Antonio 276
Vargas Llosa, Mario 226, 242
Vázquez, Tabaré 299
Velasco Alvarado, Juan 224
Venezuela 13, 242–245. See
    also Caracazo
    April 2003 popular uprising 43
    Assembly of Barrios of Caracas
        243
    Bolivarian process 244
    Caracas 67
    community organizing 244
    coup d'état against Chávez 309
    First International Gathering
        for the Rehabilitation of the
        Barrios 243
    Urban Land Committees (CTU)
        244–245
verticality 7, 34
Villa El Salvador 224, 226
violence 193–194
visibility 19, 45–46, 297–298

W
Wacquant, Loïc 201–203
wage labor
    ad precarity 202
Wallerstein, Immanuel 39, 77, 98,
    194–196, 311
Washington Consensus. See neo-
    liberalism
water 246–248
Weber, Max 211
women 17, 39, 43–44, 81, 131,
    139, 178, 207–208, 214, 215,

216, 228–230, 236–238,
241–242, 260, 310–311
feminization of society 39
work 17
and education 25
worker management 93
workers 185. *See also* labor
unions
World Bank 133, 181, 272–274,
274, 314

Y
youth 310–311
culture 232–234, 281, 282
mobilizations 234

Z
Zang, Huli 121, 123, 124
Zapatistas 8, 14, 15, 45, 48–49,
56–57, 58, 64, 81, 85, 127–
158, 259, 262, 310, 312–313,
316, 329
1974 Indigenous Congress 129
Aguascalientes 130
autonomous municipalities
128–129
Caracoles/Councils of Good
Government 128–129, 130,
131, 135–136, 136, 140,
143–144, 262, 321, 332, 333
education 136–138, 137,
138–139
EZLN 128, 130, 141–142, 144
Gatherings for Humanity and
Against Neoliberalism 130
government 139–145
health care 32–33, 132, 132–
133, 134–135
hospitals 132, 135
human rights 142
international relations 130, 141
land reform 139
La Realidad 132
law 131

March of the Color of the Earth
(2001) 130, 152
Municipal Council 130
National Democratic Convention (1994) 130
National Indigenous Convention 130
Other Campaign 127, 145–153,
298
Oventic 131
Peace with Justice and Dignity
for Indigenous Peoples' campaign 128
politics 146–147
Ricardo Flores Magón municipality 137
San Andres Talks in 1996 130
self-critique 140–141, 142
Sixth Declaration of the Lacandon Jungle 145, 146, 152
state and 152, 153–154
The Thirteenth Stele 140–141
unity from below 150–151
women and 139
Zapatista Rebel Autonomous
Education System 132
zumbayllu 8–9

Support AK Press!

AK Press is one of the world's largest and most productive

anarchist publishing houses. We're entirely worker-run and demo-cratically managed. We operate without a corporate structure—no boss, no managers, no bullshit. We publish close to twenty books every year, and distribute thousands of other titles published by other like-minded independent presses from around the globe.

The Friends of AK program is a way that you can directly contribute to the continued existence of AK Press, and ensure that we're able to keep publishing great books just like this one! Friends pay a minimum of $25 per month, for a minimum three month period, into our publishing account. In return, Friends automatically receive (for the duration of their membership), as they appear, one free copy of every new AK Press title. They're also entitled to a 20% discount on everything featured in the AK Press Distribution catalog and on the web-site, on any and every order. You or your organization can even sponsor an entire book if you should so choose!

There's great stuff in the works—so sign up now to become a Friend of AK Press, and let the presses roll!

Won't you be our friend? Email friendsofak@akpress.org for more info, or visit the Friends of AK Press website: http://www.akpress.org/programs/friendsofak